Beef Tea Gossip.

There are three forms of beef tea, suited to different stages of illness, any one of which will usually be taken without dislike by any average patient. The first is uncooked beef juice, and is often given in cases of extreme weakness, when no other food can be retained. It is made thus:

Cut into small pieces a pound of perfectly lean beef. Add five or six drops of muriatic acid, and stir for a moment. The acid, disengaging all the nutritive part of the meat from the fibre, leaves a clear red juice which is strained off, heated very hot, and seasoned with salt, and, if the patient likes it, pepper. This beef tea has frequently prolonged and saved life in desperate cases.

2d. Beef tea made in a bottle: One pound of perfectly lean beef is cut into small dice, placed in a strong quart bottle, corked, and set to boil in a pot of water. The heat disengaging the juice of the beef, gives after three hours' cooking, a strong and very nourishing liquid into which the essential principle of the meat is condensed. Let it grow thoroughly cold before using, so as to remove every floating particle of fat—then re-heat, season and serve. A teaspoonful of arrowroot stirred in while the beef tea is heating makes an excellent addition.

3d. Beef-tea for cases of lighter illness, where it is to supplement rather than replace other food: Take a pound of lean beef-steak and broil it for an instant on both sides. Chop fine as for mince meat, then add a quart of water, and boil slowly for an hour and a half. Strain it, let it get thoroughly cold, skim off the fat, and season with salt, pepper, and, if the doctor permits, a soupcon of tomato catsup. A little rice boiled with the tea makes it nice, or a sprig of celery dropped in to lend a flavor. This soup is admirable food, and almost all sick persons will be found to like it.

THE

PHILOSOPHY OF EATING.

BY

ALBERT J. BELLOWS, M.D.,

LATE PROFESSOR OF CHEMISTRY, PHYSIOLOGY, AND HYGIENE.

NEW YORK:

PUBLISHED BY HURD AND HOUGHTON.

BOSTON: E. P. DUTTON AND COMPANY.

1867.

STEREOTYPED AT THE BOSTON STEREOTYPE FOUNDRY,
No. 4 Spring Lane.

TO

THE FIVE THOUSAND LADIES

WHO, FROM 1838 TO 1858, ATTENDED MY LECTURES ON PHYSIOLOGY, CHEMISTRY, AND HYGIENE.

DEAR FRIENDS:

In the reminiscences of the past twenty-nine years many pleasant interviews at your firesides, in social gatherings, on steamboats, and elsewhere, are recalled, in which some mother or teacher has reminded me of facts or statements, physiological, chemical, or hygienic, made ten, twenty, or twenty-five years before, but still remembered; and often has the kind suggestion been made, that those teachings, which had been useful to them as mothers or teachers, when only treasured in the memory, might be more useful to their children and pupils if collected and printed.

These kind suggestions, together with the fact that the application of science to hygiene has been almost utterly neglected, have induced me to collect and condense the ideas of my old lectures, adding to them such as modern improvements in practical science have suggested, and leaving out such as have become obsolete; and the volume thus produced I take the liberty to dedicate to the friends who will be most likely to be interested in it.

With sincere regard,

Yours affectionately,

A. J. BELLOWS.

90 SPRINGFIELD ST., BOSTON,
November, 1867.

PREFACE.

WE have excellent practical treatises on Agriculture and Horticulture, and every intelligent farmer or gardener may learn what element is deficient, in order successfully to cultivate his grapes, his vegetables, or his grains; and having also chemical analyses of these fruits and grains, and of the materials from which to obtain his deficient elements, he has the means of adapting his soil to all desirable productions.

We have also treatises on raising horses, cattle, hens, pigs, fishes, and even bees and canary birds, but not a single practical treatise on raising children. We know perfectly well that our horses will not, without care in regard to their food and training, be developed in beauty, strength, or docility. Our cows must be cared for, or they furnish little milk. Our hens must have appropriate food, or they furnish no eggs. Our bees must have their proper conditions of life and health complied with, or they furnish no honey and die. All this everybody knows; but children are expected to live, and be perfectly developed, both mentally and physically, without care or consideration.

And so perfectly ignorant are people generally of the laws of nature, that they give their pigs the food which their children need to develop muscle and brain, and give their children what their pigs need to develop fat. For example, the farmer separates from milk the muscle-making and brain-feeding nitrates and phosphates, and gives them to his pigs in the form of buttermilk, while the fattening carbonates he gives to his children in butter. He sifts out the bran and outer crust from the wheat, which contains the nitrates and phosphates, and gives them also to his pigs and cattle, while the fine flour, containing little else than heating carbonates, he gives to his children. Cheese, which contains the concentrated nutriment of milk, is seldom seen on our tables, while butter, which contains not a particle of food for brain or muscle, is on every table at all times of day.

To supply this deficiency in practical science, and to correct these erroneous and dangerous habits of society, is the object of this treatise.

A. J. B.

90 Springfield St., Boston, Mass.

CONTENTS.

THE

PHILOSOPHY OF EATING.

The Human Body: Its Wants and Resources.

"And the Lord God formed man of the dust of the ground."

THIS statement, incomprehensible to the human mind as it is, is most beautifully confirmed by chemical analysis. At least it is proved, that the elements of the human system and the elements of the soil, taken anywhere on the surface of the earth, from the equator to the poles, are identical; and it is also proved that the "grass, the herb yielding seed, and the fruit-tree yielding fruit after his kind," which the earth brought forth before man was made, all are endowed with power to take from the soil these elements, one by one, and fit them to be received and appropriated directly to the supply of the human system, or indirectly accomplish the same purpose by being first appropriated by the "beast of the field and the fowl of the air," and then in their flesh to furnish these necessary elements to man.

Geological evidence is conclusive that man was not made till this whole arrangement was perfected, so that wherever he chooses to live,—in Africa or Greenland,—he finds at hand food adapted to his wants in the climate in which he finds himself. But when we attempt to trace the process by which this complicated and beautiful arrangement was made for man, we are lost in wonder and admiration. The mineral elements, which constitute the great mass of the surface of the earth, all came originally from solid rock, and must have been produced by the slow process of disintegration, by which, by the action of heat, cold, and water, particle by particle it accumulated, age after age, till the great mass was formed which should afterwards become the place of deposit for water, salt, coal, &c., which man must have, and which also furnishes the fourteen different minerals which were to make a part of the human system.

And then ages of time more must have been required to produce the organic elements, which were formed by the growth and decay of plants and trees, which grew one after another, as the appropriate elements of soil were accumulated, and gave way in turn for more perfect vegetation, till organic elements had accumulated in sufficient quantity to supply the surface of the whole earth with all that should be needed for the composition and repair of the human system.

Then other ages still were required to float these crudely mixed elements over the face of the earth, and so intimately mix them that some portion of every element necessary should be found in every foot of soil on the face of the earth.

And after all this preparation the world was not fitted for man till ages more of time were consumed in raising the hills and the mountains, so that the ocean might be formed and dry land appear, and mists, condensed into rain and dews, be collected in brooks and rivers, to carry the waters back to the ocean, to be again evaporated, and a supply be insured, and the atmosphere prepared with its due proportion of oxygen and nitrogen. And when all the fourteen necessary elements were prepared in the water, and the atmosphere, and the soil, and laws instituted by which they should be forever at his command and forever perpetuated, then man was made; and then, that he might never fail to be supplied with everything he should need, God gave him "dominion over the fish of the sea, and over the fowl of the air, and over every living thing that moveth upon the earth," which, with "every herb bearing seed which is upon the face of all the earth, and every tree in which is the fruit of a tree yielding seed," should all contain the necessary elements, so that any one of them would sustain life.

Having thus bountifully provided for every contingency of climate or circumstance, he gave man a test by which he could select that which would be appropriate and reject that which would be injurious — that article which contained the proper elements rightly organized and adapted to his condition at any time, the appetite would demand and the palate and stomach receive gratefully and pleasantly; while that which was not organized according to this plan, or had afterwards become disorganized, or contained the wrong elements, or the right elements in wrong proportions, should offend the taste, and be rejected with disgust; or, if forced into the stomach, should cause an excitement, by efforts to get rid of it, which would be more or less poisonous or injurious according to the degree of harm which it was adapted to do the system. For example, sugar contains important elements rightly organized to supply the system with requisite heat, and it is pleasant to the healthy palate, and gratefully received in proper quantities by the stomach when needed; but alcohol, which is sugar decomposed, and which contains the same elements in the same proportions, is offensive to the natural taste, and if forced on the stomach, produces an immediate excitement, which is injurious and poisonous to the organs engaged in the effort to resist it.

Fish, which was prepared with all the elements rightly organized, and in right proportions to be appropriate food, is pleasant to the taste when properly cooked, and is gratefnlly received and quickly digested; but being exposed to a hot sun for a single hour, and disorganization or decomposition commencing, it becomes disgusting and poisonous.

Phosphorus, which is valuable and necessary food for the brain, &c., when organized in fish, or peas, or oatmeal, &c., is, when once disorganized, a virulent poison; and thus in physiology as in ethics, "in keeping the commandments there is great reward." To obey the simple laws of our being is to enjoy eating, and the health, vigor, and happiness which come from the appropriate exercise of all our functions and faculties; while to seek to enhance our enjoyment by unnatural combinations of food is to clog the appetite, to lose all real enjoyment in eating, and to burden the system with untold miseries, to be suffered through life and transmitted to children "to the third and fourth generation."

If science in farming is important, as it is proved to be, may not science in eating be more important?

The scientific farmer analyzes his soil, and ascertains what elements it contains; then analyzes his grains and vegetables, and ascertains what elements they require; then analyzes the different manures and composts, and ascertains which contains, in the best combination, the elements to be supplied. This gives him an immense advantage over the unscientific farmer, who, not knowing the requirements of his soil, wastes his compost by using many materials not necessary, and too large a supply of elements that may be necessary, while many important elements will be omitted altogether.

I propose, upon the same principles, to give an analysis of the human system, — show the elements it contains, and the necessity for their constant supply, — and then to give an analysis of the food which Nature has furnished for the supply of these necessities; and I think it can be readily proved that as the scientific farmer has advantages in point of economy, the scientific eater has not only advantages in economy of living, but vastly greater advantages in the enjoyment of health and happiness. And as a matter of economy, it can be shown that in Boston and other cities more than half the expense of food is lost by want of adjustment of the proportions of requisite elements, just as all the expense of guano would be lost on the land already supplied with phosphorus and ammonia.

Chemical Composition of the Human Body.

The human body is composed of the following elements, all of which are found also in the food provided by nature, or in air or water, and all must be supplied, day by day, or some bad results are sure to follow: —

	lb.	oz.	gr.
Oxygen, a gas, in quantity sufficient to occupy a space equal to 750 cubic feet, ...	111	0	0
Hydrogen, a gas, in quantity sufficient to occupy 3000 feet, which, with oxygen, constitutes water, the weight of the two indicating nearly the necessary amount of water, ...	14	0	0
Carbon, constituting fat, and used also for fuel to create animal heat, ...	21	0	0
Nitrogen, which constitutes the basis of the muscles and solid tissues, and which is supplied by that part of food which we shall denominate Nitrates, ...	3	8	0
Phosphorus, the physical source of vitality, and the most important of the mineral elements, will represent the whole class which we shall denominate the Phosphates, ...	1	12	190
Calcium, the metallic base of lime, which is the base of bones, ...	2	0	0
Fluorine, found combined in small quantities in bones, ...	0	2	0

Chlorine, constituting, with sodium, common salt, found in the blood, ...	0	2	47
Sodium, the base of all the salts of soda, . .	0	2	116
Iron, which is supposed to give color to the blood, ...	0	0	100
Potassium, the base of all the salts of potash, .	0	0	290
Magnesium, the base of magnesia and magnesian salts, ...	0	0	12
Silicon, the base of silex, which is found in the hair, teeth, and nails, ...	0	0	2
The elements of a man weighing	154 lbs.		

Proximate Principles in the Human Body.

	lb.	oz.	gr.
1. Water, composed of oxygen and hydrogen gases, as in the preceding table of ultimate elements, ...	111	0	0
2. Gelatine, of which the walls of the cells and many tissues of the body are composed, .	15	0	0
3. Fat, which constitutes the adipose tissue, .	12	0	0
4. Phosphate of Lime, forming the principal part of the earthy matter of the bones, .	5	13	0
5. Carbonate of Lime, also a part of the composition of bone, ...	1	0	0
6. Albumen, found in the blood and in almost every organ, ...	4	3	0
7. Fibrin, forming the muscles and the clot of the blood, ...	4	4	3
8. Fluoride of Calcium, found in the bones, .	0	3	0
9. Phosphate of Soda, } found in the brain and nerves, and constituting the physical elements of vitality or vital energy, . .	0	0	400
10. Phosphate of Potash, }	0	0	100

11. Phosphate of Magnesia, found with Phosphate of Lime in the bones, ...	0	0	75
12. Chloride of Sodium (common salt), in the blood, ...	0		376
13. Sulphate of Soda, in the blood, ...	0	1	170
14. Carbonate of Soda, in the blood and bones,	0	1	72
15. Sulphate of Potash, in the blood, . . .	0	0	400
16. Peroxide of Iron, in the blood (and supposed to furnish the coloring matter), .	0	9	150
17. Silica, ...	0	0	3
	154	0	0

Classification of Food.

The fourteen elements and seventeen combinations of these elements are all being consumed every day, and, therefore, must be supplied in food, or in the atmosphere, or in water. Food may be divided into three classes. That class which supplies the lungs with fuel, and thus furnishes heat to the system, and supplies fat or adipose substance, &c., we shall call Carbonates, carbon being the principal element; that which supplies the waste of muscles, we shall call Nitrates,* nitrogen being the principal element; and that which supplies the bones, and the brain, and the nerves, and gives vital power, both muscular and mental, we shall call the Phosphates, phosphorus being the principal element. These last might be subdivided into the fixed and the soluble phosphates, — the fixed

* The terms Nitrates, Carbonates, and Phosphates, are not strictly in accordance with chemical nomenclature, these terms being generally applied to salts only; but no other single words would give an idea of the predominant element.

being a combination principally with lime to form the bones, and the soluble being combinations with potash and soda, to work the brain and nerves; but our analyses as yet are too imperfect to allow a subdivision, and as all the mineral elements are more or less combined with each other, and all reside together in articles of food, we shall include all mineral elements under the term Phosphates.

The waste, and consequently the supply, of these three classes of elements, is very different, four times as much carbonaceous food being required as nitrogenous, and of the phosphates not more than two per cent. of the carbonates. Altogether, the waste of these principles will average in a man of moderate size, with moderate heat, more than one pound in a day, varying very much according to the amount of exercise and the temperature in which he lives. These elements must all be supplied in vegetable or animal food, not one being allowed to become a part of the system unless it has been first organized with other elements of food, in some vegetable, or in water, or the atmosphere; but being appropriated by some animal, remain organized and adapted to the human system, so that animal and vegetable food contain the same elements in the same proportions and nearly the same chemical combinations, and are equally adapted to supply all necessary elements.

In Animal Food,	The Carbonates are furnished in . .	Fat.
	The Nitrates in . .	Albumen, Fibrin, and Casein.
In Vegetable Food,	The Carbonates are furnished in . .	Sugar, Starch, and a little Fat.
	The Nitrates in . .	Gluten, Albumen, and Casein.

The Phosphates, in both animal and vegetable food, are found inseparably connected with the nitrates, none being found in any of the carbonates, and generally in the proportion of from two to three per cent. of all the principles in vegetable, and from three to five in animal food.

The Carbonates of both animal and vegetable food are chemically alike — fat, sugar, and starch, all being composed of carbon, oxygen, and hydrogen, and in about the same chemical combinations and proportions.

The Nitrates, also Albumen, Gluten, Fibrin, and Casein, are alike in chemical combinations and elements, being composed of nitrogen, oxygen, and hydrogen, and a little carbon not digestible.

The Wants of the Human System, and the Reason for them.

In the foregoing tables are found fourteen different elements of which the human system is composed, not one of which is permanently fixed in the system, but each, after performing the duties assigned it for a time, shorter or longer, according to the nature of those duties, becomes effete, and gives place to other particles of the same elements, which must be supplied in food. Each organ requires different elements, and has the power of taking such as are required from the mass of elements circulated together in the blood, and of rejecting all other elements; and while these fourteen elements, all having been organized in some plant or vegetable, are supplied as they are wanted, peace and harmony prevail in the system, and perfect health is enjoyed; but let any other elements enter the circulation and an excitement is produced, and each organ makes an effort to reject them. Take alcohol, for example, and the stomach is first excited and heated by efforts to expel it. It is then thrown into the circulation so as to be expelled by the lungs, or skin, or kidneys, and the whole system becomes excited, especially the brain, in efforts to eject this enemy to all its functions.

Phosphorus, iron, and all other disorganized substances, whether elements of the human system or not, are thus rejected with more or less excitement, according to their capacity for harming the system; and thus can be clearly read the lessons of nature, teaching us to keep out of the stomach and lungs everything but these fourteen elements, and to admit them only as they are organized and prepared as in articles of natural food in Nature's laboratory — the Vegetable World. But these elements are required in very different amounts, according to the amount of exercise of the different faculties and the temperature of the atmosphere in which we live.

And here we have the foundation for a scientific adaptation of food to our different employments in life. The man who is chopping wood in an atmosphere at zero, and he who sits still, or uses only his brain, in a room at the temperature of seventy degrees, consume very different elements in very different proportions, and therefore require different elements of food. The one needs the muscle-producing nitrogenate elements and the heat-producing carbonates; while the other needs very few nitrogenates, and only carbonates enough to supply the breathing operations with fuel; but he needs more of the phosphates to keep the brain in working order, and we shall find on inquiry that nature has furnished food just adapted to these and other conditions of life, and shall find also that, following these suggestions of nature, we shall obtain a rich reward, both in the enjoyment of health and in the enjoyment of eating.

Resources for Supplying the Wants of the Human System.

The soil on the surface of the whole earth constitutes the great reservoir of crude elements of the human body, and man is kept alive as he was made by materials obtained from "the dust of the ground," but, as has already been intimated, these elements cannot be made to enter the composition of the system till they are organized — or, being organized, are eaten by some animal, and retaining their organization, are adapted still, in the flesh of the animal, to supply the demand of the human system.

These elements, becoming effete, are excreted from all animals that eat them, and, being then decomposed, enter again into the soil, to be reorganized in other vegetables; and thus, since these laws were instituted, no elements have been lost and none created — indeed, it is no more in the power of man to annihilate an element of matter than to create one. He can disorganize elements, — as he does in converting sugar into alcohol, but he only produces carbonic acid gas, &c., — which are again taken up and reorganized in some vegetable, and are reconverted into sugar; thus entering again their natural circle to go their perpetual rounds.

Every crop of corn, or potatoes, or grass, or vegetables deprives the soil of all the elements of which these crops are composed, and, if carried off and sold, impoverishes the soil proportionately. This the farmers understand, and are therefore careful to supply, with the natural excretions of animals, the elements thus removed, or with decomposed animal, vegetable, and mineral substances containing them ; and, so perfect has this knowledge of agricultural chemistry become, that it is known just what elements are needed after each crop, and just how these elements can be supplied — vegetables using only disorganized elements, while animals use only organized elements — a beautiful provision of nature. It is known also what food and management will best develop our animals, and make them subserve our interests.

Scientific laws are applied also to the care of our horses, to make them beautiful, strong, swift, healthy, and docile ; and to our cattle, and pigs, and hens, to enable them to furnish us with their invaluable contributions to the necessaries and luxuries of life ; and our farmers know just what food to give them in order best to develop these resources. We have also books on bees and canary birds, teaching what they must have and what they must not have in order to be healthy. But our children, without whom all these other blessings would be of little value, are left to die, or grow up if they are sufficiently tough, without the application of science, or even common sense, to their care or culture. What two mothers can be found to agree in regard to the diet or regimen of their children? Who studies as much to learn how to feed himself as how to feed his cattle, or even his pet dog? But are we not better then they? Did God give laws for feeding them and no laws for feeding us and our children?

Wheat—its Origin and Chemical Composition.

The plant producing wheat belongs to the order of Grasses, and undoubtedly came originally from some grass whose seeds are so unlike the grains of wheat, as developed after centuries of cultivation, as not now to be recognized. It is not found wild in any part of the world, but like the other grains, and roots, and leguminous and succulent vegetables and fruits, has been changed from the "herb of the field," which, after the fall, was the basis, or emblem at least, of all the resources that were left to man; so that almost literally, from the "herb of the field," by the sweat of his brow, he has obtained not only his necessary food, but all the choicest luxuries which he now enjoys. Wheat is the most extensively cultivated and the most generally used of any of the grains; indeed, it is grown all over the world, but it flourishes best between the parallels of twenty-five and sixty degrees of latitude. The varieties of wheat are very great, over four hundred being described by the French Academy of Arts and Sciences, and it furnishes the principal food of more people than any other grain. Of these varieties some have sharp awns or beards, and some are beardless. The grains of some are red, some brown, and some white. Some contain more carbonaceous elements, and are therefore better adapted to the supply of heat than others. Some have more nitrogenous materials, and therefore are better adapted to give muscular power. Some have more phosphates, and therefore give more mental and nervous energy.

But the average distribution of these elements more nearly corresponds with the requirements of the human system, under ordinary circumstances, than any other grain; and life and health can be continued on wheat alone for an indefinite period, with good water and good air. Wheat will, therefore, be the standard by which to compare other articles of food.

Analysis of Wheat.

The average Composition of one hundred Parts.

Water,	14.0	or,	Water,	14.0
Gluten,	12.8		Nitrates, or muscle-makers,	14.6
Albumen,	1.8		Carbonates, or heat and fat-producers,	69.8
Starch,	59.7		Phosphates, or food for brains, nerves, &c.	2.0
Sugar,	5.5			
Gum,	1.7			
Fat,	1.2			
Fibre,	1.7			
Minerals,	1.6			

These principles are made up of the fourteen elements which constitute the human system, and the proportion of the muscle-making, the heat-producing, and brain and nerve-feeding elements, are about the average proportions required, in moderate weather, with moderate exercise of physical and mental faculties. But the distribution of these elements is not equal in all parts of the grain; and this, we shall see, is very important to be understood, as ignorance of this fact has led to the sacrifice of the most important elements. This we can understand by reference to the following wood cuts: Fig. 1 being the natural size of wheat, and Fig. 2 being magnified to three or four diameters.

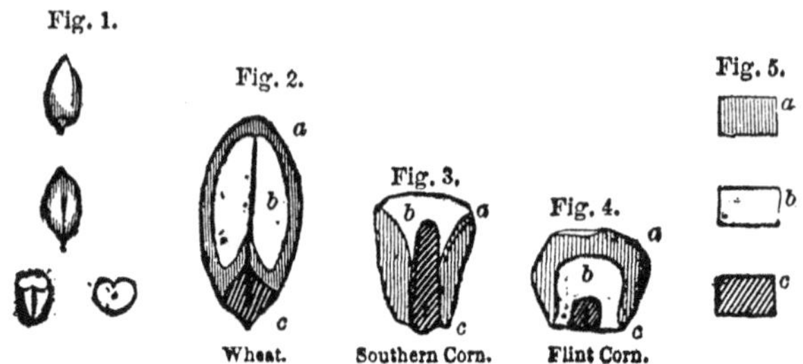

a. Nitrates, or Muscle-makers.
b. Carbonates, or Heat or Fat-producers.
c. Phosphates, or Food for Brains and Nerves.

These drawings are intended to show the position and the relative quantity of the three important principles — the muscle-makers, occupying or constituting a crust around the outside of the grain, being from twelve to fifteen per cent. of the whole grain; the heat or fat-producers, occupying the centre, being from sixty to seventy per cent.; and the food for the brains and nerves, occupying the chit or germ, being from one and a half to three per cent. The limits of these principles are not, however, as circumscribed in the grain as appears by the drawing, a small per cent. of nitrates being mixed with the carbonates, and a part of the phosphates being mixed with the nitrates; indeed, the phosphate of lime, which goes to form bones, is almost all mixed with the nitrates in the crust; while the soluble phosphates, which feed the brain and give mental vigor, are mostly found in the germ; and this arrangement is found to exist in all the grains and all the seeds of grasses, — the smallest seed under the microscope showing the same organization as that exhibited in the cut of wheat, — the smaller seeds, however, containing much larger proportions of the nitrates and phosphates, being intended for the support of birds of great activity. The practical importance of understanding this arrangement will be better understood by reference to a drawing of the transverse section of a grain of wheat magnified to eighteen diameters from the section in Fig. 1.

Fig. 6.

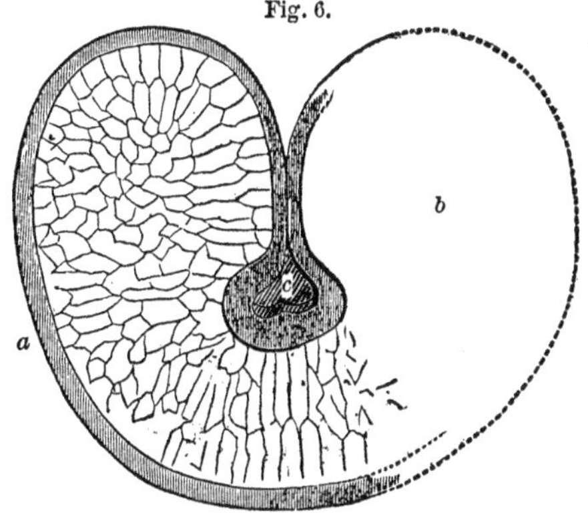

To understand how large a part of the phosphates and nitrates is lost in bolting to make superfine flour, it will be necessary to explain that gluten, which is the principal nitrogenous element in wheat, is tenacious or adhesive; while the starch, the carbonaceous element, is globular and crumbly; the consequence is, that in grinding, the glutinous crust is separated in flakes, and is sifted out, leaving the flour composed almost entirely of starch, which contains no food for brain or muscle.

The outer layers of the wheat, constituting twelve or fourteen per cent. of the whole grain, which are represented by the darkened lines, *a*, in the plates, contain a large part of all the muscle-making elements of the wheat; and, being adhesive, it is easily separated from the more crumbly particles of the starch below, which is represented by the white part within the outer lines, *b;* consequently, it is separated from it in grinding and bolting, and much of it is lost with the bran. The germ also, which contains, with the gluten, the soluble phosphates, which is represented by the darker lines, *c*, in the drawing, is also tenacious, and much of it goes off with the bran. The insoluble or bone-making phosphorus, being mixed with the nitrates, is also lost. Nothing, therefore, can be more clearly proved than that in using perfectly white, superfine flour, we sacrifice the most important elements of the wheat merely to please the eye. And yet this is the kind of flour which probably makes more than nine tenths of all the bread in American cities, besides the large amount used for cakes, puddings, and pastry.

The farmer knows that wheat will not grow in soil out of which is taken any of the essential elements that constitute that grain; and he either supplies these elements, or he makes no attempt to raise wheat. Yet how many of our citizens are attempting to raise children on superfine flour, and butter, and sugar, neither of which contains food for the muscles, or bones, or brains, sufficient to keep these organs from actual starvation!

Every one also who keeps fowls knows, that to get a supply of eggs, and raise chickens, hens must be supplied with other food than Indian corn meal, which contains too many of the carbonates, or fattening elements, and too few of the phosphates and nitrates, to supply the shells of the eggs or muscles of the future chick. They are therefore fed with ground bones and egg-shells for the one, and meat or insects for the other purpose. But how many expectant and nursing mothers, not knowing or considering their responsibilities, live on superfine flour bread, and butter, and puddings, and sweet sauce, and cakes, and confectionery, which contain little else than the three articles of food before mentioned, and in which are only found the carbonates, or fat and heat-producing elements, and only very little of food for the muscles and tissues, or bones, or brain! The results are inevitable. One half of the children die before they are five years old, and many before that age have, for the want of the phosphate of lime, defective teeth and soft and rickety bones. If they live to grow up under the same disregard to their natural requirements, their muscles are poorly developed, their tissues are weak, and susceptible to disease for the want of the nitrogenous elements of food; their bones, and brains, and nerves are weak, and subject to disease for the want of the phosphates; while, by over feeding with the carbonates, the whole system is heated and excited, and ready to be inflamed by the first spark of disease; and the inevitable results are inflammations, fevers, neuralgic pains, consumptions, defective teeth, reactive exhaustion, chlorotic weaknesses, and diseases and pains innumerable.

It seems to me that the arch fiend, who is represented as "walking about seeking whom he may devour," has never devised a more effectual plan for tormenting and devouring the human race than this.

The penalties for the breach of Nature's laws are always severe in proportion to the importance of the purposes to be subserved by them, and they must follow the transgression as effect must follow the cause. No less severe punishments than those mentioned above could be expected to follow the utter disregard for that wonderful arrangement by which in a single grain of wheat could be supplied all the elements necessary for the growth or support of all the organs and functions—an arrangement which even Infinite Wisdom could not effect but by a process that required countless ages of time. To these penalties we shall have occasion to refer again when treating of diet for the sick.

Butter, Sugar, and Superfine Flour.

The only articles, the common use of which brings upon this community the terrible evils to which I have referred, are fine white flour, butter, and sugar. These articles, made up almost entirely as they are of heat-producing nourishment, are wholesome and necessary food to the extent of more than three fourths of all our solid nutriment, that great proportion of the carbonates being required to supply fuel and fat; but they contain so few of the elements that support the muscles and solid tissues, and so few that give us vital power, that either alone, or all three combined, could sustain life only for a very limited period — probably not two months. These three important elements of food are found in abundance combined with the other important elements which the system requires, and in many they are found combined in just the proportion required; indeed, in all food in such proportions as to adapt them to the different temperatures and circumstances in which we may be placed; so that we have no necessity, or even apology, for separating what God has thus joined together.

Starch, of which fine white flour is mostly composed, is found in the entire grain of wheat, and in many other grains and leguminous seeds, combined with muscle-making and brain-sustaining elements, in just the right proportions.

Butter is found in milk, also combined with all other necessary elements in exactly the right proportions; and sugar in vegetables and fruits; and, it is a fact that our relish for, and enjoyment in, eating these different combinations of necessary food are in exact proportion to their adaptedness to our wants at the time we take them. But for the perversion of our appetites, caused by eating these three articles in an unnatural state, we should always desire most what we most need, and could always eat all we want of what we best like. And, even after our tastes have become perverted, we find, on giving attention to this subject, that the more nearly we conform to Nature's requirements in the selection of food, the more we enjoy the pleasures of eating; so that in the pleasures of the table, as in all other pleasures, they enjoy the least who most anxiously inquire, "Who will show us any good?" while they enjoy most who only expect pleasure in the line of duty.

We all instinctively desire, also, more of these heat-producing articles in cold weather than in warm, and eat, without considering the reasons for doing so, much more of the fats of animals, and butter, and buckwheat-cakes, with sirup, in winter than in summer; and as spring opens we begin to desire cooling green vegetables and acid fruits, and this desire increases till in very warm weather we loathe the food we most esteemed in winter; and if our appetites fail in warm weather it is because our housekeepers persist in supplying us with the same fat meats and the same farinaceous puddings, with sauce of butter and sugar, which were furnished in winter. Let our housekeepers just keep in mind the fact that these articles only stand in the way of gratifying our tastes and inclinations in regard to food, and they will find that the science of cooking is very simple, and the wants of a family are very easily provided for. But we need not abandon either of these perverted articles entirely. Let us only consider how to correct the errors into which we have fallen, and use "all the creatures of God which are good and not to be despised," so as to make them contribute to our health and happiness. Of this perverted trio of good things wheat is the most important,. because most extensively used, and by far the most valuable.

Microscopic Analysis of Wheat.

Fig. 7.

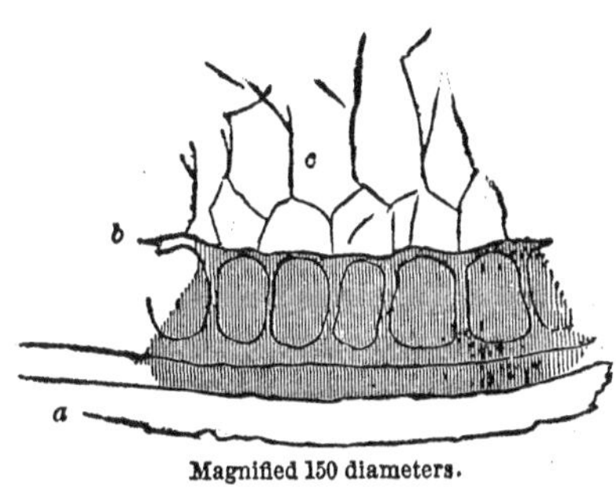

Magnified 150 diameters.

a. The outer coat, or true bran, containing iron, silica, and some other elements required in the human system, and not found elsewhere in the wheat, but composed mostly of indigestible woody fibre, which is also useful as waste to keep the bowels in action—even the outer bran should therefore be saved.

b. Gluten cells, surrounded by diffused gluten and bound by it to the true bran, so that in sifting or bolting a large portion is lost. Nine tenths of all the muscle-making elements reside in this coat or crust, and also the phosphates of lime and soda, of which bones are made; the most of which are lost in fine white flour.

c. Cells forming the central mass of the wheat, composed mostly of starch, with a little albumen and gluten intermixed, and also some of the phosphates connected with the gluten.

Starch, though a valuable element of food, and the principal element in vegetable food to keep up animal heat, is so perfectly destitute of the essential element for sustaining life, that living on that alone, as proved by experiment, any animal will die in thirty days. A glance at this plate will enable any one to understand and believe the estimate of Mège Mouriès to be true, that there are fourteen times as much of the phosphates and nitrates "in commercial bran as in commercial superfine flour;" and this important fact is proved by three separate and distinct calculations: by Mège Mouriès, in France; by chemical analysis of the bran and flour; by Dr. A. A. Hayes, of Boston, who first suggested the idea of applying tests to the whole grain, showing the arrangements of elements as delineated in Fig. 2, and other plates, the truth of these statements I have carefully tested, as have other chemists; and Mr. Thomas J. Hand, of New York, an amateur microscopist of great assiduity and skill, who has spent many years in microscopic observations on wheat, and to whom I am indebted for the original drawings of plates 6 and 7, and also for many other facts and observations, fully substantiating the facts above stated. There can be, therefore, no proof more clear and positive than that superfine white flour is deprived of a large portion of the most important elements of food.

Bread-Making.

The most important use of wheat is for bread-making. For this purpose, on many accounts, it is better than any other grain, and being better, is more extensively used in every civilized country.

As bread is the staff of life, wheat, of which it is most extensively made, is called the "queen of cereals;"

and though by producing sickness, and suffering, and death, her reign is one of terror, especially in this country and in Europe, it would not be desirable to dethrone her; but it would be desirable to inaugurate such a change as to make her reign a reign of mercy. The necessity and importance of a change in regard to the use of white bread can be understood by considering a few facts.

It is estimated that ninety-five per cent. of bread used in Boston is made of wheat flour, out of which has been taken, by the process of grinding and bolting, all but about five per cent. of its muscle-making and life-supporting elements, so that fifteen barrels are required to furnish as many of these elements as one barrel of unbolted wheat meal. This will be fully comprehended by reference to the grain of split wheat, drawn under a microscope, Fig. 6, and the proportions of nitrates, and carbonates, and phosphates, delineated by different colored lines in plates on a previous page. Carbonates white, nitrates in lines, and phosphates in darker lines. The nitrates and phosphates are inseparable by mechanical means, being bound together by gluten, of which it is mostly composed, while the carbonates, being mostly starch, which is granular, and loosely adherent, is easily separated from the glutinous crust by the process of grinding and bolting.

In making superfine flour twenty-five per cent. of the meal goes off in the siftings, of which fifteen per cent. is of the nitrates and phosphates, and ten per cent. of carbonates.

A glance at Fig. 6 will also show us the value of bran as food for horses, working cattle, and fowls, and growing pigs, and give us some hints as to the right way of using it. These animals require about the same proportions of nitrates and carbonates as man, under similar circumstances as to temperatures, &c., from twelve to eighteen per cent. of the one to sixty to eighty of the other. The microscopic analysis above referred to gives only about ten per cent. of the muscle-making elements and phosphates, while chemical analysis gives fourteen; but they are both correct, microscopic analysis recognizing only these elements as they exist in the outer shell of the grain, while chemical analysis recognizes them as mixed with the carbonates.

That superfine white flour bread does not contain all the elements necessary to keep the system in order, under any ordinary condition of life, is universally admitted by all who have given attention to the subject; and that there are objections to the usual manner of making bread, is also well known by all scientific men; and the question has become an important one, How shall wheat bread be made a reliable "staff of life," instead of the broken reed which it is now admitted to be?

Two New Plans of Bread-Making

Have been devised by scientific men, both of which have been quite extensively tried. One by Professor Horsford, of Cambridge, and the other by Mège Mouriès, of Paris.

The plan of Professor Horsford is explained in a little book published in 1861, and entitled "The Theory and Art of Bread-Making." It contains many valuable suggestions, and many important facts in regard to the sacrifice of indispensable elements in the process of grinding and bolting wheat, — the effects of fermentation, the difficulties of bread-making, &c., which, though not professing to be original, were some of them new to me, and from which I have derived great advantages in the preparation of this treatise, especially as they refer to the work of Mr. Hand, and other sources from which I could obtain important additional information. But the professor's "plan for bread-making" is open to very grave objections, and, involving as it does the life and health of those who adopt it, certainly demands a candid, but critical and faithful chemical and physiological consideration.

My first objection to the professor's plan is, that it does not attempt to restore the muscle-making elements of the flour, of which it is mostly deprived by the process of bolting, but leaves out these important parts as a sacrifice to a ridiculous caprice of the community — a whim, on account of which, flour deprived of its most important elements of nutrition, and those which give its most delicious relish, is preferred and universally used only because it is white, colored bread being unfashionable; and this idea appears the more absurd, when we consider that this same flour is frequently colored to make many common and fashionable articles of food, as gingerbread, rich cake, &c.

The first impulse of science would seem to be to teach us to use wheat, as every other gift of God, just as He made it, adding nothing to it, and taking nothing from it; and this, I propose in another place to show, is perfectly practicable.

Serious Objection to Professor Horsford's Plan for Bread-Making.

But my great objection to Professor Horsford's plan for bread making is, that, instead of recommending that the phosphatic elements usually taken out with the nitrogenous elements in bolting should be restored in Nature's own way, or rather that they should not be taken out at all, he attempts to restore them from his own laboratory, by phosphates chemically disorganized — a plan utterly at variance with Nature's laws, and therefore utterly impossible; and if it were simply a failure, the objection would be of less consequence; but, like all other attempts to thwart the purposes of God, the very effort is obnoxious to penalties.

God's plan, as clearly revealed in his book of nature, as I have elsewhere partly explained, is this: having, at infinite expense of time and labor, made the world for man,* and suppied the soil with every element which

* Writing after the manner of men.

the human system requires; and having ordained that the vegetable kingdom should be his great laboratory, in which these elements should be fitted for, and placed in harmony with the assimilating powers of the different organs, so that these elements should be gratefully received as they are wanted, to supply the requisite nutriment; God, in infinite wisdom, in order to protect the organs from all elements not thus organized in some vegetable, has made these very elements poisonous, so that they shall be rejected by the different organs at whose gate they shall call for admittance, and they are therefore made poisonous more or less according to their relative importance in the human economy.

Phosphorus, being the element on which the brain and nerves depend, and, therefore, the physical source of life itself, is, when not thus organized according to Nature's plan, the most virulent poison of any element found in the human system, indeed one of the most virulent poisons in nature; and it is susceptible of proof that the form of phosphorus which is recommended by the professor, in making his phosphatic bread, is not one of the mildest, but one of the strongest and most poisonous combinations.

Dr. J. Francis Churchill, of Paris, who has devoted more time than any one else to experiments on the different preparations of phosphorus, with a view to find the best form for the treatment of consumption, makes himself believe that while the combinations of phosphoric acid, the acid which Professor Horsford uses for his bread-making, is very poisonous — the combinations of phosphorous acid, which he (Dr. Churchill) recommends as medicine, being much milder, are perfectly innocent, if carefully used; but he has the candor to quote from Dr. Buckheim, a celebrated chemist, the following opinion from four other celebrated German chemists, in regard to his own milder form of phosphorus: —

"Woehler and Frenich, basing their opinion as much upon their own experiments as upon those of Weigel and Krug, have concluded that phosphorous acid has a poisonous effect analogous to arsenic, . . . and acts upon the economy exactly like phosphoric acid. . . . The same also holds good with the salts (phosphatic salts) of soda."

And this opinion completely covers the ground of the professor's phosphatic bread. On page 21, Professor Horsford says, "The phosphoric acid is prepared from the only practicable source of phosphorus — the bones of beef and mutton. They are boiled, then *calcined*." This burning of course disorganizes the bones, and the phosphorus is in the same condition as that used for matches, which we know to be very poisonous.

Now, if we apply to this case the law to which I have referred, that elements once disorganized can never be restored to their normal condition till they have been returned to the soil and reorganized in some plant, and, unless thus organized, can never be made to enter into the composition of any organ of the human system, we can understand how he deceives himself. Being an analytical chemist, and not a physiologist, and retaining the exploded notions of his old master, Liebig, he does not understand that chemical laws must always yield to vital laws, as all lower law must subserve the higher: the laws which control the elements of the earth must yield to the laws which control the life of man, for whom the earth was made.

If vital law had been understood as well as chemical law, he certainly would not have answered his own question, "Is bread made by the new method healthy?" by referring to articles of food in which the phosphates exist in an organized state, as in the following quotations from his book, page 23: "The French army was at one time supplied with soup-cakes, prepared from bones, with the aid of Papin's digester. The bones thus liquefied at an elevated temperature and pressure, supplied phosphates in quantity greatly beyond the normal wants of the soldiers' diet; but Nature appropriated such portions of the nutriment offered as she required, and the remainder was rejected." Does this prove that Professor Horsford's phosphates are wholesome? Then it also proves that nitric acid is wholesome: for nitrogen is known to be the basis of beefsteak as well as of nitric acid. It does, however, illustrate the dependence of chemical law on vital law.

Phosphatic salts in bones were organized there through the grass and the grain which the animal ate, which contain these elements; and the process of cooking or softening did not disorganize them. They were, therefore, ready in the soup, to be taken up and appropriated by the organs which needed these elements, and were wholesome; but the professor's phosphatic salts, made as they were from calcined bones, were of course disorganized, and, instead of being wholesome, are poisonous, just as the nitrogen in aqua-fortis, not being organized, is a poison; while the beefsteak, being composed of organized nitrogen, is eminently wholesome, although the elements of beefsteak and aqua-fortis are the same, and in not dissimilar proportions. "The advantages of the new method" of bread-making over those of the ordinary method of making it "light" with acids and alkalies mixed, or sour milk and saleratus, or tartaric acid and soda, are not to my mind obvious; while the disadvantages are in just the proportion as phosphoric acid is more poisonous than the acids in common use for that purpose.

Mège Mouriès' Plan of Bread-Making.

The other new method to which I referred — that of Mège Mouriès, now quite extensively adopted in Paris, — is not liable to the objections which have been made to Professor Horsford's plan. It neither leaves out of the flour any important elements, nor adds thereto anything injurious. It simply restores elements of the "groats and bran," as nearly as possible in their original proportions to the superfine flour out of which they have been taken; but the question to my mind is, why be at such trouble and expense to get out the bran, and then be at equal trouble and expense to get it back again?

All the object claimed to be gained by Mouriès' process is, that while it makes a ferment to raise the bread or make it light, it takes out the color of the bran, and leaves the bread white; but it also takes out the sweet natural taste of the unbolted wheat bread, and is also objectionable on the ground that the bran from mouldy and otherwise diseased wheat cannot be detected in detached bran as in unbolted flour. But thus to attempt to improve what God has made perfect, is too absurd, philosophically, to be worthy of any extended comments; and though less dangerous than the similar effort of his American contemporary, because not subject to the charge of attempting to smuggle into the system an actual poison, must still be placed in the same category, and help to show that "all human wisdom, to divine, is folly."

What advantages, then, has either the new French or new American method over the common method of bread-making by yeast?

Both make science subservient to "prejudice against color" of bread, and seem to think that, at any rate, bread must be white; while the one, to some extent, saves the evils of the loss of the muscle-making elements of wheat, and the other saves the evils of yeast, and substitutes an evil a thousand times worse than that of yeast; and while it has no advantages over the common substitutes for yeast, in the production of carbonic acid gas, as cream of tartar and soda, sour milk and saleratus, or any other mixture of acids and alkalies, is as much more injurious as phosphoric acid is more injurious than the acids in common use.

The object to be gained by using any of these materials for raising bread, is simply this: Flour, especially superfine flour, when wet becomes compact, or solid; and if thus cooked, as in some kinds of pastry, and thus eaten, will allow the juices of the stomach, which produce digestion, to have access only to the surface of the morsel, and of course must be slow of digestion; but if the particles of flour are separated from each other, as in light bread, the juices have access to every part, and the process of digestion is commenced in every part immediately.

To effect this object, some substance is intimately mixed, by kneading, so as to intervene between the particles, which, when heated in the oven, or by gentle heat beforehand, will be changed into gas, and thus separate the particles from each other; then, if the flour be sufficiently glutinous to hold the gas till the bread is baked, the particles remain separated, and the bread is light; but superfine flour is deprived of much of its gluten, and therefore is not sufficiently tenacious without the most scrupulous care to be well raised or to retain its lightness after standing. Unbolted wheat flour, having in it all its natural gluten, is much more easily managed, and indeed may be raised without the addition of any other than natural and useful elements, as we shall further explain.

In using yeast, two gases are produced by fermentation, carbonic acid and alcohol. These expand the flour and make it light, and though both are poisonous, they do no essential harm to the bread, because they are removed from it, or should be, before eating. The alcohol is all removed in baking, and the carbonic acid has such an affinity for oxygen that it unites with it on being exposed to the air, and if the bread is placed in the air, the pores will be filled with pure air instead of carbonic acid gas. Bread raised with yeast, therefore, is not unwholesome, unless eaten too soon after baking, while bread raised with phosphatic, or any other acid or alkaline salts, leave these foreign, unnatural elements in the bread after the carbonic acid gas is evolved. Yeast, however, consumes in fermentation a portion of the gluten and sugar of the flour, which, in superfine flour, are already greatly deficient; but this evil in unbolted wheat flour is of very little consequence. Unbolted flour bread, raised with yeast, loses perhaps six per cent. of its muscle-making element. Bolted flour bread, raised with phosphatic salts, has lost ninety-five per cent. of these elements.

What, then, is the True Method of making Bread?

My "ideal loaf" is made from wheat perfectly fair, and free from smut or other disease; not having been wet and moulded either before or after harvesting, and not having been heated before or after grinding; carefully kept clean after being properly ground so as to need no sifting, and, not being bolted, it retains every part that belongs to it, and needs no addition, except cold water and a little salt.

Such bread has been made light, and of course digestible, sweet and delicious to the taste, and, containing as it does in just the right proportion every element required by the human system, and being sufficiently porous to allow access to every part by the juices of the stomach, and containing in its cells neither carbonic acid gas, or in its substance any phosphorus, or soda, or potash, or other deleterious materials, is perfectly adapted to fulfil every requirement of nature, without, so far as I know for general use, a single drawback.

Such bread I have known placed on the table of a large, particular, not to say fastidious family, with the nicest and whitest family bread, and every member take it in preference. Light bread cannot be thus made from bolted flour for want of the natural gluten, and this is an additional evidence that "true bread" requires for its construction no additions to, or subtractions from, its natural elements; indeed, the conclusion is to my mind irresistible, that after such infinite pains in collecting in the soil, and making laws by which they should be collected in a single grain of wheat, all the elements in just the right proportions and combinations necessary to supply the wants of the human system, our heavenly Father would not leave this food so imperfect as to require either addition or subtraction in order to render it digestible.

Recipe for making Natural Bread.

Bread, light, sweet, delicious, and eminently wholesome, may be made by mixing good unbolted wheat meal with cold water, making a paste of proper consistence, which can only be determined by experiments, pouring or dropping it quickly into a heated pan, (that with concave departments is best,) and placing it quickly in a hot oven, and baking as quickly as possible without burning. The heat of the oven and pan suddenly coagulates the gluten of the outside, which retains the steam formed within, and each particle of water being interspersed with a particle of flour, and expanded into steam, separates the particles into cells, and being retained by the gluten, which is abundant in this natural flour, till it is cooked, the mass remains porous and digestible, and, containing no carbonic acid gas, is wholesome when eaten immediately, and of course equally so on becoming cold.

But for family bread, if not eaten till it has stood in pure air till the carbonic acid gas in the cells is exchanged for the oxygen of the air, there is no important objection to bread made from good unbolted wheat meal with fresh yeast. It contains all the elements necessary for feeding the muscles and brains, and for producing all the fat and animal heat required, and contains no materials essentially deleterious; and bread thus made from good superfine flour is only negatively deleterious, having lost its food for muscles and brains; and it need not, therefore, be discarded if at the same meal these elements are supplied in lean meat, fish, or cheese, or other food containing similar elements; but if eaten with butter or sugar only, and nothing else, would soon make of us bloated and stupid idiots.

Different kinds of superfine flour retain different proportions of food for brains and muscles, and all retain some. Indeed, bread could not be raised from flour absolutely deprived of gluten, which contains these elements.

Gluten absorbs water, and causes the paste to swell. That flour is therefore best which is most glutinous, and it is also most economical, as it will make the most bread. The proportion of gluten in wheat varies greatly according to cultivation and time of harvesting, and to the amount of nitrogen in the soil in which it grows. And by a beautiful provision of Nature, it varies also in a much greater degree according to the climate in which it grows, and this is true of all other grains. In northern climates, where more heat is required, a larger proportion of starch and other carbonates are found, so as to get with the requisite amount of food for muscle and brain more heat-producing elements.

Many hundreds of analyses have been made in Europe by different chemists with very remarkable results. In England and the more northern states the average amount of gluten in the best flour was but ten per cent., while some samples from Italian and Turkish wheat yielded as high as thirty-five per cent. of gluten. In this country, also, a similar difference, but not so great, has been observed between the nourishing qualities of flour from southern and northern wheat. Chemical analyses have not, so far as I know, been made to determine the comparative amount of gluten in southern and northern flour; but the comparison is made by a different process, and the difference between flour from Georgia wheat and that raised in Canada is at least twenty-five per cent.

The report of the Patent Office for 1848 states that Alabama flour yielded twenty per cent. more bread than flour from Cincinnati. Upon this principle the quality of flour may be tested in a tube graduated like a thermometer, only being large enough to hold an appreciable amount of dry flour, which, on being wet, will swell and rise in the tube in proportion to the amount of gluten contained in the sample used; or the experiment may be varied by noticing the degree of expansion under regular increments of heat. Upon the same principle housekeepers judge of the "strength" of flour, which is only another term for expressing the amount of gluten or strength-giving element, by noticing the height to which a given quantity will rise in a similar vessel in which it is being preparaed for baking; and when we consider that flour with the most gluten is not only twenty-five per cent. more economical than flour with the minimum of that important element, but is also sweeter and more digestible in the same proportion, it becomes a matter of great importance to be able to judge of its richness in gluten.

Another fact worthy of notice in this connection, and which may be made of some practical importance, is, that the gluten of southern wheat, or of any other southern grain, does not, to so great an extent as in northern wheat, reside in a crust around the surface of the grain, but is more enclosed in the starch in the centre — a provision of nature probably for the protection of the germ from inclement weather. This is shown in the plate, Figs. 3 and 4, in the drawing of corn. Superfine flour, therefore, made from southern wheat, is much richer in gluten than the same quality of flour from northern wheat, while the difference is much less between the unbolted flour from the different regions; and this I think accounts for the well-known fact that Italian maccaroni is much more nourishing than American.

Wheat is also made into very valuable food in the form of grits, or cracked wheat. In this form we get, in their natural state, all the elements of the human system; even the iron and silex are all there, which are sifted out of much of the unbolted flour in the outer or true bran. This bran is also the natural stimulant to keep the bowels in proper action, and, for the few exceptional cases in which it proves too irritating, the "cerealina," or grits, from wheat, deprived of its outer hull, is the very perfection of food. This new article has been lately introduced, and is used to some extent in Philadelphia.

Farina,

Also, as made by Hecker, is an excellent preparation, in which most of the elements of wheat are retained in a form very aeceptable to delicate stomachs. It is deprived of some of its gluten, but being made from the varieties of wheat which are richest in that element, is valuable, especially for those who find the grits too irritating.

Rye.

Next to wheat, especially for bread-making, rye is the best of the cereals. It is a favorite article of diet of the people of northern Europe, especially Russia, where it is called "black bread." It contains more of the heat-producing but less of the muscle and brain-feeding elements than wheat, as may be seen by comparing the following analysis with that of wheat :—

One hundred parts of rye contain

Water, . . .	13.00	or,	Water, . . .	13.00
Gluten, . . .	10.79		Muscle-feeders,	13.80
Albumen, . .	3.04		Heaters, . . .	71.5
Starch, . . .	51.14		Food for brains and bones, .	1.7
Gum, ...	5.31			
Sugar, ...	3.74			
Fat, ...	0.95			
Woody fibre, .	10.29			
Mineral matter,	1.7			

Containing more waste materials than wheat, it is more stimulating or laxative to the intestinal canal, and may therefore be useful in a constipated condition.

Maize. or Indian Corn.

Fig. 8.

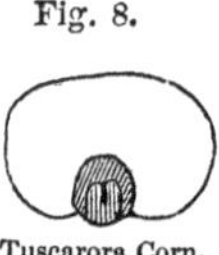

Tuscarora Corn.

Fig. 9.

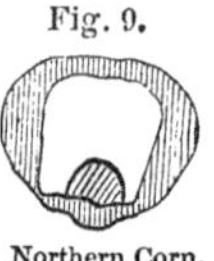

Northern Corn.

Fig. 10.

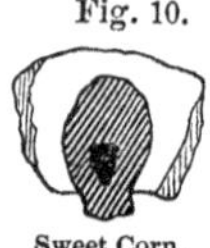

Sweet Corn.

Fig. 11.

Southern Corn.

This cereal is generally supposed to be a native of America; but having seen and planted a sample that was taken from folds that had enveloped a mummy for at least three thousand years, which sprouted and grew, and which produced the grain on a bundle of stalks like those of broom corn, or as if the seed-bearing stalks of the broom corn had been tied together and had adhered, as I have described in another chapter, I am of opinion, that, like the other cereals, it was cultivated from grass, at a period too remote to be traced to its origin, and that it came from the same species as broom-corn and sorghum. It contains less muscle-making materials and more heaters and fat-makers than wheat, and consequently is much used in fattening cattle and pigs, for which purpose it is better than any other grain.

Why this grain is better than wheat for fattening animals is seen by the fact that it contains more than six times as much oil. Starch, sugar, and fat are classed together as carbonates, or fat and heat-producers, but the effect of each is different from the other of these elements. Fat giving two and a half times as much heat as starch, there should be added at least sixteen, making the heaters eighty-nine.

The average composition of one hundred parts of Indian corn is about,—

Water,	14	or,	Water,	14
Gluten,	12		Muscle-makers,	12
Starch,	60		Heaters, Fat-producers,	73
Sugar, Gum,	3		Food for brains and bones,	1
Fat,	7			
Fibre,	5			
Mineral matter,	1			

Sugar and starch generally furnish the necessary heat, and have less tendency to be converted into fat, while the oils, as butter, the fat of meats, &c., are without much change deposited as fat. If sugar or starch alone are supplied, they will not only supply heat, but fat; but if oil be added, sugar and starch will supply the heat, and the oil the fat that is necessary, while on the other hand, if sugar and starch be deficient, and oil supplied, it will supply the heat as well as the fat of the system. Sugar and starch, and especially sugar, are supplied for keeping up the necessary animal heat in summer and the oils for winter.

Indian corn, especially northern corn, is excellent food for cold weather. Nature, however, provides that the corn of southern climates has less of the fat and heat-producing elements, as will be seen by reference to the plates, Figs. 2, 3, 9, 11.

Indian corn has too little gluten to make good light bread alone; but mixed with rye meal, which is very glutinous, the most wholesome and best of bread is made, which in many places in New England constitutes the staff of life to the laboring classes. Hominy, especially "large hominy," which is merely the grain cracked into two or three pieces, is excellent food, and if made from southern corn, as it generally is, contains a full share of muscle-making material, and is well adapted to laboring men; it also contains a large share of the life-giving principles, and is well adapted to sedentary and literary employments. "Small hominy," which is mostly used in New England, is generally made from flint corn, which contains less of the food for muscles and brains, and more of the heaters, and is therefore best in cold weather. Hulled corn also contains the elements of the corn, except those which reside in the hull; and being soaked in some alkali, the oil is removed, and it is therefore good summer food. Well washed from the alkali used to decorticate it, it is unobjectionable and wholesome to those who like it.

Buckwheat.

Fig. 12.

Buckwheat.

Buckwheat, or "brank," as it is called in England, is cultivated more for feeding fowls and birds in winter than for food for man. It is inferior to wheat in its nutritive elements, containing more heaters and not half the muscle and brain-feeders. Eaten alone, therefore, it is not much better than superfine flour; but with beefsteak or fish, to furnish requisite nutriment, it will serve to keep up the heat for a winter's day.

In one hundred parts of buckwheat are,—

Water, ...	14.2	or,	Water, ...	14.
Gluten, ...	8.6		Muscle-makers,	8.6
Starch, ...	50.0		Heaters, . . .	75.4
Gum, ...	2.0		Food for brains and bones, .	1.8
Sugar, ...	2.0			
Fat, ...	1.0			
Woody fiibre, .	20.0			
Mineral matter,	1.8			

Containing a large amount of woody fibre, which is waste, buckwheat is good for constipated habits.

Barley.

This cereal compares well with wheat in nutritive elements, but does not form light bread, and therefore is nowhere used for that purpose, but is in many places used for making barley-cakes, which are valuable for persons inclined to constipation, containing, as it does, more of waste, which is the natural stimulant of the bowels. Barley is peculiar also for the amount of phosphates which it contains,—more than twice the amount contained in wheat,—and therefore might be made useful to literary men of sedative habits, adapted, as it is, both to promote the action of the brain and bowels. For this purpose it would be useful and palatable in the form of cakes or porridge. Pearl barley, which is barley deprived of its outer coat, is also very valuable in sickness when vitality is low.

One hundred parts of barley contain, —

Water, ...	14.0	or,	Water, ...	14.0
Gluten, &c., .	14.8		Muscle-feeders,	15.0
Starch, ...	48.0		Heaters, . . .	69.5
Sugar, ...	3.8		Food for brains, &c.	4.2
Gum, ...	3.7			
Fat, ...	0.3			
Fibre, ...	13.2			
Mineral matter,	4.2			

The Oat.

This plant is found wild in the northern parts of Europe, and is the only cereal except rice that has been traced to its origin; all others having been so changed by cultivation as not to be recognized in their original seeds or plants. It flourishes in northern climates, and degenerates in warm. Unlike the wheat, its muscle-making materials are not connected with the hull, and are not therefore removed in making fine flour. Oat meal is rich in food for muscles and brains, and this may explain the fact that Scotchmen, who are raised principally on oat-meal porridge and oat-meal cakes, are remarkable for mental and physical activity. It is much used also in the northern counties of England, and furnishes the most material for hard work of any known grain. One hundred parts of oat contain,—

Water, ...	13.6	or,	Water, ...	13.6
Gluten and albumen, . . .	17.0		Material for muscles, . .	17.0
Starch, ...	39.7		Heaters, . . .	66.4
Sugar, ...	5.4		Food for brains, &c., ...	3.0
Gum, ...	3.0			
Fat, ...	5.7			
Fibre, ...	12.6			
Mineral matter,	3.0			

Some inferences of great practical importance may be drawn from these facts in regard to the adaptation of different grains for gruels, &c., in the different forms of disease, which will be more fully discussed in a chapter devoted to this subject. By comparing the above analysis with that of wheat, and that showing the loss of important elements in superfine flour, the following conclusions will be irresistible: Of heat-producing material, oat meal and unbolted wheat meal contain about the same; but in one pint of oat-meal gruel there is as much of muscle-making material as in five gills of unbolted meal gruel, and as in three quarts of fine flour gruel.

Rice.

Rice is the only cereal except oats that has been traced to its original plant. It is found wild on the borders of lakes of the East Indies, and is very extensively cultivated in marshy grounds in Asia, the southern parts of Europe, and in some of the southern states of America. It is more largely consumed by the inhabitants of the world than any other grain, wheat, perhaps, excepted; but it is poor in materials for the support of brain or muscle; and rice-eaters are everywhere an effeminate race. It contains, as will be seen by the following analysis, less than half the muscle-supporting elements of wheat, and only one quarter of the supporters of brain and nerve, and containing, as it does, a large amount of starch, can only support a life of indolence and feebleness.

One hundred parts of rice contain, —

Water, ...	13.5	or,	Water, ...	13.5
Gluten, ...	6.5		Muscle-feeders,	6.5
Starch, ...	74.1		Heaters, . . .	79.5
Sugar, ...	0.4		For brains and bones, . . .	0.5
Gum, ...	1.0			
Fat, ...	0.7			
Fibre, ...	3.3			
Mineral matter,	0.5			

Rice may be useful as a part of a meal, with beefsteak or vegetables that contain no starch; or, in some cases of sickness, when the stomach is weak, and when little is wanted of food but to keep the bellows of life blowing; but for mental or muscular strength it is the poorest article in the common lists of nutritive food; and this shows the worthlessness of "standard tables," as they are called, and as they are found in our physiological school-books and health journals, showing, as they profess to show, the amount of nutriment in different articles of food, — but making no distinction between nutriment which feeds the system and the fuel which really consumes the system. — See table of comparative "amount of nutriment," in Hall's Journal of Health, page 211, in which rice is said to contain eighty-eight per cent. of nutriment, while beans contain eighty-seven per cent.; whereas, by analysis, rice contains but seven per cent., while beans contain twenty-seven and one half per cent. of real nutriment. This table would indicate that, except in regard to ease of digestion, it would make very little difference whether we ate rice or beans; whereas one pound of beans would support life, in action, as long as four pounds of rice. This is only a specimen of articles in the "standard tables," and shows the importance of a new "standard" by which to judge of the nutritive value of articles of food.

Beans.

Having given an analysis of all the cereals in common use for food, let us now examine the leguminous seeds, or those produced in pods. These are all rich in nutritious materials; but their muscle-making element is not gluten, as in the grains, but casein, as in cheese — a substance not so easily digested as gluten, and therefore adapted to strong healthy persons with good powers of digestion.

One hundred parts of common field beans contain, —

Water, ...	14.8	or,	Water, ... 14.8
Casein, ...	24.0		Muscle-makers, 24.0
Starch, ...	36.0		Heaters, . . . 57.7
Sugar, ...	2.0		Food for brains and bones, . 3.5
Gum, ...	8.5		
Woody fibre, .	9.2		
Mineral matter,	3.5		

Two pounds of beans will therefore help do more muscular work than three pounds of wheat, and more brain work than three and one half pounds. But, as they contain less by twenty per cent. of their requisite amount of heaters, they are very appropriately eaten with fat pork, or some other heat-making food.

Different varieties of beans contain some different proportions of the same elements; but all are very nutritious. Beans are also eaten green, when the starch is not formed. In that state they are much less nutritious, and require with them butter or some other heat-giving material; but are useful food in warm weather, as are all green vegetables, with other more nutritious food.

Peas

Contain very nearly the same elements in the same proportions as beans. They are, however, more easily digested, and are too rich in true nutrition to be eaten alone, but require some less nutritive article, like potatoes, and also an addition of heat-givers, as butter, or the fat of animals.

In one hundred parts of peas are, —

Water, ...	14.0	or,	Water, ...	14.1
Casein, ...	23.4		Muscle-makers,	23.4
Starch, ...	37.0		Heaters, . . .	60.0
Sugar, ...	2.0		Food for brains and bones, .	2.5
Gum, ...	9.0			
Fat, ...	2.0			
Woody fibre, .	10.0			
Mineral matter,	2.5			

Peas also, when green, are excellent in warm weather, containing less starch and less casein, but more sugar than dried peas. They also require butter or other heaters.

Lentils.

Lentils also contain much casein, even more than peas. They are not much used for food, except at the East, where they are the favorite food in connection with rice; and they seem to be intended to supply the deficiencies of each other, rice containing too few and lentils too many muscle-making materials, in proportion to their carbonates, as will be seen by reference to their tables of analysis. Lentils contain, in one hundred parts, —

Water, ...	14.0	or,	Water, ...	14.0
Casein, ...	26.0		Muscle-feeders,	26.0
Starch, ...	35.0		Heaters, . . .	58.5
Sugar, ...	2.0		Food for brains and bones, .	1.5
Fat, ...	2.0			
Gum, ...	7.0			
Woody fibre, .	12.5			
Mineral matter,	1.5			

It will be seen that while rice contains but half its true proportion of muscle-making element, — 6.5 in 100, — lentils contain much more than their proportion, or 26 in 100. When used together, therefore, as is customary with the Hindoos, they give sufficient muscular power for such an inactive people. It will be seen, also, that both lentils and rice are deficient in food for brains; and this may likewise be a providential arrangement to adapt the proportion of food to the proportion of brain to be fed. This idea is perhaps corroborated by the fact that the higher classes in the East, who furnish brains for the lower, and do all their thinking, use food containing more of the phosphates, the little seeds of the huge grasses, of the sorghum species, called millet, which forms a large part of their food, being admirably adapted for that purpose, used in connection with rice. It is a curious fact, developed by scientific researches, that the smaller the seed in proportion to the plant of which it is the germ, the larger is the proportion of phosphates which it contains. Millet, being the small germ of the large plant sorghum, abounds in elements of food for the brain, the physical germ of human vitality.

A practical use may be made of this principle, especially with those who use much of fine flour, or butter, or sugar, in either of which is found only a trace of the phosphates, — remembering that in all our nourishment we need but two per cent. of phosphates. We can get sufficient of these elements to produce a sensible effect from the seeds of fruits and berries:

many of them, like those of the tomato, are digestible without crushing; others, like those of currants and most berries and apples, should be crushed with the teeth. The core of the apple should always be chewed, and the fibrous envelope rejected. The pits of all fruits and nuts are rich in phosphates; a small quantity are therefore useful as a dessert after a meal of too carbonaceous food.

Starch.

Of the three principal heat-giving principles of food, starch, sugar, and fat, starch is the most abundant and most important in all vegetable food. It constitutes, indeed, more than nine tenths of all the carbonaceous principles of our grains and leguminous seeds on which we mostly depend.

The ultimate elements are the same in starch, sugar, and fat, — carbon, oxygen, and hydrogen, — and their use in the system is not in building up the structure of the body or in repairing its waste, but is in fact the fuel which keeps up animal heat. This, however, is not a subordinate office, requiring, as it does, more than three fourths of all our food to accomplish it; and the adjustment of scientific principles, so as to keep the internal temperature of the body in summer and winter, in violent exercise or at rest, at just 98° Fahrenheit, is wonderful; and yet it is found that under no circumstances does it vary more than one or two degrees.

The most important principle in the production of

heat is starch, which is found in all vegetable food except the fruits.

It exists in irregularly shaped granules, varying in size from $\frac{1}{2000}$ to $\frac{1}{400}$ of an inch in diameter, in different species of plants, each plant furnishing its own peculiar granules. These granules are insoluble in cold water, but are readily diffused through it, so that by bruising or crushing the grain or potato that contains it, and washing in cold water, the starch is separated from the other principles, and, being of greater specific gravity than water, settles to the bottom of the vessel containing it, and may thus be obtained in greater or less amounts from all edible vegetables and grains. On being mixed with water of a temperature of 180°, starch becomes glutinous and loses its granular character, and in this state is much used in the arts to give firmness and inflexibility to fabrics of clothing, &c.

Starch is turned blue by iodine, and the extent of its presence in any grain can therefore be easily tested by carefully slicing and soaking the grain and applying a solution of iodine. From wheat and corn, &c., thus treated, the drawings were made for Figs. 2, 3, 4, &c. The nitrogenous and phosphatic principles may be delineated by other appropriate tests.

When starch is taken as an article of diet, its carbon is burned in the lungs in contact with the oxygen of the air, and gives out heat to warm the system, just as the carbon of wood, uniting with the oxygen of the air, gives out heat to warm our apartments; but before it is thus appropriated by the lungs, it must undergo a change in the process of digestion, so that it becomes sugar; and all starch is thus changed into sugar before it can be taken iuto the circulation to be used in the lungs or skin.

When starch and sugar, therefore, are taken into the stomach together, the sugar is first used for fuel; then the starch is converted into sugar, and used till the demand is supplied, and all that remains unchanged into sugar is cast from the system as waste, and if oil or fat of any kind be taken with sugar and starch, the fat will only be used for fuel when the sugar and starch have failed to supply the demand.

From this fact we may derive the important practical lesson of giving to the most feeble stomach sugar for fuel, and next starch, and depending on fatty substances only in the most robust, and in the cold weather, when, being more concentrated, it is useful.

Starch exists in a state of almost absolute purity in arrowroot, tapioca, and sago. These articles of food are therefore only useful by themselves when the muscles and brain are in a state of absolute rest, as in some cases of sickness. Potatoes, rice, and Tuscarora corn also contain so little nitrogen or phosphorus, that life can scarcely be sustained on them alone, but are very useful with lean meat, peas, beans, &c., which, being deficient in carbonates, need some such articles to supply the defficiency. The proportion of carbonates to the nitrates in potatoes, rice, or Tuscarora corn, is fourteen or fifteen to one; while in the standard article of food, — wheat, — it is only four to one. During the growth of plants sugar is first formed, so that in all green vegetables what little of carbonaceous food is obtained is in the form of sugar, which is converted into starch as the plant progresses, and when the grains, or leguminous seeds, are perfected, very little sugar is left, and starch is predominant; but in fruits, the sugar increases as they ripen, and, when perfectly matured, sugar is almost the only principle of nourishment.

Arrowroot

Is a form of starch obtained from the root stocks of plants. The most common source is the maranta, which is a native of tropical America and the West India islands. From these islands and Bermuda this country and England are principally supplied. Another species of the maranta is said to yield the East Indian arrowroot, and the French *tous-les-mois* is produced by another plant of the same order, which is a native of Peru, and is called *canna*. In China arrowroot is said to be obtained from the root of the water-lily.

Tapioca

Is starch from the mandioc plant, a native of South America. This plant contains prussic acid, and is very poisonous. The poison is, however, separated from the root, which, after preparation, yields cassava and tapioca. The cassava, being formed into cakes, is eaten mostly by the natives, while the granules of starch cells and tapioca are extensively used in Europe and this country for the same purposes as rice and arrowroot.

Sago

Is obtained from several plants, the most common being the sago-palm, which grows in the islands of the Indian Archipelago. The sago is obtained from the celular tissue or pith in the interior of the trunk of the tree, and some of these palms, being very large, yield sections of sago pith as large as the body of a man. A single tree, therefore, yields some hundreds of pounds of sago, and the preparation of it furnishes employment for a large part of the inhabitants of Java and the Philippine and Molucca Islands, which furnish it to all the world. In many places it is much used for the sick, it being erroneously understood to possess some peculiar virtues.

Moss and Sea-weeds.

The nutritive properties of these articles of diet consist mostly in starch, but are all too poor in any nutritive properties to be of much consequence, the gelatinous substance, on account of which it is mainly used in making blanc-mange, &c., being like the gelatine in fish and animal flesh, entirely indigestible, and only useful as waste to keep the bowels in order. The nice jellies made from calves' feet, or isinglass, or the mosses, are all destitute of nutriment.

Reindeer Moss.

Reindeer moss, however, must contain some nutritive qualities, as it seems to be a provision of nature to support the reindeer in a climate where almost nothing else grows.

In Iceland and Lapland, in spite of the extreme cold to which it is subjected, this lichen grows in great abundance, and during the winter season, which constitutes the most of the year, the reindeer has no other means of support, digging down for it with his nose through the deep snow; and some arctic navigators in their extremity have been obliged to resort to the same miserable diet, but only with temporary success, the gastronomic capacity of man being too limited to contain a quantity sufficient to sustain life but for a very limited period.

Irish Moss.

A sea-weed known under the names of carragheen moss, pearl moss, and Irish moss, grows on the rocky sea-shores of Europe, especially those of Ireland and the north of England and Scotland. It contains but little nutriment, but is used in England, and sometimes in this country, perhaps with advantage, with our too concentrated nourishment; but alone it can sustain life but for a short time. It is, however, resorted to by the poorer classes on the sea-shores of Ireland when the ordinary crops of corn and potatoes have failed, and for a time will keep them from actual starvation.

Several other sea-weeds are used in England and Scotland as gelatine, to thicken and flavor soups and ragouts, and other dishes of food; but in all there is a flavor of the sea which renders them objectionable and keeps them from general use.

Edible Bird's Nest.

In China, however, the people are very fond of sea-weeds, and many kinds are collected and added to soups, or are eaten alone with sauce. They also esteem the edible bird's nest a great luxury, making it an important article of commerce, and paying for it a great price, a large number of persons making it a trade, and doing nothing else from youth to old age but hunt for these nests in caves of rocks so difficult of access that none but adepts attempt it. They are the nests of a swallow, which are made from the gelatinous substance of sea-weeds, and are therefore valueless for nourishment, and would be almost tasteless but for the flavor imparted by the excretions of the families which have made them their home; but, having been thus occupied, they have a flavor which is relished exceedingly by the aristocracy of China, who alone can afford the expense of such a luxury.*

* Some enterprising south-shore Yankee might make his fortune by making a decoction of the gelatinous sea-weed with which he manures his land, and a decoction of old swallows' nests from the beams of his barn. Decanting, straining, and drying this decoction, he would get a *better article* than that made from Oriental nests, inasmuch as clay nests must retain more of the flavor which constitutes the value of this luxury.

Sugar.

Sugar and starch have very nearly the same chemical composition, but in some of their physical properties they are very different. Sugar is soluble in water, while starch is only diffusible through it. Sugar undergoes the process of fermentation, starch does not; sugar has a sweet taste, starch is almost tasteless. Starch, however, is convertible into sugar, and then assumes all the characteristics of other sugar, being capable of fermentation and of thus being converted into alcohol.

It is converted into sugar by the juices of the mouth and stomach, and this is the first process of digestion with starch. Sugar, therefore, is more quickly prepared to be absorbed into the blood, and better adapted as a heat-giver for the young, and in warm weather when the digestive organs are enfeebled. This is indicated in children by the almost universal love which they manifest for food containing it, and Nature furnishes it in the milk of all animals, and in the summer in fruits and berries and green vegetables, clearly indicating the importance and the appropriate use of sugar.

Sugar assumes three different forms in common articles of diet, which, though very nearly alike in chemical composition, have yet the same peculiarities. These are called cane sugar, grape sugar, and milk sugar.

They vary in composition as follows: —

	Carbon.	Hydrogen.	Oxygen.
Cane sugar,	12	10	10
Grape sugar,	12	12	12
Milk sugar,	11	12	12

They are all alike sweet and soluble in water; but the cane and milk sugars differ from the grape in that they do not ferment till they have first been converted into grape sugar.

Sugar is found in almost all plants at certain periods of their growth and development.

The Process of Malting. — Sugar is formed in the germination of seeds, as is well illustrated in the process called *malting*, which consists in placing the grain, generally barley, in a condition to favor its germination.

When in the process of growth the starch is converted into sugar, that process is arrested and the sugar is secured for the purpose of fermentation.

Alcohol.

All kinds of grain may be thus converted into malt, and used for making wine, beer, and distilled spirits; indeed, all grasses, and fruits, and vegetables, which contain sugar or starch, — and to just the extent of the sugar or starch, — can be converted into alcohol; but the process is one of decomposition, and therefore, according to principles already described, sugar and starch are then brought into a condition to be poisonous. The same elements and the same chemical combinations which in sugar are nourishing food, are in alcohol poisonous; and while the beers, and wines, and distilled spirits may afford nourishment on account of the sugar and starch, and other nutritive elements in them, and although the system may become so accustomed to the influence of the alcohol mixed in them as not to be in all cases, in their moderate use, positively or perceptibly injurious, still their habitual employment is useful or injurious in just the proportion as their carbon, hydrogen, and oxygen are organized as they came from the grain, or disorganized by fermentation.

Sugar in the Sap of Trees.

Sugar is circulated in the sap of trees and plants just before the unfolding of the buds; and in some species, as the birch and maple, is then found in such quantities as to be collected and manufactured in large quantities. The sap of the birch is collected in the spring in Scotland, and fermented, and thus birch wine is manufactured; and in the northern part of the New England States and New York sugar is annually manufactured from the sugar maple to the amount of hundreds of tons.

Vegetables and Fruits, and roots also, contain sugar, and can be fermented into intoxicating beverages; and from some, as the beet and mangel-wurzel, large quantities of sugar are manufactured, especially in France.

The Huge Grasses, as the sugar cane and sorghum, contain it, however, in the largest proportions, and are the principal sources of its supply. Treacle or molasses is that portion of the sugar which will not crystallize, and which is therefore separated by draining from the brown sugar before it is purified, and is not objectionable as carbonaceous nutriment.

Potato.

Of the class of edible roots and tubers, the *potato* stands at the head. It contains but little muscle-forming material, and a large proportion of starch, and is therefore well adapted to be eaten with lean meat, which consists chiefly of nitrogen, and has no digestible carbon.

Its native country is Chili, but it is also found wild in Mexico. Before being cultivated it is a gnarly, bulbous root, not considered edible. From this root grows a stalk, which blossoms and bears seeds. These seeds, being planted in a new soil, produce improved bulbs, which, being transplanted, improve from year to year, and form a distinctive character as to shape, color, &c., and receive a distinctive name by which the variety is known, as "kidneys," "reds," "blues," "whites," "pink-eyes," &c., each of which after a few years degenerates, and, going out of use, makes way for a new variety, produced in the same way; and thus, within the last three hundred years, it has been introduced into all Europe and America, and is an inestimable blessing to their teeming populations.

To this country especially, where every one eats meat, it is invaluable, — supplying, as it does, the elements wanting in that food, and waste material to counteract the influence of our too concentrated nutriment. It is also very valuable to the laboring classes of England, Ireland, and Scotland, used as it is with oat meal, beans, and peas, which supply the muscle-making elements in which it is deficient.

In one hundred parts of the potato are, —

Water and waste, . . .	78.2	or,	Water and waste, . . .	78.2
Albumen, &c.,	1.4		Muscle-makers,	1.4
Starch, ...	15.5		Heaters, . . .	22.5
Dextrine, . . .	0.4		Food for brains,	0.9
Sugar, ...	3.2			
Fat, ...	0.2			
Mineral matter,	0.9			

All the muscle and brain-feeding principle in the potato resides in the rose end, about the eyes or germ.

Sweet Potato.

The sweet potato is used mostly in tropical climates. It differs from the other potato but little, and that difference consists mainly in their relative amounts of sugar and mineral matters.

Water and waste, . .	68.50	or,	Water and waste, . .	68.50
Starch, . . .	16.05		Muscle-makers,	1.50
Sugar, ...	10.20		Heaters, . . .	28.05
Albumen, . .	1.50		Food for brains, &c., . . .	2.90
Fat, ...	0.30			
Fibre, ...	0.45			
Gum, &c., . .	1.10			
Mineral matter,	2.90			

Parsnips, Turnips, Carrots, Beets, Onions.

The different varieties of the roots above named are all, besides the potato, that to any extent are used in this country as food for man. So large a proportion of their bulk is made up of water and waste that the stomach of man is not sufficiently capacious to contain enough of either to support life and health alone; but for that reason they are valuable adjuncts to concentrated food, especially in warm weather, when but for these, and other similar vegetables and fruits, we should not get the bulk and waste necessary for proper digestion and intestinal action.

In one hundred parts are, —

In Parsnips.

Water and waste, ...	89.0
Muscle-makers, ...	1.2
Heaters, ...	7.0
Food for brains, &c., ...	1.0

In Turnips.

Water and waste, ...	94.0
Muscle-makers, ...	1.1
Heaters, ...	4.0
Food for brains, &c., ...	0.5

In Carrots.

Water and waste, ...	92.0
Muscle-feeders, ...	0.6
Heat-givers, ...	6.6
Brain-feeders, ...	1.0

Beets contain more sugar, and therefore more heating elements, than other vegetables, but contain the same proportions of nutrition and waste, while onions are still more nearly all water and waste.

Other green vegetable food, as cabbage, cauliflower, lettuce, cucumber, &c., and all the fruits and berries which are kindly furnished at the season in which they are most needed, are useful for the same reasons as stated above, and a choice in them can only be made by reference to the particular taste and power of digestion of each individual; that which relishes best is generally most easily digested. No one, therefore, can judge for another what is or is not wholesome.

Every article of food containing the elements of the system is wholesome if it can be eaten with a relish and be digested, and on the other hand, any article is unwholesome which contains elements not needed, and which cannot be relished or digested; and generally they are most desired when most needed, and will be digested if they can be eaten with a good natural relish.

The taste, unperverted, is a sentinel that admits no enemy and rejects no friend to the human system. It is folly, therefore, to dispute among ourselves, or to ask the doctor, whether this article or that is wholesome.

Having determined beforehand, as all intelligent providers easily may by reference to the simple principles herein explained, what class of elements is wanted to adapt the food to the circumstances of the family, they have only to select from the great variety of articles which God has given such as will be best relished, and, with very rare exceptions, nothing thus selected and properly cooked will ever prove indigestible or unwholesome, and these exceptions will only be found where the digestive organs are deranged by previous imprudence.

Animal Food.

The flesh of animals, fat and lean together, contains, as does a grain of wheat, every one of the fourteen elements of which the human system is composed, but not in the same proportions, or in the same proximate principles.

In one hundred parts of the carcass of an ox, of average fatness, are of food for brains, &c., about 4; for muscles and tissues, 15; for heat and fat, 30; water, 50. In wheat, for brains, &c., about 2; for muscles and tissues, average 14; for heat and fat 70; water, 14.

The muscle-making principles in wheat are gluten and albumen, while in beef they are fibrin and albumen; but each of these principles so perfectly agrees in chemical composition as to be considered mere modifications of the same substance, and being dried, contains precisely the same elements and in the same proportions.

The heat and fat-producing principles in wheat are sugar and starch, principally starch, with very little fat, while in beef it is fat only; and as fat produces two and a half times as much heat as sugar or starch, and beef contains more than three times as much water as wheat, the differences of the heat-giving powers of beef and wheat are much more nearly alike than would at first appear.

The five articles of animal food on which in this country we principally depend differ in their proportions of nutritive qualities, and are therefore adapted to different temperatures and different circumstances, as may be seen by the following condensed analysis of each.

In one hundred parts are, —

	Mineral matter, or food for brains, &c.	Fibrin and albumen, or food for muscles and tissues.	Fat, or food for heat.	Water.
Veal, ...	4.5	14.5	16.5	62.5
Beef, ...	5.0	15.0	30.0	50.0
Mutton, . .	3.5	12.5	40.0	44.0
Lamb, . . .	3.5	12.0	35.0	50.5
Pork, . . .	1.5	10.0	50.0	38.5

By this table it is seen that while veal contains but little more than an equal quantity of the principles that support muscle and heat, pork contains five times as much of the heaters as of the muscle-feeders. Of course pork is best adapted to food for cold weather, and veal for warm weather

Under ordinary circumstances we require four times as much of food for producing heat as for making muscle, that is, four times as much sugar or starch as albumen, fibrin, gluten, or casein; but one pound of fat contains an equivalent for two and a half pounds of sugar or starch, and therefore in animal food the carbonates, always being furnished in the form of fat, less than half the bulk of animal food is required than the best vegetable food. This, also, renders it necessary to take more animal food in winter than in summer; and hence the provision for animal heat in cold climates is the fat of animals, while in warm climates sugar is the principal provision, or sugar and starch as in fruits and vegetables.

But this table is formed on the supposition that we use an average of fat and lean meat; yet this is only true in the small meats, while in beef and pork we take very little, having an average mixture of fat and lean. In lean beefsteak we get almost all muscle-making principles, while in fat pork we get all heaters. With steak, therefore, we require some butter, or fat of pork, or some farinaceous vegetable food, as potatoes, rice, Indian corn, or wheat; while with fat pork, we require beans, peas, or lean meat, to furnish food for muscle; and if our labor or exposure to cold requires such concentrated nourishment, nothing can be more wholesome than beans and pork — the one containing heaters in the most concentrated form, and the other the most of muscle and life-giving principles of any vegetable food.

But what an absurd meal is that of beans and pork of a hot summer's day, especially of a Sabbath morning! and yet, from the landing of our Pilgrim fathers this has been the Sunday morning breakfast of a majority of New England people, and I have somewhere seen an estimate made by a quaint old divine, as a part of his sermon, of the number of tons of beans and pork preached to in New England every Sunday while the owners were asleep.

On the other hand, seeing the stupefying, and congesting, and heating, and blotch-making influence of these articles on sedentary people, some housekeepers condemn them as altogether and always unwholesome, especially pork, which is supposed to cause scrofula and all manner of diseases, and will not, under any circumstances, use it in the family. But why not use our reason, and consider what pork is, and what it was made for, and treat it as the creature of God, and therefore good, and not to be despised? The elements of the fat of pork and fat of beef, and all other meats, as also of butter, and the oil of corn and oils of the vegetables, are precisely the same, except the osmazome, which distinguishes the taste of each, and gives to one a relish for mutton and another for beef. All are wholesome or unwholesome as they are taken at the right time in the right proportion to other food, &c., and all unwholesome if taken without regard to circumstances.

"Fishes of the Sea."

"Everything wherein there is life," God gave to man "for meat even as the green herb," and of course we find in all these living things the same elements as in the products of the green herb.

An analysis of codfish and haddock gives the same elements, and in just about the same proportions, as lean beef and mutton, the only remarkable difference being in the amount of phosphates, which are much larger in the fish; but varying more in proportion in fishes than in mutton, and varying according to the habits of the fish in regard to muscular power.

Codfish, haddock, halibut, stand in relation to each other in regard to the three classes of elements — the nitrates, the carbonates, and the phosphates — as beef, mutton, and pork; halibut having less of the nitrates and phospates, and more of the carbonates, than codfish or haddock, as pork less of the former and more of the latter than beef and mutton. Fishes of the same species also have more or less of the carbonates, according to climate, being providentially adapted, as are the grains and the land animals, to supply the heat of man according to his necessities.

In regard to the nitrates and phosphates, a great difference is found in the different species, those which have the most muscular power having, of course, more of the nitrates, or muscle-making element, and those which have the most activity, the most of the phosphates, which not only furnish food for the brain, but for the nerves, and which give vitality and activity.

From a collection of facts, which I will now proceed to give, may, I think, be deduced an inference of great practical importance, both in regard to the selection of food adapted to different degrees of activity of mind and body in health, but also adapted to different degrees of vitality in sickness; and as this, so far as I know, is an application of science to dietetics not hitherto made, and as, indeed, no such effort has been made to apply the plain laws of Nature to the supply of the natural wants of the human system, as have been made by Johnston and others to apply them to the wants of vegetable, I propose to bring together facts, and show the principles upon which I deduce the corollary which I place at the head of the next chapter.

Mental as well as Physical Health, Strength, and Activity, can be regulated by, as it is to a great extent dependent on, Diet.

The vitality of plants, the muscular activity of all animals, and the mental as well as muscular and organic health and vigor of man, depend on phosphorus. These are legitimate inferences from facts, presented clearly, as you shall see, in the organization of plants, animals, and man.

In grains, and all seeds, the phosphates which give vitality, and furnish food for the brain and nerves, reside in the germ or "chit," while the fixed phosphates, which are devoted to bones, &c., are mixed with gluten in the crust under the hull, as seen in the plates of corn and wheat, Figs. 2, 3 &c.

That the phosphates are concentrated in the germ of all seeds, and that they vary in different seeds, is easily ascertained by chemical tests applied to the grain or seed, and the drawing of these plates above was suggested from experiments first made by Dr. Hayes, of

Boston, and first introduced by Dr. Jackson into his geological and mineralogical survey of New Hampshire, in colored plates, showing the extent of phosphates and other elements; but I have not been content without re-testing, and getting re-drawn, each specimen. The process is very simple, and the discovery of it very important, as I have elsewhere intimated. In this manner can be shown just the proportion of phosphates, nitrates, and carbonates each seed contains, and therefore which is best adapted to feed the muscle, and which to feed the brain, and give vitality, and which to furnish heat.

It is thus ascertained that some seeds and some grains contain two or three times as much phosphates as others. Wheat, for example, contains two per cent., while millet four per cent. Grass seed from six to seven per cent., and some, as clover and herdsgrass, from seven to nine. In all seeds, and roots, and nuts, which germinate from chits or eyes, the phosphates centre about these eyes, and what is not found there is always found connected with the muscle-making part of the grain or fruit, showing that the phosphates are connected with vitality and the life-giving principle.

The same thing is shown in animals by a test of their flesh, and by their manner of living. The flesh of quadrupeds, and birds, and fishes contain phosphorus in just the proportion to their natural activity, wild animals much more than domestic. The most active birds, like the pigeon and the migrating birds, much more than domestic fowls, and quiet and lazy birds. The migrating fishes, whose astonishing muscular power enables them to swim up rapids and over falls, contain more phosphates than the flounder and halibut, which are clumsy and comparatively dormant.

Insects abound in phosphorus in proportion to their activity and strength of muscle, and among them are the greatest gymnasts in the world. The leap of a flea is as great, in proportion to size of muscle, as if a man should jump over the Atlantic Ocean, from Boston to London; and a beetle, not weighing a scruple, will lift and move a junk bottle, with contents, weighing nearly a pound — a weight more than one hundred times as great, in proportion, as Dr. Windship could lift (and the beetle wears no yoke). Being wanted for scientific purposes, a beetle was placed, for safe keeping, under a bottle partly filled with liquid, in the inverted cup made in the bottom of the bottle. Immediately the plucky little insect was seen walking off with the bottle on his back, — as if the strong doctor, being shut up in his own office in the basement of Park Street Church, with a steeple two hundred feet high, should hoist the old thing, steeple and all, over into the cemetery.

Quadrupeds, Birds, and Insects instinctively select Food containing Phosphorus in Proportion to that of which they are composed, and in Proportion to their Activity.

The active bird lives on active insects or small seeds, which contain the most phosphorus, while the sluggish hen or robin is content with corn or worms, which contain much less of the life-giving element; and migratory birds, while they remain quiet, raising their young, live on worms and berries, but in the fall get a supply of strength for annual flight by eating seeds and active insects. The kingbird is the smartest little bird in New England, and gets his name from the fact that he governs all other birds, large and small, or drives them from his domain if they give him offence. Even the hawk, which is such a terror to other birds, seems to be a source of amusement to the kingbird. Many a time have I seen this little bird, not one tenth as large as the hawk, flying just over his back in the air, keeping out of his way by superior activity, occasionally pouncing on him, and giving him such annoyance that he was glad to leave the neighborhood to escape his little tormentor. A brace of these jolly and eccentric little kingbirds are just now affording infinite amusement to the denizens and visitors of Chester Square, in Boston. Having, according to the custom of other royal families, selected a beautiful city residence for a part of the year, and having built their nest, and the queen being engaged, *à la* Victoria, in matters pertaining to the perpetuation of royalty, the king is obliged to entertain visitors. This he does by pouncing on the backs of dogs and driving them from the square; diving at the bright buttons on the policemen's coats; knocking off tall, black, awkward stove-funnel hats, &c., &c. Looking out at my office window, which looks over an open lot to the square, the other day, I saw this kingbird pouncing with tremendous vigor into a thicket of shrubs, and soon came out a big cat, escaping, as for dear life, to the nearest shelter, with the little bird every moment striking at his back and head. This little kingbird lives on bees and hornets, — insects proverbial for their industry, strength, and persevering activity, — and on flies, whose activity keeps them up in the air for amusement, and the bird amuses himself in catching them.

The wild pigeon, which is said to fly more miles in a day than any other bird, chooses for his food, in preference to all other grain, the millet and barley, which contain three times the phosphorus of other grain, leaving all other grains untouched while these can be had. This, the boys in the country understand, and they take great pains to use barley millet or grass seed to decoy them to their nets; but the domestic pigeon, which is comparatively inactive, is content with corn, or the other grains containing much less phosphorus; and thus it is clearly established that active animals require food which contains more phosphorus than inactive animals, and the inference is conclusive that man also will have more or less activity of brain or muscle in proportion to the elements he takes to feed the brain and muscle.

In the preceding chapters we have seen that in the germ of life is found phosphorus in proportion to the future wants of the plant, and that the phosphorus is supplied by, and taken from, the soil as it is required. We have seen that quadrupeds and birds also depend on phosphorus for their muscular activity, and this element is supplied by the seeds of plants, and by insects and other animal food containing it.

We come now to consider that highest and most important order of vitality which is peculiar to man, and to see if the same element, although in a different combination, and the same law for applying it, does not pertain to that, as to the lower orders of vitality.

Of the solid matter of the brain, one twelfth, on an average, is found by chemical analysis to be phosphorus, and the proportion of phosphorus is found to be in proportion to mental development and mental activity. A celebrated French chemist has made many analyses of brains of children, idiots, and men of different degrees of intellect and mental activity, and the uniform results were, that the brains of those whose minds were most developed and active contained most phosphorus. I will transcribe one of his tables.

Composition of Brain and Nervous Substance.

	In Infants.	Youths.	Adults.	Aged.	Idiots.
Albumen,	7.00	10.20	9.40	8.65	8.40
Cerebral fat,	8.45	5.30	6.10	4.32	5.00
Phosphorus,	0.80	1.65	1.80	1.00	0.85
Osmazome and salts,	5.96	8.59	10.19	12.18	14.82
Water,	82.79	74.26	72.51	73.85	70.93
	100.00	100.00	100.00	100.00	100.00

By this table it is seen that the brain of infants and idiots contains less than half the average of that element in adults.

Another fact, established also by chemical analysis, which, with that above mentioned, proves to a demonstration that the action of the mind is dependent on phosphorus, and is subject to the same law of waste and supply as other faculties, is the following: Immediately after active mental labor the excretions exhibit a larger proportion of phosphates than at any other time, e. g., on Mondays and Tuesdays in clergymen, and at court times in lawyers. Experiments of this kind have gone to show that the amount of phosphates used up and excreted is in exact proportion to the intensity and continuance of the mental effort; and, at these times, observing clergymen and lawyers have told me their appetite calls for phosphatic food, as fish, cheese, unbolted wheat bread, oat meal, and barley cakes, &c., and some desire, and will have made for them, cakes of bran, which contain most of all the phosphorus of the grain from which it is taken.

Food for the Brain and Nerves.

That mental and nervous power is dependent on food, is an idea that may at first strike the mind as absurd, and unworthy of investigation; but the same process that proves muscles to be dependent for development, and vigor, and health on food containing nitrogen, proves the brain and nerves to be dependent for the development, and health, and the vigorous exercise of their functions on food containing phosphorus.

This subject, being somewhat new, and, as it seems to me, of vast importance, requires a little in detail the reasons for the belief that the same laws apply to the brain as to the muscular system, and that as the muscles can be trained, and their power developed by appropriate food as well as appropriate exercise, so that the brains of our children may be developed in the dining-room as well as in the school-room — the caterer and cook being important auxiliaries to the school-master.

All nature is governed by one comprehensive and perfect system of law. The law which controls the circulation of sap in one plant controls it in all other plants. The law by which the bones of one animal are so constructed as to adapt them to the conditions in which the animal is destined to live, is the law which governs the construction of the bones of all other animals, so that the naturalist will take a single bone of any animal which he has never seen, and from it will construct the animal from which it was taken, show his disposition, the arrangements of his digestive organs, his habits, and the kind of food on which he was accustomed to live.

To apply this general principle to the question under consideration, we find that wheat contains phosphorus, which it gets from the soil in which it grows, and which is necessary for its development. If the soil is deficient in phosphates the grain will be deficient in this element, and the proportions which it contains within certain limits are in exact accordance with those of the soil. Now the ultimate purpose of wheat and all its elements is evidently to supply these elements to the human system, and that a part of these elements are intended to give mental support, is proved, I think, by the fact, that the brain contains phosphorus in proportion to its activity or power of producing mental efforts, and that phosphorus is consumed and carried from the system in proportion to mental efforts, just as muscle contains nitrogenous elements in proportion to its size and power; and these elements are consumed, and must be supplied, in proportion to muscular exercise. That mental exercise does thus consume phosphorus, is proved, as I have elsewhere shown, by chemical analysis; proof of the above assertion is therefore complete. Let any man observe his feelings and mental capacity after a breakfast of white bread and butter, or griddle-cakes and sirup, or any other such carbonaceous articles of food, and I am sure he will find himself unable to perform the same mental labor as he can on a breakfast of beefsteak, or fish and potatoes, or unbolted bread and milk, or any other articles abounding in the phosphates. Brains can no more be made or worked without phosphorus than Egyptian bricks can be made without straw.

Why not, then, apply these plain laws to raising children, and cultivating their minds, as we do to the raising of wheat, and hens, and bees, and developing their properties and powers.

No man who understands his business would expect to raise wheat in soil in which is no nitrogen, lime, or phosphorus, or make hens profitable on food containing no lime for egg shells, or keep bees on a desolate island where no flowers could be found. Why, then, expect to develop brains on white bread, griddle-cakes, and doughnuts?

Precocious Children.

Many of the most promising children are sacrificed to a desire to bring them forward in advance of other children, and this desire is stimulated by natural instincts. Every living creature rejoices in the use of the faculties which God has given it, "as a strong man to run a race." The boy whose muscles are well developed will never keep still, but is ready for anything, good or bad, in which he can stir himself. To such a one study is a punishment.

But the boy whose muscles are feeble, and whose

brain is largely developed, sits still and reads, and the appetite of course conforms to the kind and amount of exercise. If he wastes his muscles by exercise, his appetite will demand the muscle-making nitrates to supply the waste. If he exhausts the phosphorus of the brain by study, he will desire phosphatic food to restore it. While the fat and stupid boy, who has neither muscles nor brain, will crave carbonaceous articles to feed his stupidity; and indulgence in these appetites will of course increase the peculiarity.

I have seen the plucky little kingbird, after an hour of extraordinary exertions in driving from the neighborhood an intruding hawk, devote the next hour to catching and eating bees and hornets, which are made up of nitrates and phosphates, as a means of restoring his muscular and vital energy; while the dormant robin would be content to live on cherries and worms, which contain very little food for either muscle or nerve. The bird is safe in following his inclinations; living as it does according to natural laws, and having no abnormal development of faculties, and no abnormal appetites, it can eat what it desires, and as much, with perfect impunity.

But the child, changed in its condition as it may be by the ignorance and folly of its parents, even before its birth, is abnormally developed, and of course has abnormal appetites.

Indulging these appetites in case of precocity of the brain, of course increases the excitement of the brain, and the result is inflammation and premature death;

and so common is this result, that it is well understood that a precocious child is short-lived. And is it inevitable that the fondest hopes of parents must always be blasted? A child with a precocious brain, or who is very forward, to use the common expression, is of course more liable to dangerous diseases of the brain than other children; but if parents would give the subject thought, and use their reason in this, as in other less important matters, these diseases might generally be warded off.

If our eyes have been overworked, or are weak and liable to inflammation, we avoid over-using them, especially in too strong light; and if so inflamed that the light, and all use of them gives pain, we shut out the light altogether, and give them rest till they recover. Both light and seeing are pleasant to the eyes in health, and absolutely necessary to give them health and strength, but when diseased, are both alike injurious, and we avoid the influence of both till they recover. And when only weak, and not absolutely diseased, we are careful to have the light, or use the eye only moderately and carefully. So of any other organ or faculty, that which is necessary to it in health, must be carefully used in tendency to disease, and abstained from in actual disease.

Apply this principle to a precocious brain. The brain is as dependent on appropriate exercise, and a supply of phosphorus in health, as is the eye on exercise and light; and as we withdraw the exercise and light from the eye in weakness and disease, so should we allow the brain to rest from exercise and phosphatic food in case of disease or predisposition to disease.

A child with a precocious brain would probably desire fish, lean meats, beans and peas, &c., in which phosphorus abounds; and while in health and perfectly developed, this desire would be an indication that these articles of food were good and necessary; but when the desire is the result of too great activity of the brain, it should be more or less scrupulously and perfectly resisted in proportion to the degree of precocity, and we should give instead cooling fruits and vegetables, with bread and milk, and other articles containing starch and sugar, to furnish the necessary heat, more or less, according to the temperature in which he lives, instead of fat, and oils, and butter, in which the carbonates are more concentrated and more stimulating.

Of the effects of diet mostly carbonaceous, we can judge from the testimony of Rev. Mr. Dall, missionary at Calcutta. In describing the character and habits of Asiatics, who live mostly on rice, an article containing, as you will see by the analysis, very little else than starch, and therefore very like our superfine flour, he says, "With the thermometer at one hundred degrees in the day time, and eighty-five to eighty-eight in the night, wakefulness is the exception and drowsing is the rule — the poor, old or young, who brings you a note from his 'master' (a word in which Asiatic reverence delights), no sooner delivers it than he flings himself on his back at full length, and is sound asleep in three quarters of a minute, so that it is hard to arouse him if you are five minutes penning your reply. This Indian faculty of literally dropping asleep used to make me smile; but I've got used to it. I now expect to see Bengal 'gentlemen' asleep in their carriages on their way to office, and less wealthy, as a matter of course, asleep in their palanquins. When the rajahs, &c., see English people dancing at the Government House, they ask, in wonder, 'Why not let your servants do this?' 'Eternal sleep is the bliss of God — and never be born again!' is Hindooism, is Buddhism, is Asianism, is the Oriental, as compared with our idea of religion."

That this stupidity is not induced entirely by the climate, is proved by the fact that the English never become so by a residence there, however long, and by the fact that other people who live on less carbonaceous food, in climates equally hot, are not thus inactive and sleepy; but it is the legitimate effect, as I have elsewhere explained, of living on food that has no nourishment for brain or muscle.

Precocity of Muscular Activity.

This is less dangerous, as the steam of vital force can be let off through the muscles till it is exhausted, without much danger, except to outsiders. Still the same law pertains to the muscles as to the brain, and, as a matter of convenience, at least to parents and schoolmasters, such boys should be limited in their supply of muscle-making materials, and might be indulged to a greater extent with the carbonates. Let them fill the stomach with crackers and milk, or vegetables and fat pork, and there would be no room for nitrogenous articles of food — or, at least, they could not be over-stimulated by them.

The daily Amount of Food necessary, and the Proportion of Nitrates and Carbonates.

Experience sustains fully the chemical and physiological deductions of the preceding chapters. Animals have been fed on pure starch, or sugar, or fat alone, and they gradually pined away and died; and the nitrates in all the fine flour bread which the animal can eat will not sustain life beyond fifty days; but others, fed on unbolted flour bread, would continue to thrive for an indefinite period. It is immaterial whether the general quantity of food be reduced too low, or whether either of the muscle-making or heat-producing principles be withdrawn while the other is fully supplied. In either case the effect will be the same. The animal will become weak, dwindle away, and die sooner or later, according to the deficiency; and if food is eaten which is deficient in either principle, the appetite will demand it in quantity till the deficient element is supplied. All the food, therefore, beyond the amount necessary to supply the principle that is not deficient, is not only wasted, but burdens the system with efforts to dispose of it. Food, therefore, containing the right proportion of heaters and muscle-makers is not only best, but most economical.

To make this statement plain, suppose we have a meal composed of roast beef, rare, with potatoes and dish gravy, and as much of unbolted wheat bread, or rye and Indian, and fruits, and cheese, and perhaps, if the beef be lean, or with green vegetables, butter or fat pork, to give them their heating principles. Of such a meal the appetite would be satisfied with just the amount of food necessary to supply either the heating or the muscle-making principles, and they would be taken in the right proportions.

But suppose, instead, we tried to satisfy the appetite with a meal composed of fried fat pork and potatoes, fine wheat bread and butter, griddle-cakes and sirup—articles almost entirely destitute of food for muscle or brain. When the stomach was filled with these articles, there would still be a demand for the nitrates or phosphates, and we should still crave some article to supply the deficiency, and all the carbonates above those which the system required would be wasted.

On the other hand, if we ate only lean meat, or fish, and green vegetables and fruits, which are deficient in carbonates, we should require a quantity of these articles in proportion to that deficiency, or the lungs would not be supplied with fuel sufficient to "run the machine." But in Boston, and probably in all American cities, a large part of the expenses of the table are for butter, superfine flour, and sugar, neither of which contains enough of the muscle or brain-feeding element to sustain life over fifty days, as has been proved by experiment with flour, while butter and sugar would not sustain life a single month without other food.

As far as we have articles of food deficient in carbonates, we can use, without loss, butter or sugar to supply the deficiency; but most of our natural food, both animal and vegetable, contains a due proportion, and if with them we use butter or sugar, they cannot be appropriated by the system, and are therefore lost.

All meats, fat and lean together, all grains and milk, contain all the carbonates that are needed or can be used to furnish heat in moderate weather. All the butter or sugar, therefore, that is added to either of these common articles of food, as they are used in making cakes, custards, pies, &c., are not only lost, but by adding too much fuel, increase the tendency to inflammations, embarrass the stomach, and induce dyspepsia, congestions, obstructions, &c.

With beefsteak, or any lean meats, or fish, or potatoes, or any green vegetables, or dried beans or peas, some oily substance seems to be needed, as all these articles are deficient in carbon, and in common use we have the choice between lard, sweet oil, or butter, or perhaps fat pork, all of which are precisely alike in chemical construction, and that one is most wholesome which is best relished.

Sugar also is needed with the acid fruits and berries, and especially with apples, which in New England are the most valuable of all fruits, either with or without cooking, and which, with sugar, furnish excellent food, especially in winter and spring, when other fruit cannot be had. But to find a good use for superfine flour, out of which has been taken nine tenths of its food for muscle or brains, is exceedingly difficult, indeed, impossible in health; and it can only be useful in disease where the irritability of the stomach or bowels forbids the use of their natural stimulant, just as inflammation of the eye makes it necessary to exclude the light.

Experiments on Prisoners as to the Amount of Food needed.

The best test of the influence of kind and quantity of food in sustaining life and health can be made in prisons, where the habits are all alike, and where the test can be made on a large scale. In five prisons in Scotland experiments were made to ascertain the smallest amount of food, and the proportions of nitrates and carbonates, that would keep the prisoner up to his weight while doing nothing, with results as shown in the following table: —

	Muscle-making Food. Nitrates.	Heat-producing Food. Carbonates.	Total Food given each Day.
Edinburgh,	4. oz.	13. oz.	17. oz.
Glasgow,	4.06	12.58	16.84
Aberdeen,	3.98	13.03	17.67
Stirling,	4.27	13.04	17.67
Dundee,	2.75	14.	16.75

Percentage of Prisoners who lost or gained Weight.

Edinburgh.—18 lost 1½ lbs. each; 82 held their own or gained weight.

Glasgow.—33 lost 4 lbs. each; 67 held their own or gained weight.

Aberdeen.—34 lost 4 lbs. 2 oz. each; 66 held their own or gained weight.

Stirling.—34 lost 4 lbs. 2 oz. each; 66 held their own or gained weight.

Dundee.—50 lost 4 lbs. 5 oz. each; 50 held their own or gained weight.

The above is the result of observations for a term of imprisonment for two months.

The Effect on Prisoners of substituting Molasses for Milk.

It is a remarkable fact, which shows the importance of connecting science with practice, that the deterioration in the quality of the diet in Dundee prison consisted in substituting molasses for milk, which had been previously used with oat-meal porridge and oat-meal cakes, molasses being entirely destitute of muscle-making material, while milk contains a full proportion of these important principles. This one experiment, and its results, are worthy of study by every mother and every housekeeper in the land. If any class of persons would suffer less than others from the use of too much carbonaceous and too little nitrogenous food, it would be that class who are idle; and yet the one hundred prisoners of Dundee, with one ounce a day more of the fat and heat-making principle than those of Edinburgh, lost two hundred and seventeen and one half pounds, while the same number in Edinburgh lost only twenty-seven pounds; the difference in their diet being, as stated in the report, that the prisoners of Edinburgh had milk with their porridge and cakes, while those of Dundee had molasses instead.

If the same experiment had been tried on men in active life, or on children, who are never still except when asleep, the results would have been more remarkable, in proportion to the greater waste of muscle in those who are active, and the greater demand for nitrogenous food; and yet how few mothers stop to consider, or take pains to know, whether gingerbread, made of fine flour, which has but a trace of food for muscle or brain, and sugar or molasses, and perhaps butter, which have none, or cakes made with unbolted wheat, mixed with milk or buttermilk, all of which abound in muscle and brain-feeding materials, is the best food for a growing, active child; indeed, the whole food of the child is given with the same want of knowledge or consideration.

But, in view of these simple experiments in the Scotch prisons, who can doubt that a want of consideration of these principles of diet is the means of consigning to the tomb many of our most promising children. An intelligent farmer knows how to feed his land, his horses, his cattle, and his pigs; but not how to feed his children. He knows that fine flour is not good for pigs, and he gives them the whole of the grain, or perhaps takes out the bran and coarser part, which contains food for muscles and brains, and gives them to his pigs, while the fine flour, which contains neither food for brain or muscle, he gives to his children. He separates also the milk, and gives his pigs the skim-milk and buttermilk, in which are found all the elements for muscle and brain, and gives his children the butter, which only heats them and makes them inactive, without furnishing a particle of the nutriment which they need.

The Amount and Proportion of Muscle-making and Heat-producing Elements of Food in Active Employments.

We see by the preceding table that prisoners, without exercise, could not be sustained with an amount of food short of four ounces nitrogenous food and thirteen ounces carbonaceous; all short of that amount being insufficient to supply the waste, and the remainder was drawn from the body itself, constantly diminishing in its weight; and that, whether the diminution was in the nitrates or carbonates.

To supply four ounces nitrogen and thirteen ounces carbon in the most concentrated food, requires of—

	Weight.	Nitrates.	Carbonates.
Lean beefsteak, ...	4 oz.	1 oz.	0 oz.
Fat pork, or fat of beef, or any meat, ...	2	0	2
Unbolted wheat bread, . . .	8	1	5
Beans or peas, ...	8	2	4
Butter, ...	2	0	2
$1\frac{1}{2}$ lbs., or	24 oz.	4 oz.	13 oz.
With active exercise, . . .	48	8	26 *
Active exercise in winter, .	58	10	31 †

Food thus concentrated would be adapted only to the most active employment in the coldest weather. Let us, therefore, make another bill of fare, in which we shall get the thirteen ounces carbonates and four ounces nitrates in a form adapted to warm weather.

	Weight.	Nitrates.	Carbonates.
Codfish, ...	4 oz.	1 oz.	0 oz.
Potatoes, ...	1 lb.	$\frac{1}{3}$ oz.	3 oz.
Wheat bread, . . .	$\frac{3}{4}$ lb.	$1\frac{1}{4}$ oz.	8 oz.
Green vegetables and fruits, ...	1 lb.	$\frac{1}{4}$ oz.	0 oz. 30 grs.
Milk, ...	1 lb.	$\frac{3}{4}$ oz.	$\frac{1}{2}$ oz.
Sugar, ...	$\frac{1}{2}$ oz.	0	$\frac{1}{2}$ oz.
Butter, ...	1 oz.	0	1 oz.
	$5\frac{1}{2}$ lbs.	4 oz.	13 oz.

* In moderate weather the waste is double.

† In New England one fifth more in winter than in summer.

This bill would be extremely diluted, as the first is extremely concentrated; but both together will show how greatly our food can be varied in quantity to get the same amount of nourishment. And with the following tables, with a little study, would enable a housekeeper to adapt the amount and variety of food to be provided to the number and circumstances of her family.

Average amount Nutriment in One Pound of Wheat.

		oz.	gr.
Water,		2 oz.	215 gr.
Gluten,	Nitrates.	2	0
Albumen,		0	146
Starch,	Carbonates.	9	215
Sugar,		1	0
Fat,		0	52
Fibre,	Waste.	0	104
Gum,		0	104
Mineral matter,	Phosphates.	0	108

Amount of Nutriment in One Pound of Rye.

		oz.	gr.
Water,		2 oz.	35 gr.
Gluten,	Nitrates.	1	318
Albumen,		0	213
Starch,	Carbonates.	8	79
Sugar,		0	262
Fat,		0	66
Gum,	Waste.	0	371
Woody fibre,		1	284
Mineral matter,	Phosphates.	0	122

The average Amount of Nutriment in One Pound of Northern Corn (Maize).

Water, ...		2 oz.	105 gr.
Gluten, ...	Nitrate.	1	402
Starch, ...	Carbonates.	9	262
Sugar, ...	Carbonates.	0	21
Fat,*	Carbonates.	1	101
Woody fibre, . .	Waste.	0	350
Mineral matter, .	Phosphates.	0	70

The average Amount of Nutriment in One Pound of Southern Corn.

Water, ...		3 oz.	0 gr.
Gluten, ...	Nitrate.	4	215
Starch, ...	Carbonates.	3	218
Sugar, ...	Carbonates.	0	200
Fat, ...	Carbonates.	0	20
Woody fibre, . .	Waste.	1	21
Gum, ...	Waste.	0	200
Mineral matter, .	Phosphates.	0	250

* Or oil, two and one half times more fattening than starch or sugar.

The Amount of Nutriment in One Pound of Barley.

		oz.	gr.
Water, ...		2 oz.	215 gr.
Gluten, ...	Nitrates.	2	110
Albumen, ...	Nitrates.	0	100
Starch, ...	Carbonates.	7	215
Sugar, ...	Carbonates.	0	215
Fat, ...	Carbonates.	0	30
Mineral matter, .	Phosphates.	0	215

Average Amount Nutriment in One Pound Oat Meal.

		oz.	gr.
Water, ...		2 oz.	100 gr.
Gluten, ...	Nitrates.	2	0
Albumen, ...	Nitrates.	0	350
Sugar, ...	Carbonates.	0	360
Starch, ...	Carbonates.	0	100
Fat, ...	Carbonates.	0	360
Mineral Matter, .	Phosphates.	0	200

The Amount of Nutriment in One Pound of Beans.

		oz.	gr.
Water, ...		2 oz.	161 gr.
Casein, ...	Nitrates.	3	368
Starch, ...	Carbonates.	5	333
Sugar, ...	Carbonates.	0	140
Fat, ...	Carbonates.	0	140
Woody fibre, . .	Waste.	1	206
Gum, ...	Waste.	1	157
Mineral matter, .	Phosphates.	0	245

The Amount of Nutriment in One Pound of Peas.

		oz.	gr.
Water, ...		2 oz.	112 gr.
Casein, ...	Nitrates.	3	324
Starch, ...	Carbonates.	5	403
Sugar, ...	Carbonates.	0	140
Fat, ...	Carbonates.	0	140
Woody fibre, . .	Waste.	1	263
Gum, ...	Waste.	1	193
Mineral matter, .	Phosphates.	0	175

Amount of Nutriment in One Pound of Buckwheat.

		oz.	gr.
Water, ...		2 oz.	118 gr.
Gluten, ...	Nitrates.	1	165
Starch, ...	Carbonates.	8	0
Sugar, ...	Carbonates.	0	140
Fat, ...	Carbonates.	0	70
Gum, ...	Waste.	0	140
Fibre, ...	Waste.	0	126
Mineral matter, .	Phosphates.	0	126

The Amount of Nutriment in One Pound of Rice.

Water, ...		2 oz.	26 gr.
Gluten, ...	Nitrates.	1	0
Starch, ...	Carbonates.	11	360
Sugar, ...	Carbonates.	0	370
Fat, ...	Carbonates.	0	30
Gum, ...	Waste.	0	40
Fibre, ...	Waste.	0	215
Mineral matter, .		0	20

Amount of Nutriment in One Pound of Potatoes.

Water, ...		12 oz.	0 gr.
Starch, ...	Carbonates.	2	205
Sugar, ...	Carbonates.	0	215
Fat, ...	Carbonates.	0	2
Albumen, ...	Nitrates.	0	142
Woody fibre, . .	Waste.	0	354
Gum, . . , . . .	Waste.	0	20
Mineral matter, .	Phosphates.	0	354

Amount Nutriment in One Pound of Sweet Potatoes.

		Ounces.	Grains.
Water, ...		10	340
Starch, ...	Carbonates.	2	249
Sugar, ...	Carbonates.	1	277
Fat, ...	Carbonates.	0	18
Albumen, ...	Nitrates.	0	105
Fibre, . , . . .	Waste.	0	35
Gum, ...	Waste.	0	77
Mineral matter, .	Phosphates.	0	210

Amount of Nutriment in One Pound of Parsnips.

		Ounces.	Grains.
Water, ...		13	53
Albumen, ...	Nitrates.	0	87
Sugar, ...	Carbonates.	0	210
Starch, ...	Carbonates.	0	245
Fat, ...	Carbonates.	0	35
Fibre, ...	Waste.	1	123
Gum, ...	Waste.	0	52
Mineral matter, .	Phosphates.	0	70

The Amount of Nutriment in One Pound of Turnips.

		Ounces.	Grains.
Water, ...		14	213
Albumen, &c., .	Nitrates.	0	77
Sugar, ...	Carbonates.	0	28
Gum, ...	Waste.	0	107
Fibre, ...	Waste.	0	168
Mineral matter, .	Phosphates.	0	35

Amount of Nutriment in One Pound of Carrots.

Water, ...		14	6
Albumen, ...	Nitrates.	0	42
Sugar, ...	Carbonates.	1	11
Fat, ...	Carbonates.	0	14
Gum, ...	Waste.	0	70
Fibre, ...	Waste.	0	231
Mineral matter, .	Phosphates.	0	70

Amount of Nutriment in One Pound of Cow's Milk.

Water, ...		13	533
Casein, ...	Nitrates,	0	350
Butter, ...	Carbonates.	0	245
Sugar, ...	Carbonates.	0	215
Mineral matter, .	Phosphates.	0	70

Amount of Nutriment in One Pound of Human Milk.

		Ounces.	Grains.
Water, ...		14	41
Casein, ...	Nitrates.	0	210
Butter, ...	Carbonates.	0	210
Sugar, ...	Carbonates.	0	300
Mineral matter,	Phosphates.	0	35

Amount of Nutriment in One Pound of Goat's Milk.

		Ounces.	Grains.
Water, ...		10	0
Casein, ...	Nitrates.	0	325
Butter, ...	Carbonates.	0	230
Sugar, ...	Carbonates.	0	280
Mineral matter, .	Phosphates.	0	70

The casein and phosphates are in larger proportions in the milk of the cow and goat than in human milk, to adapt them to the different conditions of their young. The calf and the kid, being active from their birth, require the nitrates for feeding the muscles, and the phosphates for vital power, at first; while the child, being dormant and helpless, requires less of these principles; and therefore, to substitute the milk of the cow or goat for food for the child, about one third water is required, and a little sugar — a little more for cow's than goat's milk, — but the difference between the milk of the cow and that of the goat is too little to make it an object to be at much trouble for the choice. The proportions vary in different cows, and therefore it is important, in raising children on cow's milk, to get the milk that suits, and then use the same cow's milk constantly.

The Four Principal Meats, of average Fatness, compared with Vegetable Food.

The Amount of Nutriment in One Pound of Beef of average Fatness.

		Ounces.	Grains.	
Water, . . .		8	0	
Fibrin and Albumen,	Nitrates.	1	122	Equal to same am't casein, gluten, or albumen — 1 oz. 122 grs.
Fat, ...	Carbonates.	4	340	Equal to 2½ times as much sugar or starch, or 11 oz. 75 grs.
Mineral, . .	Phosphates.	0	350	
Gelatine, . .	Waste.	1	122	

The Amount of Nutriment in One Pound of Veal.

		Ounces.	Grains.	
Water, . . .		10	9	
Fibrin and Albumen,	Nitrates.	1	199	
Fat, ...	Carbonates.	2	281	Equal to 2½ times as much sugar or starch — 6 oz. 265 grs.
Mineral, . .	Phosphates.	0	312	
Gelatine, . .	Waste.	1	82	

The Amount of Nutriment in One Pound of Mutton.

		Ounces.	Grains.	
Water, . . .		7	16	
Fibrin and Albumen,	Nitrates.	0	385	
Fat, ...	Carbonates.	6	176	Equal to 2½ times as much sugar or starch — 16 oz., or 1 lb.
Gelatine, . .	Waste.	1	52	
Mineral, . .	Phosphates.	0	241	

The Amount of Nutriment in One Pound of Pork.

		Ounces.	Grains.	
Water, . . .		6	69	
Fibrin and Albumen,	Nitrates.	0	315	
Fat, ...	Carbonates.	8	0	Equal to 2½ times as much sugar or starch — 20 oz., or 1¼ lbs.
Gelatine, . .	Waste.	0	315	
Mineral, . .	Phosphates.	0	312	

Rations for the English Soldier.—The amount and proportion of carbonates and nitrates necessary to keep the English soldier in a fighting condition, are found to be five ounces of nitrates to twenty ounces carbonates; and this amount is therefore daily furnished, both in England and in India, and the English colonies; and the English sailor has the same allowance.

Rations of the Dutch Soldier. — When in war, it is five ounces of nitrates and twenty-one ounces carbonates; but when in peace, or in garrison, it is only three and one half ounces nitrates and twenty ounces carbonates; but with this diet he is below fighting condition.

Rations of the French Soldier. — The diet of the French soldier is very different from that of the English or Dutch, they using much more of liquid food; still the proportion or amount of nitrates and carbonates is not very dissimilar. He gets about four and three fourths ounces nitrates and twenty-four ounces carbonates, and on this is always kept in a fighting condition — probably wasting three or four ounces of the carbonates.

English Soldiers in the Chelsea Hospital have their nitrates reduced to three or four ounces, but their carbonates remain the same; as also the sailor in the Greenwich Hospital; but, having no exercise, they need less carbonates as well as less nitrates, it being known that the demand for both nitrates and carbonates is equally increased or diminished in proportion to the amount of exercise.

Rations of Greenwich Pensioners. — They have three and one half ounces nitrates and twenty ounces carbonates.

Rations of Chelsea Pensioners. — They have four and one half ounces nitrates and twenty and one fourth ounces carbonates.

Rations of Old Men of Gillespie's Hospital, Edinburgh. — They have three ounces nitrates and twenty ounces carbonates.

Rations of Paupers. — In all the workhouses of England, Scotland, and Ireland, the average is daily three and one half ounces nitrates and sixteen and one half ounces carbonates.

Rations of Boys of Ten Years old. — In the English schools two and one half ounces nitrates and fifteen ounces carbonates are allowed daily.

Rations of Boys in Christ's Hospital in London. — Only two and one half ounces nitrates and fourteen ounces carbonates are allowed; but the average age is not stated.

Massachusetts State Prison. Average Number of Prisoners, 545. *Food consumed in one Week:* —

		Pounds.	Each man. lbs.	oz.	Carbonates. lbs.	oz.	Nitrates. oz.
Flour,	13 bbls. . .	2600	5	0	4	2	6
Meal,	60 bush. . .	3000	5	8	3	8	8
Beans,	9 " . .	576	1	0	0	8	5
Peas,	3 " . .	192	0	5	0	$3\frac{1}{2}$	$1\frac{3}{4}$
Rice,	$4\frac{1}{2}$ " . .	306	1	8	0	7	$0\frac{1}{8}$
Potatoes,	100 " . .	6000	10	0	2	8	$0\frac{1}{8}$
Fresh beef, ...		925	1	8	0	7	3
Fish (fresh and salt), .		1100	2	0	0	10	4
Fat pork, ...		525	1	0	1	0	0
Hard bread, ...		40	0	1	0	1	$0\frac{1}{8}$
Lard, ...		60	0	2	0	2	0
			28	00	13	$08\frac{1}{2}$	$29\frac{1}{8}$

Each man consumes in one day thirty ounces carbonates and four and one fourth ounces nitrates.

By comparing the above bill of fare with the standard already given, it will be seen that the muscle-making elements are three fourths of an ounce below the standard, while the carbonates are at least one third too high. It should be considered that living in a moderate and uniform temperature, and using only moderate muscular exercise, neither nitrates nor carbonates need be above the average, — probably not more than twenty ounces of carbonates are consumed: all the remainder is cast off as waste; and not being the natural waste, tends to derange the stomach and bowels, and clog and render dormant the whole system. The prisoners may be fat, and may look healthy, and indeed may be, and should be, with their regular habits, healthy, and the bill of mortality be much below the average; but they cannot have much muscular or mental energy.

By changing the first two articles on the bill, a saving of more than one hundred dollars would be made in a week, and a bill be made giving them more agreeable food, and giving them more of the nitrates and phosphates, and therefore more energy of mind and muscle. Half the amount of unbolted wheat flour, made from good wheat, would give more than the same amount of nitrates, with about one pound less of carbonates, and the bread would be equally satisfactory; and then half the amount of Southern corn (thirty bushels) meal, made from the variety of corn represented by Fig. 3, would give more nitrates and more phosphates than is obtained from sixty bushels of Northern corn, and the bread would be lighter and better, — which would also reduce the amount of carbonates perhaps one pound more. And the bill might be still further improved by substituting for the four and one half bushels of rice as many bushels of peas, which would add an ounce to the nitrates and subtract another pound from the carbonates, as may be seen by the analysis.

The Bill of Fare of Chinese Passengers from China to California.

		Carbonates.	Nitrates.
Rice, . . .	1½ lbs.	17 oz.	1½ oz.
Beef or fish, .	½ lb.	1½ oz.	¼ oz.
Salted vegetables,	½ lb.	1 oz.	0 oz. 87 gr.
Tea, ...	½ oz.		
Water, . . .	3 qts.		
		19½ oz.	2 oz. 87 gr.

Having a full supply of carbonates, and only half the amount of nitrates necessary for active life, probably they sleep most of the time.

American Army Rations.

		Carbonates.	Nitrates.
Pork or bacon, .	¾ lb. if all fat,	12 oz.	0 oz.
Fresh or salt beef,	1¼ lb. average fatness,	7 oz.	2 oz.
Bread or flour, .	1 lb. 8 oz. or	1 lb. 6 oz.	2 oz.
Hard bread, . .	12 oz.	11 oz.	1 oz.
Corn bread, . .	4 oz.	1 oz.	¼ oz.

8 qts. of beans in one hundred rations; or, in lieu,
10 lbs. rice twice a week; or, in lieu,
150 oz. dried potatoes and 100 oz. dried vegetables;
1 lb. tea, 15 lbs. sugar.

These rations are very unscientifically made up. If I understand the bill, a man may have three fourths of a pound of fat pork and twelve ounces of hard bread on the same day, and nothing else, and get twenty-three ounces of carbonates and only one ounce of nitrates; or he may have one pound and one fourth of fresh beef and one pound and one half of flour bread, and get twenty-nine ounces of carbonates and four ounces of nitrates; or he may have the same quantity of fat pork, which contains no nitrates, and bacon, which, if of average fatness, would give a good share of nitrates. It is evident that in any combination the rations give too large a proportion of carbonates to beget activity and energy, and a large amount of flour or hard bread must be wasted. A great improvement would be made by leaving out three fourths of the flour and all of the rice, and giving instead Southern corn bread or hominy and beans and peas. This would give much more muscle power, and would save a large amount of expense.

The great dietetic fault of the nation lies in eating too much carbonaceous food, especially with that part of the people who have followed old English habits. Probably the Massachusetts state prisoners live more nearly in accordance with physiological laws than any five hundred men outside; but we see that they waste one third of their food in superfluous carbonates.

By all the bills of fare for soldiers and prisoners, and all other tables by which it could be ascertained how much of muscle-making nutriment is required under different circumstances, it is seen that men in sedentary life, in this country or Europe, are not content with less than four ounces of the nitrogenous elements of food, and, in considerable degree of activity, they demand, and will have, five ounces; and in the same way it is ascertained that from four to five times as much of the carbonates are required as of the nitrates. If food is set before us containing these proportions of elements, we shall eat only just enough to furnish the system with the elements required; but if we have before us food containing ten times as much of the carbonates as of the nitrates, we should then eat twice as much of the carbonates as are required, in order to satisfy the demands of the appetite for the necessary supply of nitrates. We will demonstrate this proposition.

To get muscle-making food in right proportions, take natural food —

	Carbonates.	Nitrates.
1 lb. milk, . . .	0 oz. 245 gr.	0 oz. 350 gr.
1 lb. beef, roasted, .	4 oz. 340 gr.	1 oz. 122 gr.
1 lb. potatoes, . .	3 oz.	145 gr.
1 lb. unbolted bread, .	10 oz. 165 gr.	2 oz. 110 gr.
1 lb. apples, . . .	3 oz.	145 gr.
	21 oz. 313 gr.	4 oz. 335 gr.

To get muscle-making food in unnatural proportions,

take food in common use, some of which is in a natural state, others not: —

	Carbonates.	Nitrates.
1 lb. roasted beef, .	4 oz. 340 gr.	1 oz. 122 gr.
1 lb. milk, . . .	245 gr.	350 gr.
2 lbs. superfine bread,	22 oz.	370 gr.
¼ lb. butter, ...	4 oz.	0 gr.
¼ lb. sugar, . . .	4 oz.	0 gr.
1 lb. potatoes, . .	3 oz.	145 gr.
1 lb. apples, . . .	3 oz.	145 gr.
	41 oz. 143 gr.	3 oz. 258 gr.

In this bill one half the carbonates must be wasted.

Of the first bill, you may take of either of the articles as much as you please without varying the proportions of carbonates and nitrates, and consequently are in no danger of wasting food or embarrassing the system by eating too much, the appetite being satisfied when the requisite amount of nitrates is supplied; or you may vary the amount of different articles, taking more of one and less of the other, without varying the proportions of the nitrates, and therefore still eat all the appetite demands. For example, suppose, instead of a pint of milk and a pound of bread in a day, you take double the amount of milk and one and one half pounds of bread, you would then get four ounces and four hundred and twenty-eight grains of nitrates, — almost the requisite amount, from bread and milk alone; indeed, for a warm day, at rest, the amount of nitrates and carbonates would both be too large; or, with one half or one fourth of the beef, you would take more of the other articles in proportion, and could thus safely trust your appetite to the full extent of its demands without harm.

But with the last bill of fare, you must take double the quantity to get the requisite amount of muscle-making and brain-feeding nutriment, and consequently one half of all the food taken would be lost. All the sugar and butter, and more than half of the flour, would be thrown from the system as waste, and not only lost, but by giving extra and unnatural work for the excretories, embarrass their functions and render them liable to disease; while the presence of these heating articles renders every organ more liable to inflammation and disease, and the efforts of the stomach and bowels to dispose of these offensive materials, together with the fermentation of these undigested elements, would cause flatulence, acidity, dyspepsia, and the thousand and one pains, inflammations, liver and bowel complaints, which are liable to attack us, especially in warm weather, when the system is not as well able to resist these influences.

When we consider how many families, especially among the poor, live very nearly on the same kind of food summer and winter, eating in warm weather butter, fat pork, superfine flour, lard, &c., is it strange that in the height of the warm season we have bowel and liver complaints, gastric and typhoid fevers, dysenteries, dyspepsias, &c.? I think that, considering the articles wasted are among the most expensive, I am sustained in the assertion that more than one half of the expense of food in Boston, to say nothing of all the diseases, would be saved by adapting our food to the wants of the system, and that we should enjoy life, and especially the pleasures of eating, as we never can while living in disregard of Nature's laws.

Analysis of Articles of Food in a Dry State.

Articles.	Nitrates.	Carbonates.	Phosphates.	Waste.	
Wheat, ...	16.00	81	2.0	3.4	Wheat is the best grain for bread, in unbolted meal. In fine flour, only useful when the stomach and bowels are in an irritable state, as in diarrhœa, cholera morbus, &c.
Barley, ...	17.50	80	4.0	16.9	Barley is excellent for students, as it abounds in food for the brain, and in waste to keep the bowels active.
Oats, ...	19.75	77	3.5	15.6	Oats are good for active men, either with muscle or brain.
Northern corn,	14.00	85	1.3	5.0	Northern corn is fattening, containing as it does more than five times as much oil as is found in wheat.
Southern corn,	40.00	52	4.9	8.0	Hominy from southern corn is excellent food in warm weather, abounding in food for muscle and brain, and having few carbonates.

Articles.	Nitrates.	Carbonates.	Phosphates.	Waste.	
Tuscarora corn,	6.00	93	1.3	2.0	Tuscarora corn is used mostly for making starch.
Buckwheat, .	10.00	78	2.3	3.0	Buckwheat is useful only for a ride in the cold, having few nitrates for the muscles.
Rye, ...	15.5	80	2.0	15.6	Rye is excellent for persons inclined to constipation, and with corn meal makes good bread, nourishing and digestible.
Beans, ...	27.6	66	4.1	17.7	Beans and peas, containing double the amount of nitrates and phosphates, and treble of waste necessary, are appropriately used with pork or butter to supply the carbonates, &c.; and being hard of digestion, are excellent for active people whose stomachs are strong. If eaten too heartily the waste gives pain.
Peas, ...	27.00	70	3.0	19.0	
Lentils, . . .	30.00	68	17.0	19.5	Lentils and rice grow together naturally, and are evidently intended to supply each other's deficiencies. Neither, alone, would be capable of sus taining life, but for opposite reasons; the one containing double, the other one half the nitrates necessary.
Rice, ...	7.5	92	0.6	4.3	
Cheese,* about	65.	19	7.		

* Cheese has more than twice the amount of nutriment of any other known substance. It must therefore be used in small quantities, and with such articles as fruits, or fine flour, which contain little nitrogen. It is hard of digestion, but almost any one who is in good health can learn the stomach to digest it by taking very little at a time early in the day.

Articles.	Nitrates.	Carbonates.	Phosphates.	Waste.	
Potatoes, . . .	5.6	88	3.0	3.0	These and all other green vegetables and fruits, contain all the requisite elements of nourishment, but with such an amount of water and waste, that the capacity of the human stomach is insufficient to contain the necessary supply, while animal food is too concentrated to give the necessary distention and waste; but eaten together they each supply the deficiency of the other class of food.
Sweet potatoes,	4.00	80	8.8	1.5	
Parsnips, . . .	6.7	39	5.5	9.1	
Carrots, . . .	4.8	28	8.0	4.3	
Turnips, . . .	10.00	40	5.0	4.0	
Veal, ...	42.00	100	12.0	7.5	Fat being the source of supply of carbon in animal food, and supplying as it does two and one half times as much heat as sugar or starch, the true amount is obtained in this table by multiplying the figures of the next table by 2½ * While therefore beef is reported to have twice as much carbon as nitrogen, it actually has five times as much. For this reason, animal food is too concentrated, and having also too much phosphorus, requires vegetable food to dilute and modify it.
Beef, ...	30.00	150	10.0	7.0	
Lamb, ...	22.00	170	7.5	7.0	
Mutton, . . .	19.00	150	5.3	7.0	
Pork, ...	15.00	212	2.4	5.0	

* See page 124.

Analysis of Articles of Food in their Natural State.

Articles.	Nitrates.	Carbonates	Phosphates.	Water.
Wheat, ...	15.0	69.8	1.6	14.0
Barley, ...	17.0	69.5	3.5	14.0
Oats, ...	17.0	66.4	3.0	13.6
Northern corn, or maize,	12.0	73.0	1.0	14.0
Southern corn, . . .	35.0	45.0	4.0	14.0
Tuscarora corn, . . .	5.0	80.0	1.0	14.0
Buckwheat, ...	8.6	75.4	1.8	14.2
Rye, ...	13.8	71.5	1.7	13.0
Beans, ...	24.0	57.7	3.5	14.8
Peas, ...	23.4	60.0	2.5	14.1
Lentils, ...	26.6	58.5	1.5	14.0
Rice, ...	6.5	79.5	0.5	13.5
Potatoes, ...	1.4	22.5	0.9	75.2
Sweet potatoes, . . .	1.5	26.5	2.9	67.5
Parsnips, ...	1.2	7.0	1.0	82.0
Turnips, ...	1.1	4.0	0.5	90.5
Carrots, ...	0.6	6.6	1.0	87.5
Cabbage, ...	4.0	5.0	1.0	90.0
Cauliflower, ...	6.4	3.6	1.0	90.0
Cucumbers, ...	1.5	1.0	0.5	97.0
Apples, ...	5.0	10.0	1.0	84.0
Milk of cow, ...	5.0	8.0	1.0	86.0
Human milk, . . .	3.0	7.0	0.5	89.5
Veal, ...	16.0	16.5	4.5	62.5
Beef, ...	15.0	30.0	5.0	50.0
Lamb, ...	11.0	35.0	3.5	50.5
Mutton, ...	12.5	40.0	3.5	44.0
Pork, ...	10.0	50.0	1.5	38.5

Articles.	Nitrates.	Carbonates.	Phosphates.	Water.
Chicken, ...	20	35	$4\frac{1}{2}$	73
Codfish, ...	14	very little	5 or 6	79
Haddock, ...	13	very little	5 or 6	82
Sole, ...	15	very little	5 or 6	79
Plaice, ...	14	very little	5 or 6	80
Flounder, ...	15	some fat	3 or 4	78
Turbot, ...	14	very little	5 or 6	79
Trout, ...	17	very little	5 or 6	75
Whiting, ...	15	very little	5 or 6	78
Smelt, ...	17	very little	5 or 6	75
Salmon, ...	20	some fat	6 or 7	74
Eels, ...	17	some fat	3 or 4	75
Herring, ...	18	some fat	4 or 5	75
Halibut, ...	18	some fat	3 or 4	74
Oyster, ...	10	very little	2 or 3	87
Clam, ...	12	very little	2 or 3	–
Lobster, ...	14	very little	5 or 6	79
Eggs, white of, .	$15\frac{1}{2}$	none	$4\frac{1}{2}$	80
Eggs, yolk of, . .	$17\frac{1}{2}$	$28\frac{3}{4}$	$5\frac{1}{2}$	54
Butter, ...	. all	carbonates	–	–

Fishes.

Of the fishes, there has not yet been made analyses sufficiently accurate to make a reliable table. The nitrates of common white fish, like cod and haddock, are in about the same proportion as in beef and mutton, and of the phosphates rather more; while the more active fish, as the trout, pickerel, shad, &c., contain more nitrates and phosphates in proportion to their activity.

The amount of carbonates depends on the amount

of fat; the gelatinous principle, although containing carbon, is not digestible, and therefore furnishes no carbonaceous food; the nitrates consist mostly of albumen, which is easily digested, but furnish less muscular power than fibrine of red-blooded meats.

Fishes, therefore, afford better food for students and sedentary men than for those who work hard.

Except the fatty fishes, most of them require to be cooked with lard, fat pork, or butter, and to be eaten with potatoes, or some farinaceous food, to furnish the requisite carbonates. There is a class of fishes, however, like the salmon, halibut, &c., which are quite well supplied with the carbonates; they are easily digested, or not, as they contain more or less fat; and the cod, haddock, trout, shad, &c., are excellent food, if relished, for invalids, convalescents, &c.; while the fatty fishes and the preserved fishes are more suitable for those who take active exercise in the open air, and have better powers of digestion.

Preserved Fish. — Various methods are devised for keeping fish, as pickling in salt, drying, smoking, &c. Pickled fish are objectionable, having lost most of their nutritive element and their soluble phosphates. The brine in which fish as well as beef has been pickled has been analyzed, and found to contain most of the albumen and the phosphates which are adapted to give vigor to the brain and nervous system; but not the fibrine, which makes muscles, or the phosphates, which make bones. Fish, therefore, which has been in brine, is suitable for laboring men, but not for sedentary persons, or those who use their brains.

"Every moving thing that liveth shall be meat for you."

This promise was made to man on the basis of immutable law. In every living thing, life and power to move is found to depend on the same elements, — phosphorus and nitrogen, — and of course every living thing is capable of imparting life and power to move to every other living thing which has digestive powers by which to appropriate these elements; and, as has before been intimated, this power of imparting life and muscular power in any article of food is in proportion to the phosphorus and nitrogen contained in it. On the other hand, "every moving thing that liveth" contains these elements in proportion to its own vital activity and muscular power, so that we need not analyze every living thing in order to know its dietetic value. This principle is not only established by chemical analysis, but by observation on the habits of animals, and the experience of every man. (See page 84, 85.)

Who has not experienced the difference of power and activity of mind and muscle produced by different kinds of food? For example, by a dinner from the muscles of an ox, that have been developed by hard work, and one from the muscles of a dormant hog? Indeed, the difference is perceptible between the used and the unused muscles of the same creature.

The breast of the chicken or turkey, which is made up of the unused muscles of the wings, is white, dry, and comparatively insipid, containing but little phosphatic or nitrogenous food, while the muscles which move the legs are dark, juicy, rich in flavor, and contain a very much larger proportion of the life-giving and muscle-making elements. On the other hand, the breasts of the birds which live on the wing are rich in these elements, and their thighs and side bones are covered with poor, dry meat. This principle holds good in relation to all animal food, from quadrupeds, fishes, fowls, and reptiles; and it may be useful in assisting to determine the comparative value of different articles, and in adapting them to our circumstances.

A full understanding of this principle in the community will relieve the doctor from that inevitable question, which meets him wherever he goes. In the sick room or at the dinner table, in the horse cars or at the social circle, wherever he is, somebody bores him with the question, Doctor, is pork wholesome? Are potatoes wholesome? &c., &c.; questions which can be answered yes or no, or both yes and no, with equal propriety, unless, with the answer, he goes into a disquisition on the peculiar properties of each, and the circumstances which make them wholesome at one time and hurtful at another.

A rattlesnake, all but the head, would make a delicious and wholesome meal to a man who was starving, and could get nothing else, while the most delicate woodcock would be poison to a man prostrated with typhoid fever. That abstract question, then, so often asked (is this or that kind of food wholesome), is only consummate nonsense.

"Every moving thing that liveth," and "every herb bearing seed which is upon the face of the earth," is wholesome under some circumstances, and unwholesome under other circumstances.

Of Reptiles.

Crustacea and mollusks, and indeed "every creeping thing," either from necessity or choice, in some part of the world, is eaten by man; but in this country and in England only a few species are used.

Turtle.

Of reptiles, the turtle only is eaten, unless under this title we class eels. The green turtle is brought from the West India Islands and the Bahamas. It as seldom crawls on the land as the eel, and, indeed, has no feet, having in the place of them little paddles, with which it swims with great swiftness; and being very muscular and active, its flesh is very nitrogenous and phosphatic, and not being fat, is an excellent article of food taken fresh from its native element. I have eaten it cooked in four different ways—fried, broiled, fricasseed, and in soup, and found it a palatable and highly nutritious article of food. In this country it is seldom used except in soup. It is very different in its taste, and far inferior in its nutritive qualities, after being kept out of water, on its back, in the cruel manner in which it is kept on the passage. Fresh from the water, some parts of the turtle resemble the flesh of the chicken, other parts have a fishy taste, other parts are albuminous, like the white of an egg, and all parts seem to be nutritious.

Crustacea.

Many of the species of this class are esculent, and some are excellent food. In this country and England are used the common lobster, the thorny lobster or sea crawfish, the river crawfish, the large edible black-clawed crab, the common or small edible crab, the prawn, and the shrimp. They have all the same characteristics. Being active in their habits, and having powerful muscles, their flesh abounds in nitrates and phosphates, but is rather hard and compact, and therefore requires good powers of digestion, and they are adapted for food to active, healthy persons *to assist in* the labor of the day, but they are most miserably misapplied to evening entertainments in the form of salads. The lobster is the most valuable of this class of food, and is much the most extensively used.

Molluscous Animals.

In this country the only species of this class used as food to any extent are clams and oysters; and in England, besides the oyster, the mussel, the cockle, the scallop, the periwinkle, the limpet, and the whelk. But the oyster holds the highest rank in this class of food, and is used among all classes, forming a branch of trade very extensive and important.

This class of animals differs from the crustacea in this, that while the crustacea have powerful and active muscles, the mollusks have almost no muscles at all, having no motion except the opening and shutting of the bivalves, and a slight contractile power by which they imbibe their food. Of course they have not as food the muscle-making elements of the crustacea or other active fish; and although their chemical composition indicates phosphatic salts, they are mostly salts of lime, which go to form the shell and to make bone rather than afford food for the brain and nervous system. Oysters, therefore, are very unsatisfactory food for laboring men, but will do for the sedentary, and for a supper to sleep on. They contain but twelve and one half per cent. of solid matter, including fibrin, albumen, gelatine, mucus, and osmazome, and much of that is gelatine, which affords no nourishment, while butchers' meat contains on an average twenty-five per cent., and the poorest fishes contain fourteen per cent. of pure nitrates.

The nitrates in oysters are in the form of albumen, like the white of the egg; they are therefore more easily digested in a raw state than when cooked, but stewed are not indigestible, and for feeble persons and convalescents are better stewed than raw, as in this state they are relished with less stimulating condiments.

To oysters, as to all shell-fish, and indeed to all kinds of fish, there is the serious objection that great care must be used to avoid eating them after the slightest decomposition has commenced, otherwise they may occasion serious disturbance of the digestive organs, and even in some cases terrible and fatal diseases. There is also occasionally a very serious poisonous effect from fish perfectly fresh and apparently healthy, in which chemistry can detect nothing deleterious. I have known but few cases of the kind in Boston, and they were occasioned by eating mackerel; but in the Bahama Islands I saw a man, who, fifteen years before, ate a meal from a fish called there blue fish, though very different from the blue fish of New England coast, which in two hours brought on excruciating internal distress, with painful eruption of the skin, and these turns of awful distress had occurred occasionally ever afterwards, entirely unfitting him for any kind of business, and making his life a burden.

Not one in a hundred of these fishes is poisonous, but no man has sagacity sufficient to detect the good from the bad; and therefore the inhabitants eat none of these fishes till they submit them to a curious test. They place a piece of fish in the way of a species of ant which is common there: if the ant eats it, they eat it with impunity; if the ant rejects it, they of course do not eat it; — an example which gives force to the idea of Pope, —

> "Reason raise o'er instinct as you can;
> In this 'tis God directs — in that 'tis man."

Classification of Food in common use.

1st Class. — That in which the proportion of heat-producing elements is too large for the common wants of the system, and which alone would sustain life only for a time, shorter or longer in proportion to the amount of other elements which they contain. Lard, butter, sugar, or any animal fats being capable of sustaining life, without other food, only from twenty to thirty days; and superfine flour, being mostly composed of starch, has been proved by experiment on animals to be capable of sustaining life, without other food, only from fifty to sixty days. These are the Carbonates, described in another chapter.

2d Class. — That in which the muscle-making elements are too large in proportion to their carbonates. Some of these articles would be capable of sustaining life only for a limited period without articles of the first class to keep up the steam. These are the Nitrates, described before.

3d Class. — That in which the proportion of elements which support the brain and nerves, and give vital energy both of mind and muscle, is too large for the common duties of life. These are the Phosphates.

4th Class. — That in which there is too much waste material in proportion to nutritive principles, and which, therefore, if eaten alone, produces diarrhœa and debility, but which, taken with other more nutritive food, subserves the important purpose of giving distention, and keeping the bowels in action, and the system free and cool, by preventing a surplus of stimulating food.

The representative articles of these four classes are as follows:—

1st Class. Carbonates.	2d Class. Nitrates.	3d Class. Phosphates.	4th Class. Waste.
Butter and lard.	Lean meats.	Shell fishes.	Green vegetables.
Fat of all meats.	Cheese.	Lean meats.	Fruits, berries, &c.
Vegetable oils.	Peas and beans.	Peas and beans.	
Fine flour, &c.	Lean fishes, &c.	Active fishes, birds, &c.	

Under ordinary circumstances, in moderate weather, with moderate exercise of muscle and brain, the proper proportions of carbonates, nitrates, and phosphates seem to be the average proportions found in unbolted wheat meal, viz.: Sixty-five of the carbonates to fifteen of the nitrates, and two of the phosphates to seventeen or eighteen of water and waste,—or something more than four times as much of the carbonates as of the nitrates, and two per cent. of the phosphates, the amount of water not being of much consequence, as it is supplied as it is demanded, and taken as drink when it is not supplied in the food.

A consideration of this classification will help us to understand and correct many important errors in diet.

Every observing person has noticed that after a meal in which the predominant articles were chiefly composed of fat meat, fine flour, butter or sugar, he is stupid, or sleepy, and indisposed to exercise either mind or muscle; and the reason is plain: as very little food for either brain or muscle is found in either of the articles named, and this torpor will be found to be in exact proportion to the excess of these carbonates over their proper proportion. And this is the inevitable consequence of separating the important principles which God has joined together, and furnished in every article of appropriate food, in the right proportions, as nourishment for every faculty.

If the fat meat had been eaten as it was made, mixed with an appropriate amount of lean, and instead of the flour, the bread had been made of meal from the whole wheat as it was created, and milk had been substituted for the butter, and the sugar taken as it was intended to be taken, with the vegetables and delicious fruits, mixed with such other elements as the system required, then the appetite might have been indulged to the fullest extent, and no organs or faculties would have been oppressed and overburdened while others were not supplied, and every part of the system would have been prepared, without stupor or sleepiness, to perform the duties assigned it.

If we take our food as it is made, with the elements mixed by Infinite Wisdom, we need use our judgment only in cooking it so as best to develop its flavor and fit it for digestion, and our appetite would safely direct us, both as to the articles to be eaten and the amount required. But presuming as we do to know better than our Maker how to mix the different elements of food, we have spoiled some of our best articles of nourishment, and have at the same time so perverted our appetites and tastes that they are no guide, at least so far as relates to the use of the articles with which we have thus interfered.

The only articles of diet in this country which to any extent are thus perverted are wheat and milk, and these are perverted in the same way, by taking out and rejecting the nitrates and phosphates, and using the carbonates only. The effects, especially in our cities, are manifest in our liability to inflammatory diseases; in our feebleness and weakness of muscle, for want of the nitrates; in our defective, aching teeth, for want of lime, &c.; in our physical and mental debility, for want of the phosphates; and in our ash-colored, chlorotic girls, for want of the iron, — all of which elements, except the carbonates, being entirely wanting in butter, and almost all in *very nice* white flour. See plate of wheat, Figs. 2, 6, and 7.

Practical Application of the Analysis of Food to the different Conditions in Life.

Food for Out-of-door Work, with the Thermometer below Zero.

Let us first take a case requiring the most concentrated nourishment, or, in common parlance, the most hearty food.

A man works in the open air in the coldest winter weather: what articles of diet will best sustain him? Under these circumstances he must exercise his muscles to their fullest capacity or he will freeze, and he will therefore require more than twice as much muscle-making food as he would need with moderate exercise: then he would require of the most concentrated heat-producers five times as much as of the flesh-makers. Fat of animals is the most concentrated article of carbonates, and yet we are astonished at the amount necessary to support animal heat in cold climates.

It is said that an Esquimaux woman will eat a gallon of whale oil in one day, or ten or twelve pounds of tallow candles, besides the necessary muscle-making food. The stomach will not, therefore, in active life in the cold, contain food sufficient to sustain life, except in its most concentrated form. For a man, therefore, chopping wood in the cold, fat and lean meats are the articles mostly to be depended on, fat containing two and one half times the heating power of the vegetable carbonates, sugar and starch, while the muscle of meat contains, of course, the concentrated elements for working power.

Of vegetable food adapted to accompany pork and beef, beans, peas, and northern corn bread are best, as may be seen by reference to the analytical table, beans and peas containing more of the nitrates and phosphates than any other vegetable food, and Indian corn containing more carbonates, especially more oil, than other grains. Cheese is also a good concentrated article with corn bread. These articles of food are not easily digested, but are the better on that account, the stomach being subject to the same law as other organs and faculties, — "the more work to do, the more strength to do it."

Exposure to cold, without exercise, requires different and more digestible articles. Carbonates, such as sugar, buckwheat or flour cakes, rice, &c., and even the less digestible articles which cannot be eaten in summer, as cheese, beans and pork, &c., may be eaten with impunity in winter, upon the principle stated above, much more food being required in winter than in summer, proportionate powers of digestion are given to correspond. And hence we seldom find trouble from dyspepsia in cold weather, especially with those who exercise in the open air; and it is always best, in order to strengthen the stomach, to take articles of food that will tax the full power of digestion, just as it is best to take active exercise in order to strengthen the muscles. One who lives on rice, can digest nothing else; but one who can eat and digest beans, cheese, &c., can generally digest everything.

What Articles of Food are best adapted to Warm Weather?

If it be true that in cold weather we need, and the appetite demands, concentrated carbonaceous food, as has been explained in the preceding chapter, it is also true, as might be expected, and as we all know, that the appetite demands in warm weather a very different class of articles of food; and the reason is obvious.

Four fifths of our food being devoted to the production of heat, we need four times as much in cold weather as in warm. If, therefore, we ate the same articles in summer as in winter, and only what our nature required, the stomach and bowels would collapse into one quarter of their size, and could not properly carry on their functions. Nature, therefore, provides for warm climates and the summers of cold, food in which all the elements are greatly diluted, and in which the proportions of carbonates are much smaller than those provided for cold weather. This you will see in the analysis of southern and northern corn, in a very remarkable degree (Figs. 3 and 4). While the proportion of northern corn is six of the carbonates to one of the nitrates, the proportions of these principles in southern corn are nearly equal: it would therefore require six times the bulk of southern corn as of northern to support the same degree of heat; and this disparity is still more strikingly seen if we compare northern corn with some of our common vegetables. Corn contains seventy-three per cent. of carbonates, turnips four per cent., and cucumbers one per cent. Consequently it would require eighteen pounds of turnips, or seventy-three pounds of cucumbers, to furnish as much heat as one pound of northern corn meal.

The comparative proportions of carbonates and nitrates in wheat, and indeed all the cereals that grow both in northern and southern climates, as well as those of all other natural products of the soil, plainly declare the will of God in regard to summer and winter food, as do also our appetites and tastes.

In the spring we lose our desire for butter and buckwheats, and begin to crave some acid fruits and green vegetables. And yet how many thoughtless housekeepers at the north go through nearly the same routine of cooking in summer as in winter, with just about as much butter and lard and fat beef, and even pork, and fat gravy, and flour puddings, with butter sauce; not because they like it as well, or think it as wholesome, but only because "their mothers did so before them!" And so powerful is this thoughtless and absurd habit in the Southern States, that it is said that however plentiful may be the supply of milk, and cheese, and green vegetables, fresh lean beef, and fruits, &c., a southern family always has on the table a smoked ham or a "side of pork," and their vegetables are cooked swimming in fat; and to force an appetite, they use the most stimulating spices and condiments. In short, their food in the hottest weather is suitable only for the coldest northern winter weather. Is it strange that diseases prevail?

We need in summer or winter, whether using muscles or brains, or neither, every day food containing carbonates for the lungs, nitrates for the muscles and tissues, and phosphates for the vital powers, but we need them in very different proportions, according to the temperature in which we live and our habits of life. These elements are furnished at our hands, varying in proportions so as to be adapted to the different temperatures and habits; and for animals that have instincts and not intellects to guide them, from the elephant to the smallest animalcule, these different elements are so mixed and prepared, and the appetite so adjusted to them, that they always want, and always have, and always eat the right kind of food at the right time, and the right quantity.

But man, who has intellect, is expected to understand the laws of his being, and to adapt his food to the wants of his nature, varying it according to circumstances. We are creatures of habit, and our systems have wonderful power in adapting themselves to circumstances; and therefore we do not all die, however thoughtlessly we live, and however perseveringly continue the wrong habits to which we have been accustomed; and our appetites falling in with our habits, the evils of wrong living are perpetuated. Still it is true everywhere that the average amount of health and the average length of life are in exact proportion to the care we take to live in accordance with the laws of our being. This statistics show, and our own observations confirm.

But what a responsibility these considerations place upon wives and mothers, who have, or ought to have, the direction of these matters! To them, in providence, as in the word of God, the injunction emphatically is, "Keep my commandments, for length of days, and long life, and peace shall they add to thee," and to thy family. This important promise is fulfilled literally to those who study to obey physical laws, however figurative its fulfilment may be in regard to moral law.

Does any one doubt that peace to the digestive organs, and freedom from fevers and summer complaints, and many other fatal diseases, would result from a strict observance of the law, so clearly revealed, that fat meats, and butter, and fine flour, and other stimulating carboniferous food should be avoided in warm weather, while such articles should be substituted as contain the carbonates in a less concentrated form, combined with such acid fruits and vegetables, and the grains which contain less oil and starch, and more of the nitrates and phosphates?

With half the study that is required to learn a complicated piece of needlework, or a difficult piece of music, any intelligent housekeeper could learn the dietetic laws, and institute an arrangement adapting them to the mental or muscular employment of her family, so as to give them the requisite variety of wholesome food for summer and winter; for work of brain or work of muscles; and add immeasurably to the length of life and to the comfort and health of her family. But how little attention is given to this important subject!

Adaptation of Food to different Conditions and Employments in Life.

Food for Old People.

Is your fat, good-natured old grandfather living on fat beef and pork, white bread and butter, buckwheat cakes and molasses, rice and sugar, till he has lost all mental and physical energy, and desires to sit from morning till night in the chimney-corner or at the register, saying nothing and caring for nothing?—change his diet, give him fish, beefsteak, potatoes, and unbolted wheat bread, or rye and Indian, with one half or three quarters of the carboniferous articles of his former diet, and in one week he will cheer you again with his old jokes, and call for his hat and cane.

Is he lean, and cold, and restless, and irritable? — give him the fattest meats, with the best of butter, and as much sugar and molasses as he desires, not taking away entirely food for the brain and muscles, but adapting them to his circumstances. Perhaps his brain has been overworked, and exhaustion and fitful action follow. If so, he needs some form of phosphatic food to which he has not been accustomed, as oat-meal porridge, or oat-meal cake, with milk, or a diet of fish, and pearl barley, or pea soup. Or perhaps his restlessness comes from inactivity of the bowels: if so, he needs fruits, vegetables, unbolted wheat bread, &c., with care to keep his mind at ease, and to have only such company as is soothing and agreeable.

Or perhaps his irritability arises from the use of too much meat and other phosphatic food: if so, keep him on a diet in which the phosphates are deficient, as rice, flour bread and butter, &c., with other food adapted to his other conditions and habits. But that a regard to these different conditions, and an adaptation of food to conform to them, will very much contribute to comfort and happiness in the declining years of life, there is not a shadow of doubt.

Food for Children.

Is your nursing babe, eight months old, feeble and inactive, its teeth coming through the gums already black and defective, and its soft, flabby flesh indicating a want of muscular fibre? — change your own food at once, and give up butter, and fine flour, and cakes, and puddings with sweet sauce, and take instead beefsteak, oat-meal or barley porridge, with milk and unbolted wheat bread, grits, pea soup, &c., which abound in phosphates and nitrates, and in one week you shall see an improvement in the condition of the child; but if your own health will not admit of such a change, wean the babe, and give it the milk of the cow, oat-meal gruel, &c.; and for the next child, be sure and commence furnishing the material for bone and muscle at least fourteen months earlier, and its teeth will not be defective, or its muscles feeble and flabby.

Nor are defective teeth and undeveloped muscles the only or the greatest evils that accrue from neglect to furnish suitable material for the foundation of that structure which is so important as to be denominated the "temple of God." "Know ye not that ye are the temple of God, and the Spirit of God dwelleth in you?"

All nature, as well as the word of God, testifies that the crowning work of creation was man; indeed, all other creative work was but a preparation for man, and so far at least as relates to this planet, all creative work ended in making man.

But man was not created from nothing, but from elements which had for ages been collecting in the "dust of the ground;" and having at first taken these elements directly from the soil, and constructed a perfect man, God, with wisdom as incomprehensible to man as that by which the first man was created, instituted laws by which all necessary elements should be taken out of the soil by plants, and so organized as under certain laws and conditions to be able to construct other perfect human beings, and thus perpetuate the race, as we have before explained.

These fourteen elements, which were at first taken directly from the soil and atmosphere, are now all found deposited in the grains, and flesh of animals, and fruits and vegetables, and for the construction of a perfect human being must all be used, at first through the mother's system, and afterwards directly from the food in which they are deposited. This wonderful arrangement can be better understood by further explanation.

A grain of wheat, as proved by analysis, contains every one of the elements found in the human system. Plant a grain of wheat in soil in which is no lime, or phosphorus, or nitrogen, and the plant may grow from the carbon and hydrogen, and other elements which it can get from the soil, the air, and water, but the grain would not be developed, and analysis would show that phosphorus, lime, and nitrogen would be wanting in the plant and grain as it was wanting in the soil. Now, as in such imperfectly developed grain the phosphorus, and lime, and nitrogen, which were intended for forming brains, and bones, and muscles, are not there, is it not certain that such grain could not develop brains, and bones, and muscles? — for if wheat does not contain phosphorus, lime, and nitrogen, unless the soil in which it grows contains these elements, is it not certain that the human system cannot be developed by food wanting in these or any other important elements?

In soil containing as little phosphorus, lime, and nitrogen as are found in superfine flour bread and butter, the grain of wheat would not be developed at all; and can a child, for which wheat was made, be developed on white bread and butter? Milk of the cow contains all the elements of the human system, and in the right proportions; and if concentrated, or if the stomach was large enough to contain these elements in their diluted state, in sufficient quantities, would support the life and health of any man indefinitely.

Primarily it was intended to develop the calf, and it does develop every part perfectly; but feed the calf on cream alone, or butter, and it would die in two weeks. Can butter, then, develop a human being? And yet how many expectant and nursing mothers thoughtlessly provide themselves and their precious little ones with food made up mainly of superfine flour, butter, and sugar, without knowing or thinking that sugar and butter have no elements at all for muscles, or bones, or brains, and white flour very little.

If they ate nothing else, of course their children would all die within a month; and as it is, only one half in all Christendom, and not one eighth in all Heathendom, have vital power to carry them through the first five years. Those that live have a life of struggle with disease and suffering in just the proportion as they are deprived of food containing elements adapted to develop the whole system, and give power to resist and overcome disease. The inevitable effects of the diet almost universally adopted is, to stimulate all the organs by the undue proportion of carbon, of which the butter, fine flour, and sugar are composed, which form so large a part of our diet, and which render all organs more susceptible to inflammations and other diseases; while the deficiency of the nitrates and phosphates, weakening the organs and diminishing the powers of life, renders them less able to resist and throw off diseases as they occur.

Take, for example, the lungs, whose duties are to keep up the steam and "run the machine,"—duties, the importance of which is seen by the fact that, if for a single moment they cease to act, every operation of the system is suspended and life becomes extinct. Overburdened with work in order to dispose of the great excess of fuel imposed upon them, the tissues are feeble for want of their appropriate food; and is it strange that they fail, and become diseased?

Or, take the brain and nervous system, which, being overheated with carboniferous blood, and weakened by want of phosphorus, become sluggish and inactive, or act fitfully, and headache and neuralgia ensue; or, being nervous and irritable, a thousand ills, real and imaginary, render life a burden.

Or, take the liver, whose office is to eliminate effete elements from the system and assist digestion. Overburdened with work, especially in the spring, after the steam has for months been kept up to the highest practicable point, it gets tired and sluggish, and the bile becomes obstructed, and jaundice and many other bilious difficulties ensue, and thus all organs are made more susceptible to disease, and less able to resist it, by too much of the carbonates and too little of the nitrates and phosphates.

While, therefore, all animals, in their natural state, living as they do according to natural laws, raise all their young, and bring them perfectly developed to full maturity, a perfectly developed young man or woman, at full maturity, with perfect teeth and sound lungs, and well developed muscles and brains, is a rare exception to the general rule; and to every reflecting mind the reason must be obvious: we neglect to learn, and utterly disregard the plain laws of our being, and these terrible sufferings and bereavements are the natural and just penalties for our disobedience.

Can any other explanation be given, why beings supported by the same elements, and subject to the same physical laws, should be found in such different physical conditions? Mothers' milk, if the mother live on proper food, is undoubtedly the best, as it is the natural food for children till teeth are formed, which indicate a maturity that requires some other food; but sickly mothers, and those who live on white bread and butter, would subserve the interests of their children by weaning them, and substituting the milk of the cow. For young children the cow furnishes milk with too much of the nitrate element; and the reason for this provision is obvious, as I have explained.

When other food than milk is required, that containing some nourishment for the muscles and brain should always be selected, which can readily be known by reference to the tables of analysis; but starch, and arrowroot, and sugar, and cream, all of which are sometimes given in ignorance of their character, contain no element of food but carbon, and would only tend to develop torpidity and foolishness; but, on the other hand, beefsteak and oat-meal, and such other articles of food as contain large proportions of nitrogenous and phosphatic elements, tend to develop the muscles and brain too rapidly, and render the child liable to congestion of the brain; and a special regard should be had to this consideration where the child is very active and precocious. Such children always die young, unless special care is taken of their diet and general management.

Food for Children deficient in Vital Energy and Muscular Power.

That muscular power is increased by exercise has been long known. More than seven hundred years before the Christian era the Olympic games were celebrated, consisting in throwing quoits, leaping, wrestling, boxing, &c., which were held on a certain day corresponding to the 11th of July, and lasting five days, for which the competitors prepared themselves by training in the gymnasium for ten months. For a thousand years at least these games, with a few temporary interruptions, were regularly celebrated, occupying the minds of the whole Grecian nation; and at that age the training of muscles was considered vastly more important than the training of mind. Of the diet used in this training but little is now known; but Pliny says, "the gladiators ate only barley bread, and hence they were called Hordearii," hordeum being the Greek name for barley.

Jackson, the noted English trainer of prize-fighters, feeds his men on the lean muscle of fat beef and mutton, with coarse barley and wheat bread. It is not likely that ancient gladiators or modern prize-fighters understood either the chemical elements of the human system, or the adaptation of those articles of food to supply the requisite elements of muscular power; but it is interesting to notice that experience brought them to the same conclusions as chemical analysis.* The muscles of beef and mutton contain the same elements as human muscles, and are therefore adapted to nourish them, while unbolted wheat and barley furnish also a due proportion of flesh-making materials; and also in each of these articles are the phosphates, which give vital force, wheat containing them in proportions necessary for common exercise, and barley and the flesh of beef and mutton more than double the proportion of those of wheat.

If, then, both science and experience show that muscular power can be increased by muscle-making food, is it not reasonable that feeble children should be made stronger by application of the same principle? What duty, then, can be clearer than the duty of feeding our dormant, sleepy, and feeble children on food containing a full share of nitrates and phosphates, as lean meat, oat meal, barley cakes, beans, peas, &c., rather than the stupefying carbonates, as fat meat, fine flour, butter, sugar, or puddings and pies, cakes, &c., which are made up of these articles?

* Jockeys also reduce their weight by living on fish and lean meat with little carbonaceous food.

How the Blood becomes Impure.

We find by chemical analysis that the blood is composed of the fourteen elements which make up the different parts of the system, and such other elements as have been taken into the system with improper food and drink, and are allowed to go into the circulation, although not wanted for the use of any organ or function, because they cannot be removed in any other way than through the lungs, or skin, or kidneys, and must go into the circulation to get out of the system. They are, of course, not permanently found in the blood, but vary in proportions and character according to the care we take in regard to our food and drink.

If we ate only natural food, and drank only pure water, and breathed only pure air, the blood would consist of the fourteen elements only which constitute the solids and juices of the human system. It is evident, therefore, that pure blood is made from pure air, pure water, and natural food, and that while nothing else is admitted into the system, the blood cannot be impure; and if the blood in any case is found to be impure, it is because the food, or drink, or air are not plentifully supplied, or are not pure or natural, and in just the proportion as they are not pure and natural, or are not supplied in sufficient quantity.

We come, then, at once to the only way in which the blood can be kept pure, or renovated when found to be impure. If the blood is impure in consequence of additions to its natural element derived from the food, or air, or water, our first duty is to see that the source of impurity is stopped, and then Nature will soon remove the impurities. If it is impure from want of supply of its natural elements, then our duty is also plain, for every necessary element is supplied in natural food, and we have only to use our judgment in selecting the articles which contain such as are needed.

How can we know what Elements are wanted to make the Blood Pure?

Just as we determine what is wanted to supply any requisition—by comparing the supply with the demand. If a merchant was required to furnish a dozen different articles of merchandise, including gloves, and should by mistake deliver only eleven articles, he would have no difficulty in determining that gloves were the item wanted, if the other articles had all been supplied. Suppose we have a daughter of sixteen, ash-colored, feeble, and undeveloped. If we look over the list of elements, and the proportions of them required to keep the system and blood in perfect condition, as shown by the table of analysis of different articles of food, and as compared with elements of the human system, we shall probably find that, instead of the necessary elements for the blood and the vital powers, she has been accustomed to food made up to a great extent of butter, superfine flour, and sugar, which contain but very little nutriment for the blood or vital powers, mixed perhaps with other articles containing the requisite elements, but out of proportion to the wants of the system. Being supplied to repletion with carbonaceous food, there was no room for other requisite principles, and the results were inevitable. Her blood is colorless and impure, and she is feeble and chlorotic, because her food was deficient in the elements which constitute good blood.

I have investigated scores, and perhaps hundreds of such cases, and invariably find the principal cause to be, that from childhood they have been fed on white bread and butter, sweet cakes, flour puddings, pie-crust, confectioneries, &c., which had kept the system in a heated, feverish condition, with a deficiency of fruits and vegetables, that assist in eliminating from the system the impurities engendered by the excess of carbon in the system, and a deficiency of coarse bread, milk, fish, lean meat, &c., which contain the phosphorus, iron, and other mineral elements necessary for the purity of the blood; and they had generally lost their appetites for the necessary articles of food, and had acquired instead a morbid desire for something strange and unnatural, as chalk, slate pencils, pungent spices, pickled limes, &c. The evils of these habits are generally increased by want of exercise to carry off accumulated impurities, and the blood becomes too poor to be able to carry on the functions of the system. The tissues of the lungs break down under the burdens imposed upon them, consumption ensues, and we lose our daughters, murmuring, perhaps, at the mysterious providence by which we are so afflicted.

How to Purify the Blood.

We have seen that impurity of the blood consists of excess of some elements and deficiency of others, and that by comparing the list of elements required with the list habitually supplied, we can ascertain what elements are wanting and what are in excess; and having an analysis of all the articles of food in common use, which contain all the elements of the human system in different proportions, we have but to use our common sense in selecting such as will supply the deficient elements, or avoid the excessive.

The intelligent farmer finds that some of his land will not produce wheat; and by analysis he will be sure to find that the elements of wheat are wanting, or are excessive. If wanting, he supplies them in such manure as is known to contain them, and is sure of a crop of wheat; or, if excessive, he plants the ground with other crops that need the excessive elements, and after they are thus removed he can get a crop of wheat.

What should we think of the farmer whose land needed phosphorus, and nothing else, for a crop of wheat, who should follow the advice of his neighbors, as ignorant as himself, and use lime, and ashes, and salt, and a dozen other things that contained no phosphorus, because somebody else had used some of these articles on land perhaps entirely different, and had found them useful. No article in the world could do good unless it contained phosphorus, but might do harm if it contained elements already sufficiently supplied, and perhaps already in excess. But this is the method almost universally adopted by mothers, in order to purify the blood of their children. That mother is indeed a rare exception, who does not, when her daughter is pale, and she fears impurities of the blood, or perhaps to prevent such an evil, resort to something which somebody says is good for the blood, for she has tried it, without stopping to consider the absurdity of the experiment, or whether it may not, as it must, do harm by troubling the stomach with elements never intended for the human system, and therefore necessarily injurious.

In this way are annually expended millions of dollars in Purification, or Plantation Bitters, "Important Medical Discoveries, that cure all humors but the Thunder Humor," Oxygenated Gas, Compound Sarsaparilla, and the thousand and one other advertised sovereign remedies, not one of which contains a single element of the blood, or can by any possibility do good, and all must, from their want of adaptation to the plain requirements of the system, if not from their poisonous character, do more or less harm; and that they cannot as medicines do good, can be shown by principles as simple. But this subject will be considered elsewhere.

All Elements of Food must have been organized in some Vegetable, or they are rejected.

Not only is it impossible to purify the blood by the use of articles recommended by ignorant empirics, as we have endeavored to show, and useless to attempt any purification except by the common-sense expedient of supplying deficient elements, and removing or withholding redundant ones, statements, the truth of which will be understood and appreciated by all, learned or unlearned; but it is also true, as I shall endeavor to prove, that no element, however much it may be wanted in the system, can be made to become a constituent of the blood, or be appropriated by any of the tissues, unless that element has been organized in some plant, and is thus fitted to be received according to the law of nature.

I make this proposition with diffidence, because it has not been considered by our scientific physicians; and every day, chlorotic girls and other patients are furnished with disorganized iron, and other elements from the shops, with the expectation that they will supply the deficiency of the elements which are supposed to be wanted to restore the blood to its normal condition; and one learned professor, as I have before stated, is endeavoring to supply the posphorus, which had been taken out of the wheat, where it was organized and prepared to supply the system with that important element, by adding to the flour salts made from disorganized phosphoric acid.

I have elsewhere referred to the great plan of nature, by which all the elements necessary to be used in making or repairing the system were deposited in the soil before man was made, to be taken up in the sap of plants, and vegetables, and fruit trees, and deposited in the seed, and fruits, and juices of these trees and plants, in just the proportions necessary to supply every organ and function; then to be eaten, and digested, and made a constituent of the blood, and appropriated by the organs and tissues; then to be cast off by the excretions, and again deposited in the soil, to be again taken up by vegetation, and continue their rounds perpetually.

Now this is undoubtedly the best arrangement for supplying the human system with all necessary elements that even God could make — an arrangement, to short-sighted man, wonderful and incomprehensible; and is it for us, who have not intellect sufficient to understand one of the processes by which this plan is executed, to say that any part of it is unnecessary? — that iron and phosphorus, prepared from crude, unorganized materials, in the laboratory of any chemist, are just as well adapted to supply the wants of the human system, as these elements prepared in Nature's own laboratory? Why not, then, take carbon and nitrogen, or the other elements, directly from the ground, and repair the whole system, or make a new man, by a shorter and cheaper process?

The Penalty for taking into the Stomach Elements of Food not organized.

After such infinite pains to perfect a plan for supplying the human system with every necessary element, it seems to me reasonable, and perfectly consonant with Nature's other laws, that an ordinance should be instituted requiring that no elements should be admitted into the system except in accordance with this arrangement, and that every attempt to introduce them should be visited by punishment, more or less severe, according to the importance of the element; and this we find to be true.

Not an element is allowed to be incorporated into, and become a part of the blood, or any organ or tissue, that is not fitted for digestion in some vegetable; and if any element is offered that is not thus prepared, a rebellion ensues, more or less energetic and severe, according to the importance of the element. This rebellion, or excitement, is injurious to the system, and all the organs and functions involved; and this is what is meant by the word *poison*, and constitutes the penalty.

Phosphorus, for example, is a very important element, being the element on which the action of the brain depends, and the physical source of vitality, and an important constituent, as well, of bones and other solid tissues. In a common-sized man there are found to be nearly two pounds of solid phosphorus, doing its important work quietly and harmlessly; but take two grains of the two pounds which have been disorganized as can easily be done by calcining a bone, and attempt to put them back and reorganize them, by giving them at once to a healthy man, and such an excitement is produced, especially of the brain, that delirium, inflammation, and death might ensue within a single hour; but give ten times that amount, organized in oat-meal or barley cake, or any other natural food containing it, and the system will quietly and gratefully appropriate what it needs, and reject the remainder without excitement or harm.

And can we resist or gainsay the evidence thus furnished, that oat-meal and barley cakes, and unbolted wheat flour, are the appropriate means of introducing phosphorus into the system, rather than phosphatic bread, the phosphorus in which was taken from calcined bones?

The Penalty of taking Disorganized Iron.

Iron is a necessary, but less important, element of the human system than phosphorus. It is found in the bran of wheat and other grains, and vegetables, and, being transferred from them, is found also in the muscles and blood of animals, and in the curd of milk, and other natural food, in quantities as large as can be appropriated by the system; and this is proof to my mind that Nature intended it to be furnished through these articles of natural food.

Being less important than phosphorus, the penalties for attempting to introduce it in any other way are less severe and less manifest, but are still sufficiently apparent to corroborate my position.

Dr. J. Francis Churchill, a French author, who has given great attention to the effects of different mineral elements on the human system, in an article headed "Danger of Iron in Consumption and Chlorosis," says, that M. Trousseau, another very celebrated French physician, whose authority in this country to-day is as high as that of any man living, has carefully investigated the effects of iron, and from a synopsis of a report of these investigations he makes the following quotations: "M. Trousseau has just given utterance to an authoritative and positive statement, which will, no doubt, surprise the profession everywhere. He declares that iron in any form, given in chlorotic affections, to patients in whom the consumptive diathesis exists, invariably fixes the diathesis, *and hastens the development of the tubercles.* The iron may induce a factitious return to health; the physician may flatter himself that he has corrected the chlorotic condition of his patient; but to his surprise, he will find the patient soon after fall into a phthisical state, *from which there is no return.* This result, or at least its hastening, M. Trousseau attributes to the iron. The assertion is a most startling one. M. Trousseau is nevertheless so certain of what he says, that he denounces the administration of iron in chlorosis as *criminal in the highest degree.*" (The Italics are as in the quotation.) This opinion is confirmed by my own observation in a practice of forty years, and furnishes proof sufficient that iron as well as phosphorus must be introduced into the system only as organized for digestion in some plant, or a penalty must be paid. The excitement that follows the taking of iron is less active and less dangerous than after taking phosphorus, because it is less important to the system to reject it immediately; but it illustrates the arrangement of Providence, and establishes the same principle.

Can phosphorus, iron, oxygen, hydrogen, nitrogen, carbon, or any other of the fourteen elements which constitute the human system, be made to form a constituent of the blood, or any organ or tissue, unless introduced as they are organized for that purpose, in the atmosphere and water, and in vegetable and animal food, before they have become fermented or decomposed?

To comprehend the importance of this question, let us first glance at the various methods in which important elements are forced upon the human system, with the expectation that they will be received and appropriated as if they were introduced in accordance with natural laws, keeping in mind what I have endeavored to prove in the preceding chapters, that all elements offered are either kindly received and appropriated, or are rejected as poisonous.

Thousands of invalids, feeble children, and especially feeble girls, are taking every day some preparation of

* Since making this quotation M. Trousseau has deceased.

iron, with the expectation that it will supply the supposed deficiency of that element, and thus give them health and strength.

Phosphorus, also, is introduced in superfine flour bread, with the understanding that it can be made to take the place of that element, which had been bolted out; and it is also used to supply the supposed deficiency of that element in consumption and other diseases. Oxygen, likewise, in the form of gas, is taken to purify the blood and give vigor to the system.

Carbon and hydrogen are taken in the form of alcohol, with the expectation that they furnish natural heat to the system.

These ideas seem to have come from Liebig, a very learned German chemist, who gave to the world much valuable information on the subject of the chemistry of food, and whose ideas for the last twenty years have been very generally adopted, but who ignored the vital law as controlling chemical laws, and classed alcohol with sugar and other carbonaceous food, because it contains the same elements, and who offered the analytical table of alcohol and sugar which I have copied in another chapter, as proof that alcohol must be nutritive because sugar was nutritive, notwithstanding the fact that the taste and smell, and perceptible effects of the two articles, were no more alike than any other two articles containing different elements. The same argument is still used by eminent chemists, which may be condensed from an argument already quoted, as follows: Phosphorus, taken from bones without decomposition, is wholesome, as proved by experiment; therefore phosphatic bread, although containing phosphates chemically decomposed, cannot be unwholesome.

Arguments relied on to sustain the Use of Disorganized Elements, and to prove that such Elements may be and are incorporated into the Blood and Tissues.

Practically, as has been said, it is generally conceded that elements wanted by the human system can be supplied, and will be received, whether they have been prepared in any vegetable organization or not; but when the question is put directly to our chemists and scientific physicians, as it lately was before the committee of the Legislature on licensing the sale of alcohol, "Is alcohol, or any other disorganized element, actually appropriated by the organs or tissues as food, and incorporated into them as nutrition?" the answer is, "That question is not settled;" very few being ready to make the assertion that it is.

And the reason is obvious. There is no proof that a single element ever was made to enter into the blood, or any organ or tissue, as a part of their constituents, unless it was taken with, and formed a part of, some food organized directly or indirectly by passing through some vegetable. I find but one author who claims to bring such proof, and this proof I think can be clearly shown to be fallacious.

Frederick William Headland, of the Royal College

of Physicians in London, has written a book on the action of medicines, which has recently been published in this country, and which is adopted as a standard work. It goes more thoroughly into the subject than any other author.

He places alcohol as a stimulant and narcotic, without the pretence that it can be appropriated by the system, to make any part of its tissues or fat, or even be used as fuel to produce animal heat; but in proof that iron from the shops does enter into the blood as a part of it, he says, "In some cases of chlorosis the blood was analyzed before giving iron and after it had been given for a few weeks, and the blood was found to contain more of red globules after taking the iron than before." And this is accepted as proof positive that the red globules, or at least the color of the globules, were produced by the iron thus introduced.

But scores of cases can be brought, where, under a different treatment, the results were the same, and even more striking, without using a particle of iron; and my explanation is, that the effect of the iron was that of a mere stimulant, promoting sanguification, from food taken in the mean time containing iron. Of abundance of testimony on that point, I will bring only one witness.

Dr. Churchill, whom I have already quoted as condemning iron on account of its tendency to develop tubercles, says, in his book on "Pulmonary Phthisis and Tubercular Diseases," that phosphoric acid and its preparations "are the most valuable blood-creating agents known, as is shown by the fact that more rapidly than any other medicine it increases the quantity and color of the blood;" and he gives cases to prove it quite as remarkable as those referred to by Dr. Headland, and thus the proof that iron produces the red globules directly is entirely neutralized.

Now let us bring into one view the different parts of that wonderful, and to us incomprehensible arrangement, made "in the beginning," when "God created the heavens and earth," by which all the solid elements that man should ever require should be placed where, by laws ordained for that purpose, they should be pulverized, and mixed, and scattered, and deposited, and after countless ages be fitted to supply all his physical wants. And then "the Lord God formed man of the dust of the ground," and instituted laws by which the elements of which he was made, and which would ever afterwards be needed for his repair and reconstruction, should be taken up in the sap of herbs, and grasses, and fruit trees, and deposited in seeds, and juices, and grains, and fruits, or in the flesh of animals, and birds, and fishes, in such abundance and profusion over the face of the earth, that anywhere, and in all circumstances, to the end of time, these elements should be ready at his hand, requiring only the use of his intellect and physical faculties to procure them and fit them for his digestive organs.

With this arrangement, so perfectly adapted to all the exigencies of human life, so clearly revealed as the plan of Infinite Wisdom, is it reasonable that we short-sighted beings should presume to say that any part of it is unnecessary or unimportant, and that elements not prepared in accordance with it are just as good, and this on no other ground than that they have the same chemical character as organized preparations of the same elements? — while the evidence before us is abundant that the same elements, with the same chemical combinations, are wholesome food or virulent poisons as they are or are not organized according to this wonderful plan? Beefsteak and nitric acid both owe their active properties to nitrogen, and the chemical combinations in both are nearly the same; the one is nourishing and the other poisonous in proportion to the amount of nitrogen it contains. What folly, then, to attempt to decide on the influence of any substance on the human system by its chemical combination! Chemical must always obey vital law, as lower law the higher.

WATER.

We have seen that mineralogy, geology, and natural history all corroborate that incomprehensible statement of the word of God, that man was made from the "dust of the ground;" and I have endeavored to delineate also the great law of nature by which the solid elements of the human system are constantly supplied; and we have seen that less than one quarter of the weight of the system is composed of solid matter, more than three quarters being water.

We come now to consider the arrangement, equally wonderful, and above human comprehension, by which water, without which life could not have been begun or continued for a single day, should, with unfailing certainty, always be supplied. And here we shall also find in the book of nature the same interesting and complete corroboration of the word of God.

Away back in the ages of eternity, farther than the imagination of the human mind can reach, — "in the beginning, God created the heavens and the earth," the sun, moon, and stars, and every element of matter contained in them; but for ages the condition of things was such that all we could understand, and therefore all that is revealed, is, that the "earth was without form and void."

The first intimation we have of the particulars of its construction, is made concerning water, in this statement: "And the Spirit of God moved upon the face of the waters." And this is all we know, or could be made to understand, and therefore is all the explanation given till the first day, or period, when "God said, Let there be light, and there was light." This, too, being incomprehensible to the human mind, unenlightened by scientific developments, is not explained.

In the description of the second day, or period, we begin to get a glimpse of the condition of things. "And God made the firmament, and divided the waters which were under the firmament from the waters which were above the firmament." "In the beginning," the earth was made of molten rocks: this is clearly understood by the condition in which we find it; and of course the water existed only in a state of vapor, or in gaseous elements. To "divide the waters from under the firmament from the waters above the firmament," was, therefore, to cool the outside and form a crust of the earth, so that the vapor could be condensed into water, and thus be separated from the vapors in the regions above the earth. The second day, or period, seems, therefore, to have been devoted to a preparation of the supply of water for man, who was not to be created till the sixth day, or period, when all necessary preparations for him should be completed.

The third period seems to have been devoted to the same work of perfecting an arrangement for the supply of water. "And God said, Let the waters under the heaven be gathered together in one place, and let the dry land appear." How this was accomplished can now be read much more clearly in the "book of nature" than in the written word.

The internal fires of the earth, pent up as they were by the solid crust that enclosed them, began, in their efforts to escape, to throw up the surface of the earth into ridges, and hills, and mountains, and of course the waters retired from these ridges, and hills, and mountains, and they became dry land; and one third of the earth being thus raised, the other two thirds were of course depressed, and there the waters gathered into oceans, and seas, and lakes: and thus was completed the third period of preparation for supplying man with water.

That the mountains were once raised from level layers, or strata, which had previously for ages been covered with water, there is not in the mind of any reflecting man, who knows the facts, a shadow of doubt. Look into any cave, or excavation, or mine, in any mountain on the face of the earth, and we can see that the strata of different materials, such as coal, slate, &c., which must have been formed under water, and of course on a level, have been pushed up from a level to the position in which they are now seen, by some power from beneath, as if the wet leaves of a pamphlet had been pushed up into an inverted cup, and there left to dry. Finding such a semi-globular mass of printed matter afterwards, and separating these leaves, it could be seen that they once were on a level, and that in that position the words must have been imprinted on them. In a similar manner can be seen, in the leaves or strata of sandstone, evidence, in the position of the strata, and in the shells and other materials imbedded in them, evidence unmistakable that these strata were for ages under water, and of course on a level, and had been pushed up to their present position, and there left to dry and consolidate.

Thus was so far accomplished the work of supplying water for man, that some vegetation could grow; and before the close of the third period we find "the herb yielding seed after his kind, and the tree yielding fruit, whose seed was in itself after his kind." But the earth was not yet ready for man, for mists and clouds in the heavens had not yet dispersed, so that the sun had ever shone, or even penetrated but imperfectly the darkness that shrouded the earth, "for the Lord God had not caused it to rain on the earth, but there went up a mist from the earth, and watered the whole face of the ground."

But the fourth period of creation seems to have been devoted to clearing off the mists from the face of the earth, so that the rays of the sun could penetrate through them, and divide the day from the night; and then for the first time appeared the sun and the moon in the revelating vision to Moses, as if they had just been created and set there, "the greater light to rule the day, and the lesser light to rule the night;" and as if then "He made the stars also," their light having never before reached the earth. Then came the fifth period, when the sun, having cleared off the mists and clouds from the earth, a system of distillation could be commenced from the surface of the ocean and the earth, and pure water be taken up to be condensed, and fall in dews and rains, and be collected into rivulets, and streams, and rivers, and the great system be inaugurated which to the end of time shall circulate the waters from the ocean to the air and from the air to the ocean, supplying men, and animals, and the minutest insect, without cessation, with this necessary element.

Then, and not till then, was the earth prepared for animals, whose life depends on a constant supply of water for the circulation of the food, for perspiration, and the necessary secretions; and not till then were created "every living creature that moveth," "and every winged fowl after his kind," that could in any way contribute to the support or comfort of man. And then, everything being made ready, God said, using for the first time the plural pronoun, as if the councils of heaven were called for the crowning work of creation, "Let us make man in our image, after our likeness; and let them have dominion over the fish of the sea, and over the fowl of the air, and over the cattle, and over all the earth, and over every creeping thing that creepeth on the earth."

Let us now review the history of this preparation for the advent of man, and notice the perfect harmony between the revelation to us through Moses, twenty-five hundred years after the work was finished, and the revelation to us in the mountains, and rocks, and rivers, and the chemical character of the elements that compose them.

This harmony is the more striking when we consider that Moses knew nothing of astronomy, mineralogy, geology, or chemistry, as is evident from his descriptions, in all of which he gives us not the actual condition of things, or the actual development of events, but only a description of things and events as they appeared to him, or as by a kind of panoramic vision they were revealed, to be described in his own words.

Thus, in his description of the sun, moon, and stars, as they appeared when the mists had cleared off so as to reveal them, as if they were then created, he says, "And God made two great lights, the greater to rule the day, and the lesser to rule the night;" "and he made the stars also." "And God set them in the firmament of the heavens to give light upon the earth." This was on the fourth day, but on the second day, he says, "God said, Let there be light;" and this was when "God moved upon the face of the waters," and the mists were so far condensed that light from the sun began to shine through them. It is evident, therefore, that Moses wrote in his own language a description of appearances, as revealed by a kind of panorama, as suggested by Hugh Miller in "The Testimony of the Rocks."

First, he saw the earth, so enshrouded in mists that not a ray of light could penetrate to its surface, and it appeared "without form and void;" then, next, as it appeared when the mists were partly condensed into water, so as to let in a little light; then, as the mountains and hills were raised, and the waters settled into seas and oceans; and finally, when the arrangement was fully perfected, so that every blade of grass, and every little insect should be sure of a supply of water, and the earth was fully prepared for the advent of man, for whom all this preparation was made. Now, astronomy, geology, and chemistry all demonstrate that all that was thus revealed to the vision of Moses, and all he describes as appearances, were in perfect accordance with, though not a revelation of, scientific truth. The earth must have been enshrouded in darkness, for water cannot exist at a temperature above 212°; and of course a temperature sufficiently high to melt the rocks must have driven all the water into vapor around the earth. Now, if the little fog which gathers over a city, as it sometimes does over the city of London, can so obstruct the light as to leave the inhabitants groping in darkness, what must have been the darkness when the whole ocean was in vapor around the earth?

And as the surface of the earth cooled, and the vapor condensed, after a while the light of the sun must have begun to shine through, according to the description of the first day, and there would be a manifest division between the water and the fog, described as the firmament dividing the waters below from the waters above, which constituted the work of the second day. And when the hills and the mountains were raised, as geology teaches they were raised, to form the dry land of every continent, then the waters must necessarily have been "gathered together in one place." The sun must have been in the heavens when "darkness was upon the face of the earth," but it could not "divide the day from the night," and "be for signs and for seasons, and for days and for years," till the mists should have been dispersed so that its light should shine on the earth. And then, to complete the harmony of the testimony of Moses and the testimony of nature, in the chemical composition of plants and animals, we find a description of the earth as being covered with vegetation, and the animals as being created, which was to finish the preparation of the earth for man, just when the arrangement was completed by which vegetation and animals could be perpetually supplied with water. If, then, we take the view of Dr. Kurtz, that the narrative of Moses was "simply prophecy described backwards," and of Chalmers, Pye Smith, and Hugh Miller, and other Christian philosophers, "that the Mosaic account of creation can only be regarded as a record of appearances," we find in the record of Moses respecting the formation of water, and the arrangements for its perpetual supply, and in the records of geology and chemistry, the most perfect harmony and consistency. That this view is true, not only of the revelations of Moses but of all Old Testament revelations, is now almost universally admitted by all Christian philosophers; and, being admitted, there is no longer among them the least anxiety lest the truth of the Bible should be overturned or weakened. But until this was understood, there was a constant jealousy lest some astronomer or geologist should discover some discrepancy between the written word of God and the book of nature. Thus, when Galileo announced the discovery through his telescope that the earth revolved around the sun, the Christian philosophers of his day, with that strange perversion of intellect by prejudices which always characterized the human mind, demanded as security for their precious Bible that he should retract his opinion, and let the sun go on its revolutions around the earth, and even demanded that he should do so on pain of death. Not one of them dared to look into the telescope, lest they might be convinced of the revolution of the earth; for if the earth did revolve, then Joshua's testimony was not true. Joshua said, when "the sun stood still in the midst of the heavens, and did not go down about a whole day," . . . "there was no day like that before it or after it." Galileo said the sun had always stood still, and the revolution of the earth divided the day from the night; and so determined were these philosophers to preserve the Bible from harm, and so darkened were the minds of these the best men of the age, that they deliberately concluded to take his life as a choice of evils,—the life of one man, even one of the best of men, being considered of little value compared with the value of the precious word of God. But now that it is understood that Joshua only described a miraculous event, as it appeared to him, there is no difficulty on that point in the mind of any intelligent Christian, whether philosopher or not.

In our day, also, we have seen the jealousy awakened among intelligent Christian men, and even philosophers, upon the statement being made that the earth, according to its geological construction, could not have been formed in a single week. All Christendom was thrown into alarm and excitement again, lest the Bible might be discredited, and many an anathema was heaped on the names of good men who dared to interpret the Bible by the revelations of Nature. I remember, as if it were but yesterday, though now forty-five years since, the day and the room in which I began to read the then recently published "Book of Nature," by J. Mason Good, in which the idea first struck my mind that the six days of creation, as recorded by Moses, really meant six periods, or ages, of indefinite and inconceivable length. The idea did literally *strike* my mind with such force as to produce an effect almost stunning; and for that day I read not another word in the book, but gave up my mind to the strange reveries which it excited. I trembled lest the Bible should fall under such a plausible statement of geological revelation; but, looking into the subject, I found that the record of Moses and Joshua must be understood as a record of appearances; and since then I have felt no apprehensions for the revelations of the Bible, and no difficulty in reconciling them with the revelations of geology or chemistry.

12

Uses of Water in the Human System.

By the table of analysis of the human body, we see that three fourths of its weight consists in water. Without water no vital process could be carried on for a single moment. The blood must be liquid or it could not circulate, and not circulating, no elements could be supplied, and none could be removed; and then oxygen and hydrogen are very important elements in the composition of the organs as well as the blood. And thus water occupies a position in the economy of the system which fully explains the importance which seems to be attached to it in nature, rendering it necessary to institute that complicated arrangement for its production, circulation, and minute distribution over the face of the earth which we have been considering.

But one of the most important, and to me the most interesting purposes subserved by water, is that chemico-vital process by which the temperature of the body is regulated so as, under all circumstances and external temperatures to which it can be exposed, internally to remain of the same temperature. That certainly is an admirable adjustment of vital and chemical principles, which, without regard to external clothing, or external temperature, or the kind of food taken, or the amount of exercise used, shall keep the internal temperature at 98°, so that in the same individual, under all ordinary circumstances in health, it will not vary from that point more than one or two degrees, in summer or winter, at rest or in violent exercise.

In a series of experiments on one hundred and fourteen individuals, of both sexes, of different ages, among various races, in different latitudes, and under various temperatures, Dr. J. Davy found that a thermometer placed under the tongue indicated a temperature varying only from 96.5 to 102—only $5\frac{1}{2}^{\circ}$; and the extremes of these cases were found very rarely, and always in individuals of great peculiarities of constitution.

The process by which this adjustment of temperature is made, as I have said, is partly vital and partly chemical. That part which is vital I will not attempt to explain; but the chemical process is in accordance with a law instituted "in the beginning," and instituted especially for this very purpose (if we believe that the earth was made for man, and all the laws which govern it). This law is easily understood, and is worthy of particular consideration.

If a solid is changed into a liquid, or a liquid into a gas, heat is required, which is taken from surrounding objects to supply it. If you place a pot of cream within a vessel, in which it will be surrounded by ice and salt, both of which being solid, the action of the salt on the ice changes it into water, which, requiring more heat, takes it from the cream, which is the nearest object, and freezes it into ice-cream.

If you allow moist clothing to remain touching the surface of the body, the moisture, by the heat of the body, or by the atmosphere, is changed into vapor, and produces a dangerous sensation of cold. I have often amused the class to whom I was lecturing by an application of this law, in freezing water in a warm lecture-room. Take two watch crystals, and put in one a little water, and in the other a little ether, which being light, boils at the temperature of the atmosphere when the pressure is taken off. Put these together, under an air-pump, and take off the pressure: the ether will boil, and give off vapor, which, abstracting the heat from the water, causes it to freeze; so that in the same temperature we have the processes of boiling and freezing at the same time.

This principle is used in warm climates in cooling water and other drink. A porous jug, called a *monkey*, or a bottle with a wet cloth around it, is always seen hanging in the window where the breeze is drawing through, and the evaporation from the surface of the jug or bottle abstracts the heat from the water within; and I have drank it as cool as was desirable, with the sun directly overhead.

We have seen also the operation of this principle in heating and boiling water. Apply heat to water, and its temperature increases till it comes up to 212°; then a violent agitation commences, and steam is evolved more or less rapidly in proportion to the heat applied; and this evolution keeps the water at the same temperature, so that no amount of heat in the open air can raise the temperature above 212°.

And this is the principle which regulates the temperature of the human system, and keeps it at 98°, regulated by the operation of a vital law which we do not understand, and the evaporation of water, as before described, so as to keep the internal parts of the body at 98°, while water, under the regulation of physical law alone, is kept, when boiling, at 212°.

By this law all animals can, to some extent, adjust themselves to different temperatures; but each species, being intended to occupy only a limited range of heat and cold, each being limited to a few degrees of latitude, have not the necessity for that power to a very great extent. But man, who is destined to have dominion over all animals in all latitudes, must have power to adapt himself to a great range of temperature. In many parts of the tropical zone, the thermometer rises every day, through a large portion of the year, to 110°, and in British India it is occasionally recorded at 130°; while the arctic voyagers frequently record it as low as 55° below, and Captain Franklin at 58°, and one record by Captain Back is made as low as 70°; making a range of temperature in which men live from 130° above to 70° below — two hundred degrees.

Workmen in furnaces are accustomed, in some places, to enter a room where the floor is red hot, and the temperature of the air stands at 350°; and the "Fire King" Chabert was in the habit of entering an oven, at a temperature of from 400° to 600°; and it is not an uncommon feat to take beefsteak into an oven and wait for it to be cooked; indeed, the temperature which Chabert was accustomed to endure would crisp a steak to charcoal.

This almost miraculous power of resisting the effects of heat is evidently not purely chemical, as is shown by the different effects of the same temperature on the living and dead muscle; but that chemical law comes into play in this power to sustain extraordinary heat, is shown by the fact that the evaporation of water on the surface of the body is in proportion to the degree of heat to which it is exposed, and of course the heat is evolved from the body according to chemical laws. It is, therefore, a power partly chemical and partly vital, — great changes can therefore be endured with impunity only by persons with good vital powers and in good health. Young children suffer greatly by changes of temperature, and many an infant is killed by treatment which would be safe at maturity, the nurses or mothers exposing them to the influence of cold air or cold water, not knowing their want of power to resist the cold, or perhaps having the idea that exposure will render them tough.

Old people also suffer from exposure to changes, and statistics show that from the age of eighty and upwards more than twice as many die in January and February as in July and August; indeed, the mortality of all ages is greater in winter than in summer.

M. Quetelet gives, as the results of a large number of statistical observations in Brussels, the following table of the mean monthly mortality at different ages, reckoning the average of the whole year at one hundred per month: —

Mean Monthly Mortality in Brussels.

	First Month.	2 to 3 Years.	8 to 12 Years.	25 to 30 Years.	50 to 60 Years.	90 Years and above
January,	139	122	108	105	130	158
February,	128	113	106	104	122	148
March,	121	130	127	111	111	125
April,	102	127	134	106	102	96
May,	93	112	121	102	93	84
June,	83	94	99	102	85	75
July,	78	82	88	91	77	64
August,	79	73	82	96	85	66
September,	86	76	81	95	89	76
October,	91	78	76	93	90	74
November,	93	91	80	97	100	103
December,	109	101	96	97	115	129

This difference in the rate of mortality in summer and winter physiologists have generally supposed to depend on the changes of temperature and the want of power to resist them, especially in infants and old people, and to a great extent this explanation is undoubtedly correct; but experiments to which I have elsewhere referred, made in the Foundling Hospital and in the Zoölogical Garden of London, thirty-five years ago, by which the length of life of infants and monkeys were increased one hundred per cent. in two years, by a new system of ventilation, would seem to indicate another reason for the difference of mortality in infants and old people in summer and winter. Probably in Brussels, where the winters are long and cold, as a matter of economy in heat the houses are not well ventilated, and infants and old people, not being able to go out, are exposed constantly to impure air, which would help to account for the facts presented in M. Quetelet's bill of mortality. In July and August old men and infants breathe pure out-of-door air; in January and February that luxury perhaps cannot be afforded.

There is, however, no doubt that the power of generating heat and of resisting cold is very different at different ages; and this depends entirely on the degree of activity. The young Guinea pig, which can run about and pick up food for itself as soon as it is born, is no longer dependent on its mother for heat, or the power of resisting the effects of cold; but young dogs, cats, and rabbits, which are born blind, do not for some weeks acquire the power of resisting the effects of cold, and would die but for the warmth imparted by the mother. The infant is the most helpless of all animals, and is longest in arriving at maturity sufficient to resist the cold air, and it cannot be too carefully protected, unless in our care to protect it from cold we deprive it of pure air, which is quite as essential as a regular temperature.

Demand for Water in the Human System.

Besides the great demand for water, especially in warm weather, for the purpose of evolving heat, as I have described, it is wanted in large quantities to supply the excretions, and thus carry off effete matter from the system. Three quarters of the system is water; and if the waste of water was no more rapid than that of the solids, we should require half a gallon in a day, the waste of solids being reckoned at nearly two pounds, but the waste of water in warm weather and in active exercise is many times greater than the waste of the solids.

The amount of water excreted by the kidneys varies, being to some extent in the inverse proportion to the excretions from the skin. In summer it is less than in winter; the quantity, therefore, excreted in twenty-four hours cannot be exactly ascertained. It is estimated at about thirty ounces in summer, and forty ounces in winter, for a person who only drinks what nature requires; but many persons drink, from mere habit, twice as much as is needed, which must of course pass off in excretions. From the skin is excreted, in ordinary circumstances, from one pound and three fourths to five pounds in twenty-four hours, and in extraordinary circumstances, as in the case of glass-blowers, furnace workmen, &c., it has amounted to sixteen or twenty pounds. More than half as much as the ordinary excretions from the skin is also excreted from the lungs, besides an indefinite and very variable amount from the bowels. We require, therefore, from four to twelve pounds of water daily to keep all the organs and functions in healthy working order.

Importance of Using Pure Water.

Water, to perform perfectly the duties assigned it in the human economy, must be perfectly pure; nothing but oxygen and hydrogen combined can pass through the system to accomplish the various purposes which I have described, and every element combined with them in water must be disposed of by the excretories, and must be a source of embarrassment and disease to the delicate organs whose duty it is to expel all intruding elements from the system. Our study, therefore, should be to get water as pure as possible. Nature has provided, in two ways, never-failing sources of supply of pure water, — in the juices of all natural food, animal or vegetable, and in the condensation of vapor in the atmosphere. By comparing the analysis of the human body with that of different articles of food, we shall be interested to find on an average as much water in the different articles in their natural state as in the system, and that to compensate for the increased expenditure of water in summer, the amount of water in the fruits and vegetables intended for summer food is vastly greater than is found in the grains and fat meats that are intended for winter. The average amount of water in fruits, and vegetables, and berries, is more than ninety per cent., while seal oil, of which an Esquimaux will eat a gallon in a day, contains no water at all. This interesting provision of nature will be impressed on our minds by bringing together the different articles of food, with the amount of water in each, as in the following table, from analyses already given: —

Quantities of Water in One Hundred Pounds of Vegetable Food.

	Pounds.		Pounds.
Indian meal, . . .	14	Potatoes, ...	75
Rye, ...	13	Carrots, ...	86
Peas, ...	14	Turnips, ...	87
Rice, ...	13	Parsnips, ...	79
Beans, ...	14	Mangel-wurzel, . .	85
Lentils, ...	14	Cabbage, ...	92
Buckwheat, . . .	14	Apricot, ...	75
Barley, ...	14	Green Gage, . . .	71
Oatmeal, ...	13	Peach, ...	80
Oyster, ...	87	Cherries, ...	75
Egg, ...	67	Gooseberries, . . .	81
Milk, ...	87	Cucumber, . . .	97
Beef without fat, . .	74	Apples, ...	84
Veal, " . . .	75	Pears, ...	84
Mutton, " . . .	71	Butter, ...	None.
Pork, " . . .	76	Lard, ...	"
Chicken, " . . .	73	Almond oil, . .	"
Codfish, ...	79	Olive oil, ...	"
Haddock, ...	82	Mutton suet, . . .	"
		Fat of all meats, .	"

From the above table it will be seen that five sixths

of the food usually eaten consists of water; and therefore, using an average amount of vegetable food, we get more water than the natural proportion of that element in the human system. And if our liquid excretions were no greater in proportion than the solid, we should need no drink. Noticing this fact, some of our ultra dietetic reformers have inferred that the intention of Nature was that water should be supplied through food alone; and Alcott succeeded in abstaining entirely for a whole year from all kinds of liquids except such as were furnished in natural food, as milk, vegetables, fruits, &c.; but I often thought, when seeing him moping about the streets, looking like a walking mummy, that his personal appearance did not very highly recommend his principles. He said, however, that he did not experience the sensation of thirst more than two or three times, and that after copious perspiration from working in hot weather. His food was entirely vegetable, and he ate six pounds in a day, which would give him five pounds of fluid daily, — an amount, it would seem, abundantly sufficient for such a desiccated specimen of humanity. — He needed more nutriment rather than more water, his gastronomic capacity not being sufficient to contain, in such food, the requisite amount of nutrition.

But that Nature intended partially to supply water to the system through the medium of food, is evident from the fact to which I have before alluded, that food produced in warm climates, and intended for warm weather, when water is most needed to supply the excretions, contains a much larger proportion of water than food intended for cold climates and cold weather. This is seen in the above table, the green vegetables and fruits showing from eighty to ninety-seven per cent. of water, while the fat of all animals contains none. Still, there are very few animals, whatever their food may be, who do not drink water. Mice, quails, parrots, and a few other birds and quadrupeds, are said to drink no water; but cattle, which live on grass alone, containing more than ninety per cent. of water, still require drink, and perish without it; which to me is proof positive that food was not intended to supply all the water needed in the system.

It is, however, best to use as far as practicable food containing water, especially in places where pure water cannot be obtained, as water combined in natural food is absolutely pure, and perceptibly different from the purest water obtained outside of this natural organization. This, in regard to milk, has been proved by experiment. Carefully add to a dish of pure fresh milk a few drops of pure Cochituate water, and almost immediately, under a microscope, can be seen commencing a change which will result in decomposition. Place a dish of pure milk, containing eighty-seven per cent. of water, as it came from the cow, where it will keep sweet twenty-four hours, and place beside it another dish of the same milk, adding only one per cent. of pure water of the same temperature, and the milk last named will be changed in less than twelve hours. When our milkmen, therefore, dilute their milk, they not only defraud by selling water for milk, but they actually adulterate it in the true sense of that term. From this fact housekeepers and milkmen may get an important hint. It is not only necessary, in order to keep milk from changing, to have the dish or can containing it well scalded and sweet, but also perfectly dry, a single drop of pure water being sufficient to start the process of fermentation, or change, and the more impure the water the greater will be its influence.

No water can be obtained perfectly pure, as even that which comes directly from the clouds contains slight traces of mineral, animal, and vegetable matter. Carbonate and muriate of ammonia have been obtained by distillation from pure river water, and this ammonia is the cause of that feeling of softness which is even greater than in pure distilled water.

Collected in the cleanest and purest vessels, it also contains organic matter and the germ of animal and vegetable life sufficient to produce putrefaction, animalcule and vegetable moulds; and when collected in large cities it is less pure than in the country, containing as it does, besides the impurities already mentioned, creosote, carbonic acid gas, and other materials resulting from combustion, decomposition, and evaporation. Still, next to water contained in milk, and the juices of fruits, rain water is the purest.

Snow Water.

Snow, being rain congealed, contains the same ammoniac impurities; but being congealed in the upper and purer regions of the atmosphere, it brings down with it less of the organic impurities, but being in other respects the same, cannot be injurious to health, as is commonly supposed. It will not, however, quench thirst unless melted before it goes into the mouth, the loss of heat in melting counteracting entirely the natural effect of water, so that the natives of arctic regions, according to the testimony of Captain Ross, "prefer enduring the utmost extremity of thirst rather than attempt to remove it by eating snow;" but after it is melted it is as nearly pure as any water, and quenches thirst as well.

Spring Water.

Water falling in rain on the surface of the earth percolates through the soil and substratal gravel or sand, till it comes down to an impervious stratum, carrying with it of course all soluble substances that have been taken up but not filtered out by the sand through which it passes. It passes along this impervious substratum till it comes to some opening in a valley, or remains to be obtained through a well. It is of course affected by the salts of the soil, and by the soluble minerals in the gravel, or sand, or rock through which it passes, and the quality of the water depends on the character of the soil and the gravel. If the soil be thin and poor, and the foundation rock and gravel be granite, as in New England, there are few soluble salts or minerals to be taken up, and the water is pure; but if the soil is rich, and the subsoil and rocks are mixed with soluble mineral compounds, as in most of the rich valleys of our great rivers, the water is filled with organic and mineral matters, and is the source of many diseases.

River Water

Is generally a mixture of rain water and spring water, and of course varies in its impurities according to the character of the soil of which it is the wash, and rocks and gravel through which it is filtered, and according to the amount of impurities which it receives in its passage to the ocean.

From water the system obtains nothing of value but oxygen and hydrogen. This, I think, has been shown by the explanation of the law which makes provision for the fourteen elements in pure air, pure water, and in organized vegetable matter. I cannot, therefore, agree with Dr. Lankester in his "Guide to the Food Collection in the South Kensington Museum." * That waters from rivers, surface wells, and deep artesian wells, containing saline and mineral matters in solution, "provided they are not in quantities so large as to act injuriously on the system, may become a source of supply of these constituents to the body." Having proved, as I think I have, that Nature accepts of no

* I take pleasure in acknowledging my indebtedness to Dr. Lankester for many analyses of grains, &c., and for many other interesting facts which have been of great service in the preparation of this treatise; also to Drs. Johnston, Pereira, and other distinguished English authors.

supplies of elements but in accordance with her own definite provision for these elements, as before explained, I cannot think that she trusts to chance supplies, and would allow the human system to depend for the supply of any elements on waters, some of which contain no inorganic elements, and some quite too many. On the contrary, the first process in the use of water in the system is to remove all elements but oxygen and hydrogen from drinks of any kind as soon as they are taken into the stomach. If the drink contains sugar, or the juice of meat, or any other appropriate element of food, these elements are first abstracted and digested, and if it contains inorganic substances, or organic substances not needed in the system, they are first cast off by the excretories, so that whatever we drink, nothing but pure water is used, or can be used, by the system. If we take brandy, or wine, or beer, or coffee, or tea, or whatever else we take, it quenches thirst because it contains water, and to just the extent of the water. It is therefore important that our drinks should contain nothing deleterious.

The following are the constituents of the waters of the Thames and Colne, as used in London and other cities in England, according to analysis made by Mr. R. Phillips, and accepted by Dr. Pereria, reported in 1843.

One gallon of Thames water, of 70,000 grains, contains, in grains, —

	Inorganic.	Organic.	Total.
At BRENTFORD, the source of the Grand Junction Works. — Solid matter,	19,400	368	19,768
BARNES, source of the West Middlesex Water Works. — Solid matter, . . .	18,600	368	18,968
CHELSEA, source of the Chelsea Water Works, — Solid matter, . . .	19,400	238	19,638

Colne Water.

	Inorganic.	Organic.	Total.
OTTERPOOL SPRING, near Busby. — Soluble matter, ...	21,485	185	21,485
MAIN SPRING, the supply of the Colne. — Soluble matter, ...	21,800	268	22,062
COLNE ITSELF. — Soluble matter, ...	21,300	126	21,426

Analyses of London water, by different chemists, accepted by Dr. Lankester in 1860.

River Water.

	Inorganic.	Organic.	Total.
AT GRAND JUNCTION WATER WORKS.—Soluble matter,	21,500	1,500	23,000
NEW RIVER.—Soluble matter, . . .	21,000	1,000	22,000
THAMES at WICKENHAM.—Soluble matter, ...	20,000	2,000	22,000

Surface Wells.

	Inorganic.	Organic.	Total.
BELGRAVE MEWS, .	110,000	15,000	125,000
GREFTON STREET, .	115,000	26,000	141,000
WADSWORTH ROAD, .	72,000	19,000	91,000
SPENCER'S COURT, .	172,000	14,000	186,000
BROAD STREET (Golden Square), . .	102,000	5,000	107,000

Artesian Wells in Chalk.

	Inorganic.	Organic.	Total.
TRAFALGAR SQUARE,	68,000	0,000	68,000
RICHMOND, . . .	27,200	0,800	28,200
LONG ACRE, . . .	57,000	0,000	57,000

Waters used in American Cities.

	Inorganic.	Organic.	Total.
Croton Water, NEW YORK. — Soluble matter, . .	11.34	7.37	18.71
Schuylkill Water, PHILADELPHIA. — Soluble matter, ...	7.29	2.13	9.42
Cochituate Water, BOSTON. — Soluble matter, . .	2.90	2.45	5.35

The above analyses are by Professor Horsford, and are from one hundred thousand parts, while the analyses of London water were from seventy thousand parts, making the contrast greater than appears in the figures by nearly one third. Professor Benjamin Silliman remarked in his report on Cochituate water, that it is so nearly pure as to answer very well for chemical purposes, for which distilled water is generally used. The reason of its purity is evident. Cochituate Lake, being supplied mainly from springs coming through pure granite sand, and resting also on pure sand, and not being much exposed to the influence of decaying vegetable matters, it has no source of supply either of organic or inorganic material.

The importance of pure water, as a means of preserving health, will be understood by all who have given attention to the laws which I have endeavored to explain, by which all elements not organized in pure water, pure air, and appropriate food, are rejected by the system as poisonous; but we have also facts which place the subject in a very strong light. In a case at the Nottingham Assizes, in July, 1836, it was proved that dysentery in an aggravated form was caused in cattle by the use of water with putrescent vegetable matter, produced by the refuse of a starch factory; proving my position true, that nutritious elements, if disorganized, become poisonous. The fish (perch, gudgeon, pike, roach, and dace), and even frogs in the pond through which the brook ran, were destroyed. All the cows, calves, and horses which drank of this water became sick, and in eight years the plaintiff lost twenty-four cows and nine calves, all of dysentery. It was also shown that the mortality was in proportion to the quantity of starch made at different times, and that when the water containing the putrescent matter was not allowed to pass into the brook the mortality ceased, and the frogs and fishes were restored.

Dr. Bell, surgeon to the barracks at Cork, found dysentery prevailing among the soldiers, till he suspected that it arose from water contaminated by the drainage from the city, and, changing the water to that of pure spring water, had no more of the disease; and in our late rebellion, it was found that whenever the soldiers were obliged to drink water containing organic impurities, as in the swamps of Chickahominy, they soon became sick of dysentery, or some other disease of the digestive organs.

Waters containing Inorganic Substances usually denominated Hard Waters.

Those waters which are usually obtained from wells, contain salts of various kinds, derived from the soil and subsoil through which they percolate, and of course are more or less injurious as they contain elements and combinations more or less active. The most common salt found in hard water is sulphate of lime, the elements of which and the elements of soap have a mutual affinity for each other, and when soap is used with such water a double decomposition takes place, — the sulphuric acid unites with the alkali of the soap, setting free the fatty acids, which, uniting with the lime, form an insoluble earthy soap, which floats on the surface, and the soap losing its influence, the water feels hard and very imperfectly performs the functions of ablution. These salts also have a very unfavorable effect in the animal economy, as the elements not being wanted in the system have to be cast out through the excretories, causing, in their passage out, diseases of the kidney and of the skin, and it is found that gravelly deposits and eruptions of the skin are frequent in proportion to the inorganic substances in the water habitually used. Horses seem instinctively aware of the evils of hard water, and prefer even turbid river water to hard well water. Mr. Youatt, an English writer, in his book on the Horse, published in London, 1831, says, "Hard water, drawn fresh from the well, will assuredly make the coat of a horse, unaccustomed to it, stare, and it will not unfrequently gripe and otherwise injure him." And Mr. Chadwick, in his report to her Majesty's principal Secretary of State for the Home Department from the Poor Law Commissioners, on an inquiry into the sanitary condition of the laboring population of Great Britain in 1842, observes that "water containing animal matter, which is the most feared, appears to be less frequently injurious than that which is clearest, namely, spring water, from the latter being oftener impregnated with mineral substances." These considerations are sufficient to show that pure water is important for the preservation of health; but in one respect pure waters are more dangerous than those containing salts, especially the salts of lime. Pure water will, under some circumstances, corrode lead pipes, and dissolve more lead than those containing salts of lime, especially carbonates, which form a crust on the surface of the pipes, and thus protect them from the action of water, while even rain water, on surfaces of lead exposed to air and water alternately, as in lead gutters, cisterns, pipes, &c., acts with considerable energy, as may be seen by examining any pipe at the surface of a cistern of water, or any cistern lined with zinc or lead, at the surface of the water, or the top of a closed cistern, where the steam or moisture gathers. The drops of water which condense on the top of a cistern of water are impregnated with the oxide of zinc or lead (both nearly equally poisonous), and dropping into the water, impregnate the whole mass, and render it unfit for drinking purposes. There are also places in all lined cisterns, and all pipes where two metals are united or come in contact, forming a galvanic battery — as in soldered joints, supporting bars of iron, copper faucets, &c., and the action on the water, however pure, in these parts will cause decomposition of the metals; and thus in the purest water, if we obtain it through lead pipes, or zinc-lined cisterns, or copper boilers, we get some very deleterious mineral matters, which affect the system, even though we get them in very minute quantities.

The worst of this influence is, that it is cumulative; and no particular effects being perceived, perhaps, for a long time, we come to doubt whether water which we have used with apparent impunity for months, and perhaps years, can in any way be injurious; and many a disease, such as colic, numbness, pain in the bones, constipation, fits, spasms, cramps, &c., is charged to something else, or the cause of which is not known, is really induced by the cumulative influence of lead, zinc, or copper from our water pipes or cistern linings, &c. Cases frequently occur in which whole families are afflicted with some mysterious and complicated diseases, from which they suffer for months and years, and which destroy all their comfort and all their usefulness, and even the life of some of the members, before they suspect the cause; but when scientific investigation is finally obtained, the cause is found to be lead pipes, from which they had used water from the same well for years, much of the time enjoying good health. Not one half of the evils from metallic water pipes are known, or ever can be known, till they are utterly discarded, and we experience the blessings of health which come from pure water.

Every scientific man, and every other man who realizes these evils to the community, ought to "cry aloud and spare not," till our city authorities, and every individual householder, shall open their eyes to see them, and shall banish forever all unprotected metallic service pipe. Let the people once make up their minds they will drink no water poisoned with lead, or zinc, or copper, whatever it may cost to get pure water, and there will be found means of procuring pure water; but as long as we deceive ourselves as we do with the idea that however others may suffer from water impregnated with lead, or zinc, or copper, we are safe, — our well of water, and our Cochituate, or Croton, or Schuylkill water does not corrode pipes, — we shall continue to take water poisoned with lead and other mineral matters.

The truth is, we who laugh at the silly ostrich for poking her head under the sand, and thinking herself safe because she can see no danger, are after all but little wiser. We blind our eyes to a thousand evils, and bear their consequences rather than take the trouble to remove them.

Ask a man who lives on the border of Chickahominy Swamp, or any other notoriously vile and sickly locality, about the health and comforts of his home, and he will tell you he has "a heap" of good and pleasant things about him, and no annoyances or sickness of any kind. "They have the dysentery and bilious fever over the other side, a few miles off, and the mosquitoes are awful;" but he has none of these troubles.

Ask a man, as I did, who had always lived on the Mississippi River, and always drank water so thickened with organic and inorganic impurities that it looks like gruel more than like water, why he did not filter the vile stuff, and he will tell you, as he told me, "There was never sweeter, or better, or more healthy water drank in the world; it is much better without filtering, as it has more *body to it.*" I asked him if in his neighborhood they were not subject to dysenteries, bowel complaints, bilious fevers, and the like. He said, Yes; but the water had nothing to do with such troubles.

Ask the Cochituate Water Board about Boston water, and they will tell you truly that it is the purest water used by any large city on the face of the earth; that, according to Prof. Benjamin Silliman, it is capable of dissolving only forty-six hundredths of a grain of lead in a gallon, and therefore cannot corrode leaden pipes; but they will not tell you that, open any cistern or any pipe that is not all the time full, and you will find the lining coated with carbonate of lead, and that near the soldered joints a galvanic and chemical action is constantly going on, so that the pipes are eaten off and burst very frequently (in my house the pipes are eaten off and burst five or six times a year, and always near some soldered joint).

Deceive ourselves as we may, there is no water incapable of acting on lead, or zinc, or copper, under some circumstances, and these metals should never be used for, or connected with service pipe; and the sooner the people fully understand this fact the better. But how shall we protect ourselves in the mean time? It takes a long time for the most palpable truths to get control of corporations, proverbially conservative. Meantime we should never use water to drink or for cooking that has stood for any length of time in the pipes, and never use at all for these purposes water that comes from a leaden or zinc-lined cistern.

Water containing organic matters can be filtered through sand and charcoal. Boiling also purifies water, the salts that are held in solution by carbonic acid, as the carbonate of lime, or carbonate of iron, or lead, the heat of boiling water driving off the carbonic acid, and leaving the lime, or iron, or lead deposited on the vessel in which it is boiled. In travelling in regions where the water is impregnated with lime, or organic materials, it is a good precaution to drink no water that has not been boiled, and a better plan still, to get as much as possible of the necessary supply for the system from milk, and vegetables, and fruits, from which we get water absolutely pure, and fitted to be appropriated, without any process of purification, in the stomach. Another reason for not drinking water which contains organic matters, without boiling, is, that all such waters contain animaculæ, and the eggs of insects and vermin, some of which are capable of resisting the action of the gastric juice, and will live and grow in the stomach; thus leeches, and snakes, and other disgusting creatures have been known to be taken in impure or stagnant water in which they are hatched, and live in the stomach for a long time, causing great annoyance and distress. No animalcules are found in water absolutely pure, and none are known to exist that are not destroyed by boiling water.

And now, having explained the process by which, at such infinite expense, water is furnished to every living thing, everywhere and at all times, and having shown that pure water, and nothing else, can dilute the blood and prepare it to circulate, carrying to every part the nourishment needed, and taking from every part the effete materials no longer wanted, and that nothing else can supply the hydrogen, and other elements, as they are needed in the system, and that, therefore, all other drinks subserve these different purposes because they contain water, and in just the proportion as they contain water, all other drinks might be summarily disposed of as useless and injurious; but wedded, as every nation is, to some artificial drink, and biased, as scientific men are, in favor of that to which they themselves are accustomed, there is need of applying chemistry, physiology, and common sense to our drinks, as well as to our solid food. For, though it be true, as we have said, that pure water is the only true drink, and that therefore there can be no substitute for it; and though it be true that all the living creatures which

God has made, some of which, as we have seen, are subject to the same physiological laws as man, and take the same kind of food, all take water alone for drink, and are all contented with it; still, to conform to his cosmopolitan character, man sometimes needs some modification of water for drink to avoid and counteract the influence of impure water, to which, in our present ignorance of the means of correcting the evil, we are sometimes subject. Even a teetotaller ought to be excused for breaking his pledge if so situated that he could get nothing else, and must choose between wine, although it did contain a little poisonous alcohol, and impure waters, containing materials a thousand times more deleterious than a little alcohol.

The substitutes for water, commonly adopted in civilized nations, are alcoholic drinks, including distilled spirits, beers, cider, wines,—and tea, coffee, and chocolate; each of which deserves, and shall have, a passing notice.

Tea.

That infusion which is usually denominated Tea, which is used by five hundred millions of the inhabitants of the earth, is made from the leaves of several varieties of a small shrub found in China and India, and now cultivated in many other parts of the world. The leaves are not gathered till the plant is four years old; and the plant is renewed every tenth or twelfth year. The shrub is closely allied to the well-known

Camellia Japonica. The difference between teas of the two general classes in common use — the green and black teas — is accounted for in different ways by different authors. Lankester says the difference is partly the result of soil and growth, and partly from the mode of curing. "Black tea consists of leaves slightly fermented, washed and twisted. Genuine green tea is made of exactly the same leaves, washed and twisted without fermentation; but commercial 'green' teas are often black teas colored with Prussian blue." While Mr. Reeves, whose opinion, according to the authority of Pereira, is entitled to great weight, expresses his surprise "that any person who has been in China, or indeed any one who has seen the difference in the color of the infusions of black and green tea, could suppose for a moment that they were the product of the same plant, differing only in the mode of curing, particularly as they do not grow in the same neighborhood of each other." But whether the difference consists in the manner of preparing, or the species or varieties of plants, chemical analysis shows that green tea, as it comes to us, contains more tannin, and more of that peculiar principle which is found combined with tannin, which is called theine, or theina, which is the same principle found in coffee, and called caffeine. The tannin is injurious on account of its astringent effects, and the theine and caffeine are injurious to many people on account of their peculiar influence on the nervous system, inducing restlessness and wakefulness. On that account green tea disagrees with more people than black tea, and, in this country, is almost given up for black tea.

Dr. Lankester estimates that in the United Kingdom above thirty-two thousand tons, or seventy-three millions of pounds, are annually used, or about two pounds and three quarters for every person in the kingdom; and he has given a table showing the relative consumption of tea in different countries; and I transcribe below his estimate for the United Kingdom, France, Russia, and the United States.

Annual Consumption, in Ounces, per Head of the Population.

United Kingdom, ...	35¼ oz.
France, ...	1 "
Russia, ...	4 "
United States, ...	16 "

The property which distinguishes the different kinds of teas from each other, and gives them their flavor, is found in the form of volatile oil. This flavor, or osmazome, is, as I think can be shown, the source of all the benefits that can be derived from tea, and the source of one class of evils which arise from its use in excess. By the chemical analysis of pure tea, of any variety, we find no elements capable of doing harm to the system, except tannin and osmazome. Osmazome in tea seems to be a flavor universally admired, and therefore the cause of its extensive use all over the world. It is only injurious when taken in excess, being the element diffused through all natural food, and which is useful in giving a relish and in promoting digestion; but in excess, produces nervous excitement and subsequent depression. These effects are, however, evanescent, and soon pass away unless the cause is continued. But tannin, or tannic acid, is a medical agent, permanent in its effects, and undoubtedly injurious to the system in proportion to its use. It is found combined with theine, the peculiar principle of tea, and constitutes more than twenty-five per cent. of the dry leaf.

According to Dr. Lankester, one pound of good tea contains —

Water, ...	0 oz.	350 gr.
Theine, ...	0 "	210 "
Tannic acid, ...	4 "	87 "
Casein, ...	2 "	175 "
Aromatic oil, ...	0 "	52 "
Sugar, ...	0 "	211 "
Fat, ...	0 "	280 "
Woody fibre, ...	3 "	87 "
Mineral matter, . . .	0 "	350 "
Gum, ...	2 "	385 "

The chemical difference between black and green teas may be seen by the following table from Mulder, comparing two kinds of green tea with two kinds of black: —

	Chinese.		Javanese.	
	Green.	Black.	Green.	Black.
Chlorophyll, ...	2.22	1.84	3.24	1.28
Wax, ...	0.28	.00	0.32	.00
Resin, ...	2.22	3.64	1.64	2.44
Gum, ...	8.56	7.28	12.20	11.08
Tannin, ...	17.80	12.88	17.56	14.80
Theine, ...	0.43	0.46	0.60	0.65
Extractive matter, . .	22.80	19.88	21.63	18.64
Apotheme, ...	.00	1.48	.00	1.64
Ext. obtained by hydrochloric acid, . . .	23.60	19.12	20.36	18.24
Albumen, ...	3.00	2.80	3.64	1.28
Fibrous matter, . . .	17.08	28.32	18.20	27.00
Volatile oil, ...	0.79	0.60	0.98	0.65

By this table we see why green tea is more injurious than black, containing as it does nearly one third more tannin, and from one third to one quarter more volatile oil, while of the other important element, theine, there is a little more in the black tea. That it is not theine, but tannin and volatile oil, that produces tremor, anxiety, sleeplessness, &c., is therefore proved, black tea containing most theine, and yet producing least of these nervous symptoms. On the other hand, I cannot believe with Liebig that theine or caffeine have any important influence in the change of the tissues or in the composition of the bile, and "are better adapted to this purpose than all other nitrogenized vegetable principles."

We have seen that every principle, important to the human economy, is so carefully provided for, that wherever man may choose to live, he finds all these principles prepared for his use ready at hand; but caffeine and theine are only found in tropical climates, and are indeed quite local in their production. We find, also, that more than three quarters of all the people in the world live and enjoy health without ever tasting these principles. Liebig's theories, therefore, in this matter, as in many others, are not sustained by facts or general principles. Theine, caffeine, or any other peculiar principles found in tea or coffee, cannot be proved to be essential to health in any circumstances or conditions of life; but I am not, on the other hand, prepared to prove that to everybody they are essentially injurious.

The truth, it seems to me, lies between the extremists, on the one hand, who think theine and caffeine, to use again the words of Liebig, "are capable of supplying the place of the nitrogenized product produced in the healthy state of the body," and the extremists, on the other hand, who condemn tea and coffee "as evil, and only evil, and that continually." Tea and coffee are sometimes useful; but not for nutriment, or to take the place of nutriment: Nature furnishes no substitutes. They are useful for their osmazomes, and are useful or injurious as they are used or not used in accordance with the purposes of that principle; and here, perhaps, as well as anywhere, I may explain what is meant by osmazome, and its purposes in the economy of nature.

The Principle which gives Relish to Food and Drink.

Much too little has hitherto been thought by physiologists, and almost nothing has been written on that beautiful provision for our happiness by which everything that is useful as food or drink is made agreeable to the palate, so that the higher our relish for any given article, the more perfectly is it digested and made to supply the wants of the system, we have therefore a natural guide to the right kind of food at the right time, and, on the other hand, have a disrelish for articles which, not being suited to our condition, would be injurious. But a little reflection will show us that, in this adaptation of our palates to the peculiar taste or osmazome of every distinct article of food, we have a faithful sentinel, inviting the admission of friends and protecting us from the approach of enemies.

Place before a child, who has never tasted of sugar, or butter, or superfine flour, or any other elements of food that have been separated from their natural connections, and whose tastes are therefore unperverted, milk, unbolted bread, meats, fruits, or any other natural food, and he will choose just that article which is best adapted to his condition at the time, and may be trusted to eat as much as he pleases.

At first, after being weaned from his primary milk, he will prefer the milk of the cow, and after a while need, and choose with it, some more concentrated food, as unbolted wheat, or other bread from grains in their natural state, and then meats, and potatoes, and fruits, according to their season; and he never will desire any other than natural food till his appetite is perverted by sugar, or butter, &c., which, being separated from their natural elements, contain their osmazome in a state too concentrated. After that, his bread will be insipid without butter, and his milk must have sugar, and the natural relations of his tastes to natural osmazomes is broken up. And so dependent are the digestive organs on the osmazome to which they are used, that, after becoming accustomed to butter, sugar, tea, coffee, or any other food or drink in which is a concentrated and agreeable flavor, they will not readily digest food without them. Thus we become accustomed to, and dependent on, articles of food and drink which are temporarily useful, but permanently injurious.

Many a man becomes so accustomed to alcoholic drinks, as wines, beers, and even laudanum, that he suffers from indigestion and loss of appetite unless they are constantly supplied; and this, as I understand it, is the source of benefit from tea and coffee. The agreeable osmazome promotes digestion, as all other agreeable flavors do; and with a dinner or breakfast of food which, from improper cooking, or for any other reason, is not relished, a small cup of pure aromatic coffee or tea is undoubtedly a real benefit.

The French people seem to understand this principle better than the English or Americans, not only in regard to tea and coffee, but in regard to all kinds of food and drink, adjusting the articles to each other, so as not to burden the system with redundant carbonates while the nitrates and phosphates are deficient, and always making them relish by delicate condiments. Instead of drinking with a breakfast three or four cups of coffee or tea, boiled so as to extract all the tannin and lose most of the aroma, they take only moderately of an infusion made so quickly as to extract only the aromatic properties, while the more deleterious tannin remains with the dregs. And this, after all, to my mind is a solution of that vexed question which has so puzzled and deceived Liebig and other physiologists.

That coffee, tea, fragrant wines, and other alcoholic drinks, &c., do under some circumstances take the place of food, or at least enable men to keep the flesh and strength with less food than without them, there is no doubt; but that this is done according to the theory of Liebig, "by retarding the metamorphosis of the tissues," or by furnishing actual nourishment from alcohol or any peculiar principles in coffee or tea, there is not a shadow of proof. On the other hand, the evidence is clear, that not in proportion to the alcohol, or theine, or caffeine contained in these articles is the benefit to be derived from them, but in proportion as the osmazome of each is agreeable to those who take them; and the benefit is derived from the perfect digestion of food which is caused by this agreeable osmazome. No man of careful observation has failed to notice that a little food, well relished, will keep us in better condition than large quantities of the most appropriate elements so badly cooked, or so miserably served, as not to be eaten with relish; and this explains the well-known fact that Frenchmen live and keep in good condition at one third less expense than Yankees or Englishmen.

Having now given my views of the sources of benefit to be derived from tea, coffee, and all other agreeable beverages, and shown that they are useful in promoting digestion by their osmazome, and not by any special principle contained in them, it will be useless to go into an analysis of each beverage. The whole matter may be summed up as follows: The system needs the three classes of elements included in the terms Nitrates, Carbonates, and Phosphates, and pure water; and these elements, to be rightly appropriated, must be presented to the digestive organs flavored so as to be agreeable to them; and this flavor is as important as the other elements.

The experiment has been tried of shutting up a dog, with good natural food, containing all needed elements but osmazome, but having been cooked and re-cooked till all taste and smell were removed; the stomach would not receive it, and the dog pined away until it was evident he would starve without this element, although all others were supplied. And this one experiment, it seems to me, is worth more than a volume of commentaries on the importance of osmazome. It shows us not only that it is duty to eat good food, containing nutritive elements in right proportions, but it is duty to eat it also with a good relish.

Does any one say he cannot afford to eat good ripe fruit, and berries, and well-flavored meats, and vegetables? let him make a calculation, comparing the amount of fine flour, butter, sugar, and other carbonaceous food consumed by his family, with the requisite amount of that class of elements, as shown by the tables, and calculate the amount of money thus uselessly expended, and he will find that, by bringing his commissary department under physiological rules, he will have surplus funds sufficient to procure every natural luxury which is needed to enable him to enjoy, to the fullest extent, the very highest gustatory pleasures of which he is capable.

And here again we are liable to err. Our gustatory pleasures are not in proportion to the amount of osmazome in our food or drink. Nature's flavors are very delicate, and the very choicest relish is that produced by very slight traces of osmazome. For example, take nutmeg, a very slight grating of which will flavor a large bowl of porridge. Attempt to increase the relish by increasing the quantity of the spice, and you utterly fail, making your beverage less and less agreeable as you increase the quantity of nutmeg, till it becomes disgusting, and positively injurious to the digestive process; and this is true of all other condiments, and indeed all other good things. Delicate flavors are agreeable and useful in promoting digestion; but every article which is capable of promoting health and happiness, in appropriate quantities, is capable of doing harm in unnatural quantities, just as every other blessing is converted into a curse by being perverted and misused.

Just here human nature, especially Yankee human nature, is prone to deceive itself. A man finds himself very happy with his family in a little tasteful cottage home, with an income sufficient to meet his expenses, and save a little every year for future contingencies; but he wants a larger income, that he may increase his conveniences, enlarge his establishment, and lay up more money. But does his enjoyment increase with his means? On the contrary, his cares increase, and his real enjoyment diminishes at every step, till long before he becomes a millionnaire he is decidedly miserable.

The doctor thinks by taking medicine twice a day his patient may get well in two weeks; but the patient prefers to wait only one week, and therefore takes his medicine four times a day: but if the directions were judiciously given, the patient finds himself worse and not better at the end of the week.

A cup of very weak, well-flavored tea or coffee may be very agreeable, and promote digestion, and be of real service, especially if taken with food which is not well relished; but if we follow our inclinations, and attempt to increase the enjoyment and the advantage of the beverage by increasing its strength or its quantity, we may get instead nervous excitement, restlessness, and indigestion, and a thousand other troubles, and the evils will increase, while the pleasures and benefits will diminish, pro rata. And thus we find everywhere the same law, encouraging us to be content with Nature's simple arrangements for our welfare and happiness, and warning us of the danger of disregarding them. My position in regard to condiments and aromatic drinks is this: If we could always get good natural food, adapted to our constitutional condition, and have it cooked so as best to develop its natural osmazome, and if we could get with it pure water, we should need nothing else to enable us to enjoy to the fullest extent our gustatory pleasures, and the enjoyment arising from the highest degree of health and activity of all our faculties; but that, with unsavory food and impure water, we derive great benefit from delicately flavored condiments and aromatic beverages in moderate quantities; that a choice in these beverages is to be determined by consulting the taste of each individual; that in preparing these beverages the question is how to get the osmazome without getting the deleterious qualities with which it is connected; and that the advantages to be derived from osmazome are never in direct proportion to the amount taken, but are more nearly in the inverse proportion, while the deleterious elements connected with almost all the beverages in common use increase in direct proportion to the quantity used.

The deleterious element in tea and coffee we have already shown to be tannin, and this element can be avoided by making these beverages quickly, never allowing but a few moments in steeping. By this process the osmazome, being volatile, is all obtained, while the tannin, being extractive, remains with the dregs. Made in this way, and used moderately, there are very few individuals to whom they are injurious.

Beer, Cider, Wine, &c.

Of the other aromatic beverages in common use,— beer, cider, wine, &c.,—the deleterious principle is alcohol; but the principle which distinguishes each, and constitutes its value, is osmazome; all other principles of any consequence, are sugar, starch, &c., which they hold in common with articles of food, and which are derived from the grains and fruits from which they are made; but the osmazome in these beverages, as in those already considered, constitutes their commercial and their real value. The only chemical difference between the highest and the lowest priced wines consists in the "bouquet," or osmazome, but alcohol is the principle for which these beverages are universally demanded; and as there has been, and is still to some extent, a difference of opinion among chemists and physiologists respecting the relation of this principle to the human system, it will be necessary to give it a careful consideration. (See page 220.)

Cocoa and Chocolate.

The chocolate plant, of which cocoa is the seed, is a small tree, with dark green leaves, growing in Mexico, Caraccas, Demerara, and other places. It produces an elongated fruit, in shape like a cucumber, but more blunt, which grows from the stem or main branches. The seeds, or beans, that furnish the cocoa, are imbedded in the fruit in rows, in a spongy substance, and are about fifty or sixty in each fruit. When ripe, the seeds are taken out, cleaned and dried. The best cocoa is made from seeds shelled and roasted, but inferior cocoa is made by grinding with the seeds a part of the shell. *Cocoa-nibs* are made from seeds merely roasted and crushed after being shelled; *Cocoa-paste* is the seed ground down, and mixed with sugar; and if flavored with vanilla, it is called CHOCOLATE.

Cocoa differs from tea and coffee in that it is rich in nutritious food, and having in it no tannin or other deleterious elements, its theobromine, or characteristic property, being connected with albumen — a muscle-making element; as the characteristic element of tea, theine, is connected with tannin. Containing also a large share of butter, and four per cent. of phosphates, it is supplied with all the requisite elements of food, and to those who like its flavor, it is a very agreeable and useful beverage, having all the advantage of tea and coffee, without their deleterious qualities. Its nutritive elements are, however, too concentrated to agree with very delicate stomachs, as may be inferred from the following analysis. One hundred parts *cocoa* contain, —

Water, . . .	5.0
Albumen. . .	20.0
Theobromine, .	2.0
Butter, . . .	50.0
Woody fibre, .	4.0
Gum, . . .	6.0
Starch, . . .	7.0
Red coloring matter, . . .	2.0
Mineral matter, .	4.0
	100.0

or,

Water, . . .	5.0
Nitrates, . . .	22.0
Carbonates, . .	69.0
Phosphates, . .	4.0
	100.0

One pound of Cocoa-nibs, or two pounds of Cocoa-paste, contain, —

Water, ...	0	350 gr.
Nitrates (Albumen and Gluten), . .	3 oz.	85
Theobromine, ...	0	140 gr.

Alcohol.

I have already adverted to alcohol as being the result of the chemical decomposition of sugar. (See page 70.) We come now to consider and establish the fact that, though sugar and alcohol are composed of the same elements, viz., hydrogen, oxygen, and carbon, the one is a useful carbonaceous food, while the other is a poison.

Alcohol is sugar disorganized by the process of fermentation, and is subject to the same law as phosphorus and iron. It is composed of carbon, hydrogen, and oxygen, as is also sugar, from which it is made, — elements which are wanted in the system, as well as phosphorus and iron, and if taken into the stomach organized, as in sugar-cane or beet, are all gratefully received and easily digested; but taken in a disorganized state, as in alcohol, they cause immediate excitement, by the efforts of all the organs to expel them as intruders.

Let us see how nearly alike, chemically, are sugar and alcohol, and the change effected by the process of fermentation.

One atom of sugar contains, —

Carbon.	Hydrogen.	Oxygen.
12 atoms.	12 atoms.	12 atoms.

These are converted, by fermentation, into two atoms of alcohol, containing, —

Carbon.	Hydrogen.	Oxygen.
8 atoms.	12 atoms.	4 atoms,

and four atoms of carbonic acid gas, which accounts for the lost carbon and oxygen, the carbonic acid gas containing, —

Carbon.	Hydrogen.	Oxygen.
4 atoms, and	None.	8 atoms, and
8 "	12 atoms.	4 "
12 atoms.	12 atoms.	12 atoms.

Thus we see that the same elements are found in sugar as in alcohol, and combined in the same proportions; but sugar, being organized for digestion, is agreeable to the natural taste, and is readily appropriated as carbonaceous food, while alcohol, being disorganized, creates a rebellion, and is rejected from the system as an intruder; so that we find in alcohol, as in the preparations of phosphorus and iron, the elements are agreeably and usefully appropriated by the system or rejected as poisonous, as they are or are not organized in Nature's own laboratory. And this consideration, it would seem, should forever settle the question whether alcohol is nutritious, and clearly show that vital law is higher than chemical law, and must control it; and that therefore the same chemical combinations of elements may be poisonous or nutritious as they are or are not subject to vital law, as we have before seen in combinations of phosphorus and iron.

Liebig's Theory respecting the Nutritive Qualities of Alcohol.

It is now more than twenty-five years since Liebig commenced his valuable chemical investigations of food, and its relations to the human system. He discovered that some elements of food—carbon, hydrogen, &c.—were appropriated for the purpose of producing heat, while others were devoted to the growth and strength of the muscles; and finding sugar and alcohol both to be composed of these carbonaceous elements, he classed them together as heat-producing articles of food; and that idea has since been adopted by many, perhaps most chemists, and some physiologists; but I have endeavored to show (pages 37–41) that the same combination of elements may be, and are, nutritious or poisonous as they are or are not organized by the process which Nature has provided; and that while sugar is a valuable principle in food, alcohol contains no power of sustaining life, but, on the other hand, produces in the human system "evil, and only evil, and that continually;" and this I shall endeavor to prove.

Professor Carpenter, of the London University, has published a book on physiology, which as late as 1860 has been republished in Philadelphia, edited by Professor Francis Guerney Smith. From that Physiology, which is now the standard work in this country and England, I copy these words: —

"It may be safely affirmed that alcohol cannot answer any one purpose for which the use of water is required in the system, but, on the other hand, it tends to antagonize many of those purposes."

"Alcoholic liquids cannot supply anything which is essential to the due nutrition of the system."

"The action of alcohol upon the living body is essentially that of a stimulus, increasing, for a time, the vital activity of the body, but being followed by a corresponding depression of power, which is the more prolonged and severe in proportion as the previous excitement has been greater."

The U. S. Dispensatory, compiled by Professor

Wood, of Philadelphia, the standard work on that subject in the United States, also expresses similar opinions on the character and effects of alcohol. Professor Bigelow's Materia Medica, the standard work when I was a member of Harvard School, expresses a similar opinion. All agree that alcohol is a stimulus which, literally, means a *goad*, a *whip*. When a horse gets stuck with a load too heavy for him, we use the goad or whip to excite the muscles to take the load up the hill. But, when once up, the careful driver will be sure that next time the load shall be lighter, or the horse made stronger with oats. What should we say to the teamster who persisted in the opinion that the whip afforded nourishment to the horse because he could be made to draw a heavier load by whipping, and therefore persisted in whipping him more severely as his strength became exhausted? But if this is not the position of those who think that alcohol is nutritious I cannot understand them.

Is alcohol useful in promoting digestion, or in consumption or general debility?

Keeping in mind the fact that, upon the highest medical authority alcohol is only a stimulant, I have no difficulty in determining how far alcohol is useful and how far injurious.

I have sat by the bedside, and, watching the sinking pulse, and fearing lest Nature might not be able to carry the load, have put in the goad, and in three minutes have felt the circulation rise; but in a few minutes more it would sink again, and the stimulant must be renewed, or it would sink lower than before. By careful watching and spurring I have kept up the heat and circulation till a little nourishment could be digested, and perhaps the patient saved. But this is all the use I have ever made of alcohol as a medicine.

To whip and spur poor human nature all the way down through consumption to the grave, increasing the stimulus at every step as nature flags, seems to me absurd, cruel, and unphilosophical in the extreme. If stimulants should be thus applied to a jaded horse, its owner would be tried for cruelty to his beast; and yet there are said to be hundreds and thousands of men, women, and even children, now subjected to a similar mode of treatment in Boston and vicinity.

In an essay which obtained the prize of two hundred dollars, and which, Dr. Churchill says, displays great research upon the subject of the effects of alcohol, Dr. Bell comes to the following conclusions: —

"1. The opinion so largely prevailing as to the effects of the use of alcoholic liquors, viz., that they have a marked influence in preventing the deposition of tubercle, is destitute of any foundation.

"2. On the contrary, their use predisposes to tubercular deposition.

"3. Where tubercle already exists, alcohol has no effect in modifying the course usually run by that substance.

"4. Neither does it mitigate the morbid effects of tubercle upon the system in any stage of the disease."

Professor Wood, in his Dispensatory, says the

habitual use of alcoholic drinks produces deplorable consequences. Carpenter's Physiology says the physiological objection to the habitual use of even quite small quantities of alcoholic drinks rests upon the following grounds: "They are universally admitted to possess a poisonous character." "They tend to produce a morbid condition of the body at large." "The capacity for enduring the extremes of heat or cold, or mental or bodily labor, is diminished rather than increased by their habitual employment."

In a lecture of Professor Jacob Bigelow, in 1825, he used the following words, which I recorded at the time: —

"Alcohol is highly stimulating, heating, and intoxicating, and its effects are so fascinating that, when once experienced, the danger is that the desire for them may be perpetuated." "Many patients have become gradually and imperceptibly intemperate under the sanction and guidance of a physician."

How often has my heart been saddened by witnessing illustrations of Professor Jacob Bigelow's statement concerning patients being led to intemperance by the guidance of their physician. Not long since an interesting lady, not thirty years old, came to me for advice. She had been subject, for two or three years, to terrible internal cramps from indigestion, and was advised by her physician to take gin. At first she only took it when the cramps occurred, and it relieved her, but soon she took it to prevent their recurrence, and it seemed for a time to succeed; but as she never knew when the pains were coming, she never knew when to stop the gin: and after two years her system had become so accustomed to the stimulus that no quantity short of that which produced actual inebriation would either prevent or relieve the distress. In that condition I found her, and of course advised to break off the habit at once, and take appropriate remedies. In two days she returned, and said she had had no return of the cramps, but felt as if she should die unless I allowed her gin, or a substitute. I put the case as it plainly stood. She must break away from gin then, or be a slave to it for life. She braced herself up to the resolution — "I will die now, sober, rather than live to be a drunkard;" and many a time since has she thanked me for assisting her in that resolution. And many a similar case has come under my observation, only differing in this, they never were able to break away from the snare that had caught them.

Is alcohol useful by preserving the tissues, and thus increasing the term of life?

There may be a sense in which this question may be answered in the affirmative, but it seems to me difficult to conceive a case in which tissues thus preserved would be of value sufficient to pay the expense of the process; but this idea having been recently advanced by a learned professor, deserves a passing, though not a serious notice.

Professor Yeomans, of New York, says, "It has been demonstrated that alcoholic drinks prevent the natural changes going on in the blood, and obstruct the nutritive and reparative functions."

Carpenter's Physiology says, "Alcoholic drinks diminish the waste of the tissues." That is, alcohol suspends the action of the whole system, brain and muscle, and tends to bring us down to a state of torpidity, like snakes and toads, who have wonderful powers of preserving their tissues by masterly inactivity. The professor did not prescribe the form in which alcohol should be taken, nor the regime to accompany it in order best to succeed in preserving the tissues; but, "holding the mirror up to nature," I think I can see and supply the deficiency.

In the first place, you should sit perfectly still, for every motion tends against the preservation of the tissues; then you should live in the most impure air possible, for every breath of air containing oxygen burns up the waste of the tissues, and counteracts the desired influence; and then you should keep the tissues well preserved in lager beer, this form of alcoholic drink being best adapted to bring us into a state of torpidity.

You have seen, perhaps, a toad, a motley-faced, blubber-lipped toad, sitting in the corner of the garden, in one spot, hour after hour, and day after day, with just energy enough to wink, and to catch a fly if he comes within an inch of his nose; — a perfect personification of a bloated, beer-drinking, Pennsylvania Dutchman, who will sit, it is said, in the chimney-corner from morning till night, with just energy sufficient to raise the beer to his lips, and to call for more when his mug is empty. How long he can succeed in preserving his tissues has not been fully ascertained; but his prototype, the toad, sometimes succeeds wonderfully. Before a rain, a toad will sometimes muster up energy sufficient to crawl up into the fork of a tree, and there fill his big mouth with air, and blowing it through his lips, will utter a kind of trumpet sound, to notify us that a rain is coming; and when it comes, he crawls under the rough bark in the fork of the tree, and there waits and winks till the rain is over. Now it is said to have happened that, waiting too long, and the old bark becoming dry, he is bound in and can never get out. Year after year he stays there, winking in summer and suspending his work in the winter. Meantime the tree grows over him, and after many years, perhaps, is cut down, and there the toad is, still alive and winking.

Now this is not exactly an illustration of the power of alcohol to preserve the tissues, unless the toad has the power of manufacturing his own alcohol out of the carbon and hydrogen with which he was all the time surrounded, but it does illustrate the condition towards which all tissues must be brought to be preserved by alcohol. And the question comes up, What is the use of such tissues? What is a Dutchman good for who does nothing but drink lager beer? Professor Jackson's cabinet of morbid tissues is too small to accommodate him, and that is the only place for morbid tissues preserved in alcohol.

The professor's predecessor used to teach us that it

was not desirable to preserve the tissues; that the more we exercised and wore out the tissues, and the purer the air we lived in, and the more we avoided the stupefying influence of alcohol, the oftener the tissues would be renewed, and the more healthy and useful we might become.

The only argument now depended on to prove that alcohol in any beverage is useful to the system, is founded on experience, and experience in this case, as in all others in which there is no careful observation, is merely "the *post hoc ergo propter hoc* error" which imputes the cause of everything to that which comes just before it. This was the reliance in the recent struggle in the Massachusetts legislature to establish the character of alcohol for usefulness as nutriment, and the eminent counsel referred to the extraordinary case of Cornaro, who lived fifty-eight years on twelve ounces of solid food and fourteen ounces of light wine each day, and he quotes Professor Lewes as saying, "he wonders that intelligent men, in view of such facts, can doubt that alcohol is nutritious." The wine which Cornaro drank, as indeed all other sugared alcoholic beverages, contained excellent aromatic nourishment. Why then impute the results to alcohol, of which in light wine there is but very little? All we can say in favor of the little alcohol in light wines is, that it would probably do no harm, as the stomach may become accustomed by habit to the presence not only of alcohol in moderate quantities, but other poisons, as opium, tobacco, and even arsenic, so as to digest food and perform its functions in spite of them, and those who take these poisons may live perhaps as long as Cornaro; but does that prove that opium and arsenic are nutritious? I once heard of a farmer who claimed that sawdust and Indian meal would fatten hogs, for he had tried the mixture; but when asked what proportions were best adapted to the fattening process, he said he thought the less sawdust and the more meal the better.

Let two starving men have nothing but alcohol and water, and let one drink the pure water and the other a mixture of alcohol and water, and the water drinker will live the longest — the experiment has been tried many a time, accidentally on man, and for the sake of experiment on other animals.

The opinion of Liebig, that "alcohol is burnt in the lungs, giving off carbonic acid and water, and serving to support the temperature of the body," is proved to a demonstration to be wrong. All arctic explorers concur in the opinion that alcohol has a decidedly injurious effect on men exposed to the cold.

Sir John Ross testifies that he experienced in his own person the beneficial effects of abstaining wholly from spirituous drinks, and he proposed to his men that they should try the same experiment, which was done with very gratifying results. He says, "When men under hard and steady labor are given their usual allowance or draught of grog, or a dram, they become languid and faint, losing their strength in reality, while they attribute that to the continuance of their fatiguing exertions. He who will make the corresponding experiments on two equal boats' crews, rowing in a heavy sea, will soon be convinced that water-drinkers will far outdo the others."

Rev. W. Scoresby, before a committee of the House of Commons, testified as follows: "My experience has been in severely cold climates, and there it is observable that there is a very pernicious effect in the reaction after the use of ardent spirits. I did not use them myself, and I was better, I conceive, without the use of them. I am well assured that such beverages as tea and coffee, or, I doubt not, milk and water, are in every way superior, both for comfort and health, for persons exposed to the weather, or other severity. Spirits are decidedly injurious in cold climates. The men who have been assisted by such stimulants, have been the first who were rendered incapable of duty. They became perfectly stupid, skulked into different parts of the ship to get out of the way, and were generally found asleep. In case of a storm, or other sudden difficulty, I should most decidedly prefer the water-drinkers to those who were under the influence of any stimulant."

Dr. Rush says, in his "Medical Inquirer," "There cannot be a greater error than to suppose that spirituous liquors lessen the effects of cold on the body. On the contrary, they always render the body more liable to be affected and injured by cold. The temporary warmth they produce is always succeeded by chilliness."

Backus gives some striking facts illustrating this point, which I will quote. "In the winter of 1796, a vessel was wrecked on an island off the coast of Massachusetts. There were seven persons on board. Five of them resolved to quit the ship during the night, and seek shelter on the shore. To prepare for the attempt, four of them drank a quantity of spirits, and the fifth drank none. They all leaped into the water: one was drowned before reaching the shore; the other four came to land, and, in deep snow and piercing cold, directed their course to a distant light. All that drank spirits failed, and stopped, and froze, one after another; the man that drank none reached the house, and about two years ago was still alive."

"A few years ago a brig from Russia, laden with iron, ran aground upon a sand bank near Newport, Rhode Island. The master was desirous to unload and get her off. The weather, however, was extremely cold, and none could be found to undertake the task, as the vessel was at a distance from the shore, covered with ice, and exposed to the full effects of the wind and cold. A packet-master of Newport, who abstained from the use of spirituous liquors, at length engaged to unload the brig, and procure his men to do the work. Six men were employed in the hold, which was full of water. They began to work with the free but temperate use of ardent spirits, supposing they would need it then if ever; but after two hours' labor they began to give out, chilled through. After having warmed and refreshed themselves, they proceeded to make another attempt, using cider only through the day. They now succeeded better, but still suffered much from the effects of the cold. On the second day the men consented to follow the direction of their employer, and drank nothing but milk porridge, made rich, and taken as hot as the stomach would bear it. Although the weather was equally as severe as before, they were, after this change in their diet, enabled to continue their work from four to seven hours at a time, and then come up from it not at all chilled. With this same beverage, handed round every half hour, they continued their work from day to day, with not one drop of intoxicating liquor, until the iron was all handed out and brought on shore. Not one of them had a finger frozen."

"In the winter of 1825 two vessels were coming into the harbor of New York during an extremely inclement night, the temperature being several degrees below the freezing point. The captain of one of these vessels supplied his crew with warm alcoholic drinks during their exposure, while that of the other dealt out nothing but hot coffee to his men. The result was, that on arriving next morning, a large proportion of the crew of the former vessel were severely frost-bitten, while that of the other wholly escaped, not a single man having suffered any injury from the cold." These facts were published in the New York papers at the time, and are within the recollection of many of our readers. (See Appendix to American edition of J. Pereira's Treatise on Food and Diet. Appendix by C. S. Lee.)

That alcohol *per se* is not nourishing, but poisonous, I have never known questioned except where some point is to be made, as in the late struggle for a license law in the Massachusetts legislature.

Professor Yeomans, of New York, in a very able paper on Alcohol and the Constitution of Man, says, "Chemical experiments have demonstrated that the action of alcohol on the digestive fluid is to destroy its active principle, the pepsin, thus confirming the observations of physiologists, that its use gives rise to the most serious disorders of the stomach, and the most malignant aberrations of the entire economy."

"It is evident that, so far from being the conservator of health, alcohol is an active and powerful cause of disease, interfering as it does with the respiration, the circulation, and the nutrition; nor is any other result possible." "Nothing can be more certain than that it is a powerful antagonist of the digestive process." "It prevents the natural changes going on in the blood." "It impedes the liberation of carbonic acid, a deadly poison." "It obstructs the nutritive and reparative functions." "It produces disease of the liver." "It has a powerful affinity for the substance of the brain, being, indeed, essentially a brain poison." If these effects do not prove alcohol poisonous, where shall we look for proof that any substance is poisonous? But experiment can never settle this question, nor any other question pertaining to vital chemistry. He who made man and knows how to keep him in repair, has plainly given us laws of nutrition, and, as in all other important matters, has fixed a penalty for the breach of His laws.

If alcoholic drinks are useful then, they are useful not on account of, but in spite of, the alcohol contained in them, and are useful in proportion as sugar, starch, and other nutritious principles, together with osmazome, predominate over alcohol; and thus we have a standard by which to test the value of alcoholic drinks. That article is best which contains the most agreeable osmazome and the least alcohol, the elements of nutriment being of little consequence, unless, as sometimes happens, the stomach will receive nutriment through the medium of aromatic beverages better than in any other combination. This, however, in my experience and observation in a practice of forty years, is never only a temporary expedient, and in cases of extreme debility, which give place to more substantial nutriment, containing no alcohol, the moment the digestive powers so react as to be able to bear them. It may therefore be desirable to have an analysis of the wines and other beverages in common use.

Wines.

European wines, in one imperial pint, contain, according to Lankester, —

	Water.	Alcohol.	Sugar.	Tartaric Acid.
Port, . . .	16 oz.	4 oz.	1 oz. 2 grs.	80 grs.
Brown Sherry,	15½ oz.	4½ oz.	360 grs.	90 grs.
Pale Sherry,	16 oz.	4 oz.	80 grs.	70 grs.
Claret, . .	18 oz.	2 oz.	—	161 grs.
Burgundy, .	17½ oz.	2½ oz.	—	160 grs.
Hock, . .	17¾ oz.	2¼ oz.	—	127 grs.
Moselle, . .	18¼ oz.	1¾ oz.	—	140 grs.
Champagne, .	17 oz.	3 oz.	1 oz. 133 grs.	90 grs.
Madeira, . .	16 oz.	4 oz.	400 grs.	100 grs.

These wines are prepared from the juice of the grape by direct fermentation. The juice before fermenting is called "must." Wines vary according to the flavor of the grape from which they are made, the sugar and acid they contain, and the degree of fermentation by which the sugar is changed into alcohol. Those with much sugar are called "sweet" wines; those with little, dry wines. To some wines sugar is added to correct their acidity; others are sweet because fermentation has not exhausted the natural sugar. On the degree of fermentation also depends the amount of alcohol. To Port Wine, Sherry, and Madeira, alcohol is added to give them strength; but not to Claret, Hock, and the light wines from Europe. The acid in grape wines is the tartaric, which forms an insoluble salt that collects on the wine-casks; and is the source of our cream of tartar and tartaric acid. Wines from apples are called cider, and those from pears are called perry; each having its distinctive taste from the osmazome of its own fruit.

Analysis of Distilled Spirituous Beverages.

	Water.	Alcohol.	Sugar.
Brandy, ...	9½ oz.	10¼ oz.	80 grs.
Gin, best, . .	12 oz.	8 oz.	—
Gin, retail, . .	16 oz.	4 oz.	½ oz.
Rum, ...	5 oz.	15 oz.	—

Distilled spirits are made by applying heat to fermented liquors, and collecting the alcohol as it condenses in cold pipes and runs back into a receiver. Alcohol is thus obtained from molasses, from malt, from all the grains and fruits, and also from potatoes; and anything, indeed, which contains either starch or sugar, can be converted by fermentation into alcohol.

As it is employed in the arts in its concentrated form, *it has no* special *flavor*, and is then called "Spirits of Wine."

Gin is obtained from fermented grain, to which is added the berries of juniper, which give its characteristic flavor. It is sometimes flavored also with cinnamon, cloves, &c., and is then called "Cordial" or "Cordial Gin."

Whiskey is distilled from grain, mostly in this country from corn, and obtains its flavor from fusil oil, which gives it a peculiar smoky taste.

Rum is distilled from fermented sugar and molasses, which, in the West Indies, is flavored with pine apples. In New England it has been extensively made without the flavor of pine apples, and is known all over the world as New England Rum.

Brandy is distilled from wine, and its peculiar taste is imparted by the addition of peach kernels while it is distilling. This taste is, however, imitated by the use of sorrel and other vegetables that contain prussic acid.

Arrack is obtained from fermented rice, butternuts, and the sap of various species of palm.

Analysis of Beers and Ales.

	Water.	Alcohol.	Sugar.	Acetic Acid.
London Stout, .	18½ oz.	1½ oz.	281 grs.	54 grs.
London Porter,	19½ oz.	¾ oz.	267 grs.	45 grs.
Pale Ale, . . .	17¼ oz.	2½ oz.	240 grs.	40 grs.
Mild Ale, . . .	18¾ oz.	1¼ oz.	280 grs.	38 grs.
Strong Ale, . .	18 oz.	2 oz.	2 oz., 136 grs.	54 grs.

The above analysis of beers and ales is made from beverages containing no elements but those which are derived from malt, hops, and water, the alcohol being obtained from starch, which, in the process of malting, is changed into sugar, and then, in the process of fermentation, changed into alcohol, the sugar also coming mostly from starch, but partly from the barley, as it is found there, and is not all changed to alcohol by fermentation. The color and flavor of the different beers and ales is obtained by roasting, more or less, the malt.

Acidulous Drinks and Fruits.

That vegetable acids perform important services in the human system is evident from various considerations. They are found in almost all fruits and vegetables, and all nations, savage and civilized, make constant use of them in some form, and this has been true in ancient as well as modern times. Moses speaks of vinegar as being in common use in his day, and Boaz, smitten by the charms of "the Moabitish damsel that came back with Naomi out of the country of Moab," and desirous of expressing his appreciation of her kindness to her mother-in-law, said to her, "at meal time come thou hither and eat of the bread, and dip thy morsel in the *vinegar*." (Ruth ii. 14.) This universal appetite, however, only goes to show a demand of the system for some acid, but it does not prove the wholesomeness of vinegar as produced by the process of fermentation, as we shall see on further investigation.

It has been clearly proved by repeated experiments that some vegetable acid is necessary for the preservation of health, or, at least, that the complete abstinence from succulent vegetables or fruits, or their preserved juices, is the cause of scurvy — a disease which nothing will cure but the vegetable acids.

It is also proved that acids that are organized in fruits and vegetables are much more efficient in preventing or curing scurvy than acetic acid (vinegar,) or any other acid not thus naturally combined with esculent principles; indeed, it is certain that some such organized combinations are necessary either to prevent or to cure scurvy; and I think it is evident further that an abundance of these acids are furnished in organized food, so that if we took every day apples or other fruits, either green or preserved by desiccation, or exclusion from the air as in canned fruits, or ate with our meats every day plenty of potatoes, squashes, or other vegetables, we should need no vinegar, or any disorganized or concentrated acids. But with a diet deficient in these subacid and succulent principles, vinegar is, to some extent, beneficial.

Vinegar, like alcohol, is the product of fermentation, and, like alcohol, comes also from the same element. Sugar and starch, and everything that contains sugar or starch, will, by a fermentation called the vinous fermentation, produce alcohol, and by a second or acetous fermentation the same material will produce vinegar. At first sight we seem to have here an exception to the law, which I have elsewhere described, which makes all substances which are disorganized poisonous, in order to protect the system from their deleterious influences; but the exception is only apparent, and goes to illustrate still further the design of nature in making such elements only poisonous as are injurious if they could be admitted into the system. Vinegar is not admitted into the system as a principle to supply any organ with nutrition, or to furnish heat; but only as a chemical agent, to combine with the alkalies evolved from the liver and other excretory organs, to eliminate these effete elements from the system, and thus purify the blood and cleanse the system from the impurities which would otherwise remain in it. Vinegar, therefore, is merely a chemical agent, and, as such, useful in the absence of natural, organized acids, and not a nutritive principle; but alcohol is neither a chemical agent in the system nor a nutritive principle—the one being useful is received, if taken in proper quantities, without exciting the system to reject it, while the other, having no useful purpose to subserve, produces an excitement, and is expelled as an intruder. Still, vinegar is not an organized element, and not harmless.

Vinegar, therefore, is not necessary, and not useful as a beverage or a condiment, except in cases where the organized acids are not to be obtained, and cannot take the place of them either as a preventive or curer of disease. The liberal use of lemon juice, or tomatoes, or any other organized acid fruits will prevent the scurvy for an indefinite period, as has been proved on sailors in very long voyages; but we have abundant testimony that on similar voyages the liberal use of vinegar will not prevent this terrible disease. These experiments show that vinegar is not the form of acid naturally adapted to the requirements of the system, and that it should only be used when the acid fruits and succulent vegetables cannot be obtained.

The best vinegar in this country is obtained from the cider of apples, and in farming communities each householder makes his own vinegar by exposing a barrel partly filled with cider to the sun and open air; fermentation is started by a little of the mucilaginous coat or skin which forms on the surface of vinegar, called "mother," and which consists of myriads of exceeding minute vegetables, in which are generated the microscopic animalcules called eels, which may be the cause of some of our obscure diseases; at least, there is no evidence that the heat of the stomach or the gastric juice is capable of destroying them; and no heat short of boiling water will kill any animalcule, and we seldom use vinegar except on cold food. There is evidence that some animalcules are capable of resisting the gastric juice, and of living, and growing, and producing many troublesome diseases in the stomach and intestine canal. It is at least safest, therefore, to depend for our necessary acids on the fruits and vegetables, of which we can always procure an abundance at an expense vastly less than that of the superabundant carbonates which we waste in using flour, sugar, and butter, which are not only wasted, but which produce a state of the system *that makes these acids necessary*. If we should give up all superfluous carbonates, therefore, we should need no vinegar, as all necessary acids would be furnished in the food that would naturally take the place of these articles. In England, vinegar is mostly made from malt or new barley subjected to acetous fermentation, which produces the same acid, the acetic, as that of the cider vinegar; but to give it life and character a little sulphuric acid is allowed in England, by law, to be added. This is much more injurious than acetic acid, having a stronger affinity for many elements in the system, especially for the lime in the teeth, than acetic acid.

Vinegar in large quantities is known to be injurious, and in the long-continued use of small quantities; by disturbing the functions of digestion and preventing the proper formation of chyme, it stops the supply of nutriment, and produces paleness and wasting. On this account it is in repute among such silly young ladies as prefer to be pale and sickly, rather than rosy and plump, and many such, by its constant use, succeed most lamentably in reducing themselves to their own foolish standard of beauty.

The following case is quoted from Portal by Pereira: "A few years ago a young lady, in easy circumstances, enjoyed good health; she was very plump, had a good appetite, and a complexion blooming with roses and lilies. She began to look upon her plumpness with suspicion; for her mother was very fat, and she was afraid of becoming like her; accordingly she consulted a woman, who advised her to drink a small glass of vinegar daily. The young lady followed her advice, and her plumpness diminished. She was delighted with the success of the remedy, and continued it for more than a month. She began to have a cough; but it was dry at its commencement, and was considered as a slight cold, which would go off. Meantime, from dry it became moist; a slow fever came on, and a difficulty of breathing; her body became lean and wasted away; night sweats, swelling of the feet and legs succeeded, and a diarrhœa terminated her life. On examination all the lobes of the lungs were found filled with tubercles, and somewhat resembled a bunch of grapes."

Now that fruits can be so well kept by simply canning them and excluding the air, and such abundance and such a variety of fruits are now produced, we can have, at an expense very trifling compared with their value, all the acids the system requires, at all times of year, in a form at the same time agreeable and wholesome; and have, therefore, no necessity for using acid in the form of vinegar, which certainly has no advantages over fruits and vegetables, and which has, to say the least, some very suspicious characteristics as a sanitary agent. The expense of one of the half dozen barrels of flour which almost every family wastes in the year would do much towards supplying the necessary acids of any family, if judiciously expended in pleasant sour apples or good ripe tomatoes, with cans or bottles to keep them in, and dried apples from carefully selected fruit. Let every family have these agreeable acids on their table every day, morning and noon, during the whole season in which the summer fruits are absent, and let every member, young and old, eat all they will, and there would be no necessity for vinegar, or any other objectionable acid, which a morbid appetite only will crave.

Inquire into the habits of the school-girls who flock

to the grocers at every recess, for lemons, pickled limes, and cucumbers, and you shall find every one of them living on fine flour, butter, sweet cakes, and confectionery, with no natural acids to eliminate these carbonaceous principles from the system; or if they do have any of these acid fruits, they are taken with the last meal at night, when the powers of digestion are exhausted, and not able to get from them their appropriate elements; and taken then, perhaps, in the shape of some jelly, between two layers of rich cake, the carbonaceous elements of which are more than sufficient to counteract any benefits that might be derived from the acid.

Fruit, as I have elsewhere explained (see page 211), and in fact every other class of food, is most wholesome in the condition in which it has the richest and most agreeable flavor. Fruits have the best flavor uncooked. There may be some exceptions, in which the osmazome is best developed by cooking, of which, to my taste, the tomato is an example; but apples, peaches, pears, and almost all the fruits and berries, have their richest flavor developed by Nature's own culinary process; and science has now devised so many means of preserving fruits, and all other articles of food, that no good reason can be given why we may not, at all times of year, have a constant supply of natural acids in a variety sufficient to satisfy the most fastidious tastes. And it is to be hoped the time will speedily come when all fruits, vegetables, or meats preserved in vinegar, salt, sugar, smoke, or alcohol, will be discarded as being unnatural and unwholesome articles, either as necessaries or luxuries of life, either imparting, as they all do, injurious elements, or chemically changing or withdrawing the nutritive elements, or at least changing their relative proportions, so as to be unfit for digestion. And with the arrangement described in the next chapter, which is applicable to ships as well as houses, and can be secured from the influence of all climates, the disease of scurvy need never be known, or the many other diseases induced by salt, vinegar, pyroligneous acid, carbonaceous food, or alcohol.

Plan for Preserving Fruits and Vegetables.

Professor Nyce, of Cleveland, Ohio, has perfected and patented a plan for preserving fruits, vegetables, &c., which seems to me of great interest and importance, not only as a means of applying practically the principles of science to the useful purposes of life by adding to our luxuries, but, as I have endeavored elsewhere to show, of adding to the supply of elements actually necessary for the preservation of health, and of avoiding the injurious articles now used in preserving food. And as this plan strongly favors my "Philosophy of Eating," and my humble efforts to induce men to return to the primitive use of natural food as the means of enjoying, to the highest degree of which they are capable, the pleasures of health and "the pleasures of the table," I shall transcribe what is known, and already to some extent published, on this subject. The first public notice of this plan of preserving fruits and vegetables, so far as I know, was given in a

"*Report of the Cincinnati Horticultural Society on certain Early and Summer Pears, kept in the Conservatory of Benjamin M. Nyce, from August till December* 15, 1861.

"*No.* 1. *Rousellet Stuttgart.* — Juicy, and of a rich saccharine taste; reminds one of the Belle Seckel.

"*No.* 2. *Bartlett.* — Has been kept a little too long; is still juicy; somewhat more saccharine than usual, and quite good.

"*No.* 3. *Belle Lucrative*, or something else. — Has the extraordinary fine flavor, and melting, buttery lusciousness, which have given the Belles their reputation.

"*No.* 4. *Unknown.* — In good condition, is of a somewhat insipid, sweetish flavor, evidently natural, sound, and without blemish.

"*No.* 5. *Belle Lucrative.* — Is in perfect condition, plump, juicy, and well-flavored; fully up to its reputation, very juicy, and very buttery.

"*No.* 6. Also the well-known *Beurre Bosc.* — It retains, in every respect, all its well-known characteristic excellences.

"In conclusion, we may say that all the above-named fruit attained its natural color at maturity, and seemed to be free from all foreign flavor and taste which usually adheres to fruit that has been preserved by other means beyond its natural season.

"ROBERT REILLY, *Chairman.*

"CINCINNATI, Dec. 15, 1861."

To this report is added a letter from Benjamin M. Nyce, July 20, 1861, with specimens of fruits of the growth of 1860, preserved in his fruit-house, together with some strawberries gathered seven weeks before, and found in a state sound and fresh.

Apples, of the growth of 1860, preserved in his patent preserving fruit-room: Pennock, Romanite or Gilman, White Winter Pearmain, White Bellflower, Rhode Island Greening, Pryor's Red, Northern Spy, Rane's Janet, Rambo, Campfield.

Potatoes, growth of 1860: Perfectly sound, showing no disposition to sprout, or grow, or wilt.

And the chairman adds, —

"These products furnish further evidence, if any such were needed by this society, that the ingenious application of scientific truths has enabled our enterprising friend Nyce to arrest the natural process of decay in our perishable fruits, most of which appear before us in a perfectly sound condition, after months of isolation from the parent trees, upon which they acquired their growth and perfect maturation."

Principles of the Fruit-Preserving House.

The objects to be attained are coldness, dryness, purity, absence of light, sameness of temperature, exclusion of oxygen, — it being proved that all these conditions are necessary in order to prevent decomposition and retain the natural osmazome, without the addition of any foreign flavor.

Coldness is attained by the constant use of ice, and

it is found that in order to fix the condition of the fruit in the state in which it is put into the house the temperature must be kept at about 34°. Some fruits will bear a lower temperature than others. The Catawba grape, for example, will suffer no harm at a temperature of 26°, while lemons will suffer at 32°. Sour fruits will not bear as much cold as sweet ones. In a dry atmosphere the process of change towards decomposition is very slow at a temperature of 40°, unless the fruit is too ripe when put into the house. Fruit fully ripe cannot be absolutely fixed, so that no change will go on at a temperature short of the freezing point. The difference between fruit fully ripe and that as it comes from the tree as soon as it has ceased to receive any virtue from the tree or vine, is this: the one contains starch, which is not subject to decay, and the other contains no starch, but sugar, into which starch is changed in the process of ripening, which is subject to decay, more or less rapidly, down to the freezing point. From unripe apples or pears grated to a pulp, and washed in cold water, and the turbid liquor left to subside, a deposit of starch will be found on the bottom of the vessel; but from the juice of the fruit when perfectly ripe and fit for the table, not a particle of starch can be found. Fruit, therefore, to be fully preserved from change, must be placed in a low temperature immediately after being gathered, and the thermometer must never be allowed to indicate a rise above 36°. And the preservation is more perfect if kept at 34°.

The second object — *dryness* — is more difficult to

attain, and constitutes one of the most important points of Professor Nyce's improvement. This is accomplished by the use of dried bittern, or chloride of lime, which is obtained from salt-works, being the residuum of the brine after the salt has been concreted. This bittern, evaporated to dryness, has a strong affinity for water, and being spread on the floor of the fruit-room, absorbs the moisture from the atmosphere.

Purity is attained in the usual way, by removing and keeping out all sources of impurity; and this is found to be necessary, else the flavor of the fruit is affected by it.

Darkness is effected by excluding the light; or making the house without windows, except a single light of glass in large houses, in each apartment enclosed by a shutter, so as to afford light, when required, sufficient to examine a thermometer and hygrometer, and ascertain the temperature or moisture; and this arrangement is necessary, because light is known to favor decomposition.

Evenness of temperature is necessary, because the expansion and contraction of the skin and the cellular structure, produced by only a few degrees of change in temperature, tend to disorganize the structure of the fruit, and thus favor decomposition.

Exclusion of oxygen is necessary, because oxygen is the principal agent in all decomposition. This is effected by filling the apartment with carbonic acid gas, which has no effect on the fruit. This is as easily accomplished as to exclude air from any vessel by filling it with water, and upon the same principle, as can be proved by a simple experiment. Put into an open jar a little chalk or marble, and pour on it a little vinegar, or any other acid. The acid combines with the lime of the chalk or marble and sets the carbonic acid free, which, being specifically heavier than air, fills the jar, and remains in it, although the top or mouth may be open. There seems to be nothing in the jar, because the gas is invisible; but tip the jar over a lighted candle, as if to pour water upon it, and the light is extinguished as quickly as if immersed in water. This simple experiment would show that, as vinegar poured into a jar of pickles would fill all the interstices between them and exclude the air, so a room filled with carbonic acid gas, by filling all the interstices between the apples or pears, &c., would exclude all the air which contains oxygen. Thus all the conditions are complied with necessary to preserve the fruit.

If kept in a cold, dry, pure, and dark atmosphere, having nothing in contact with it that has an affinity for any of its elements, fruit and all other organized elements remain unchanged as long as that condition is kept perfect. And thus the season of the different kinds of fruits may be so prolonged that we may have the year round the most delicious fruits and the succulent vegetables. And every family who should desire to return to the primitive "Philosophy of Eating" may do so, and have all the luxuries that Adam and Eve enjoyed in Paradise, at an expense absolutely less than is now incurred in living on superfine flour, butter, and sugar, to say nothing of the expense incurred on doctors and drugs in efforts to counteract the influence of fever and inflammation-producing articles. Indeed, the plan ought to be recommended as a matter of economy, as well as for the enjoyment of life and the luxury of health to be derived from it. The cost of an arrangement sufficiently large for a family to preserve all their vegetables, fruits, eggs, meats, &c., could be saved in a single year, by enabling them to lay in their stock when each article was most plenty and cheapest. They could have also wines from all the varieties of grapes, and the juices of all the delicious fruits with their health-giving acid, without alcohol or vinegar. And this I say, not being an officer, or member, or stockholder of the Massachusetts or any other Fruit Preserving Company, or having any interest in the patent, or ever having had a word of conversation on the subject with any of its members.

The Cost of a Preservator.*

A house, with room fifteen feet square, eight feet high, twenty-two feet square on the outside, would hold five hundred bushels, and its cost is estimated as follows: —

* It is called "Fruit-preserving House," and "Patent Fruit-House," but I take the liberty to introduce a name quite as significant and more symphonious.

Common iron, at $7\frac{1}{2}$ cents per lb., . . .	$210.00
Galvanized iron, No. 26, at 20 cents per lb., ...	105.00
Galvanized iron, No. 20, at 18 cents per lb., ...	80.00
Other materials to make the whole cost,	800.00

A house seventeen feet square outside, ten feet inside, is estimated to cost four hundred and seventy-five dollars, and will hold two hundred and fifty bushels.

Large houses, with an entry through the middle, with five or six rooms on each side, cost about one dollar for every bushel they hold. Preservators for family use may be made or placed in the cellar, shed, in the yard, or any where else where there is room at an expense but little above that of a common refrigerator, except for the patent, which need be but a trifle to give the inventor a fortune.

The Cost of Running a Preservator.

In one holding seven thousand bushels of fruit, the whole cost for a year was but one hundred and fifty-five dollars, except for ice, and ice costs less than in a refrigerator of the same capacity, as ice may be put in all at once for a whole season, and work from one winter to another without one hour's additional labor, until the last pound is melted, and if the construction is perfect, the temperature in the preservator not vary a single degree. Besides the expense of ice, that of bittern is the principal, and that costs almost nothing except the expense of transportation from salt-works, as two men can dry in a single week enough that is running away as useless to supply a house of the capacity of ten thousand bushels for a whole year. All that is afterwards required is once in two months to take out the bittern and dry it in the sun, which requires but a few hours of labor.

There is no expense in exhausting the oxygen or supplying the carbonic acid gas. The chamber is simply closed, and the fruit in the process of ripening consumes entirely the oxygen, and gives off in its place the carbonic gas to supply its place, and then, as long as that condition remains unchanged, the fruit remains in a fixed condition. Then if the lower part be made perfectly tight, fruit could be taken from the upper part without disturbing the lower, the carbonic acid gas being heavier than air, remains, as I have before explained, at the bottom, as vinegar remains in pickles, while the pickles are removed from it.

Flavor.

Apples, as well as other fruits kept in this manner till the next spring and summer, are heavy, juicy, and rich in flavor, and are even better than when ripened in the open air, as the evaporation goes on very slowly at 34°, and gives time for the more complete separation of the atoms of water from those of the sugar contained in the fruit, and a larger proportion of water and less of the osmazome escapes than when the temperature is higher and the evaporation more rapid. Fruits are therefore sweeter, and richer in flavor, kept in this way, at the end of six months, than when only kept a few weeks in an open atmosphere.

Keeping Fruit after it is Removed from the Preservator.

Fruit, such as apples, taken from the preservator in July, will keep as well as the same fruit would have kept in December in the same temperature. No fruit will keep long in a temperature of 70° or 80°, whether in a warm room or in an open-air July temperature.

The keeping will depend on the soundness of the fruit and the temperature of the weather, from two or three days to two or three weeks.

To get the fullest benefits from this means of preserving fruit, each family, or at least each neighborhood, should have its own preservator, and then they could have not only all our native fruits and vegetables, but fresh butter, eggs, fish, fresh meats, birds, and the choicest luxuries in this or from foreign countries, ready at hand at all times of year and for all special occasions, and thus have no excuse for resorting to vinegar or any other disorganized principle, or for abstaining from fresh fruits and vegetables and other articles, not only as luxuries, but as they are proved to be necessary for the preservation of health. Fruits, however, like apples and pears, have been brought from Cincinnati and Cleveland to Boston in

June and July, in a good condition and of delicious flavor; also grapes, as fresh as when they came from the vines, and even improved in flavor.

The Length of Time that Fruits, &c., can be Kept.

Some articles can be preserved for years, while others only for a few weeks. Strawberries can be kept fresh from four to six weeks, thus prolonging the season of this delicious berry to three or four times its natural length; and other berries also can be preserved much longer, enabling those who have a preservator to lay in a stock of his favorite berries while they are plenty and cheap, and prolong the enjoyment of these luxuries indefinitely.

Bartlett pears can be preserved in the most perfect condition until midwinter and later, and other later pears and apples can be preserved the year round without losing their flavor; indeed, the flavor is improved by keeping.

Foreign fruit, as oranges, lemons, pine-apples, &c., could be bought when they first came in the winter and early spring at less than half their cost later in the season, and this would be at a time when our domestic fall fruits and vegetables had been used, and room for them left in the preservator.

Eggs can be kept fresh a whole year, making a saving of more than half their expense by purchasing in the spring when they are most plenty.

As a matter of economy, therefore, every good liver should have in his own house or shed or yard a preservator sufficiently large to supply him with all the perishable articles of food which his family needs. This would also lead to a consideration of the "Philosophy of Eating," and thus be of incalculable advantage, not only as a means of enjoying, to the highest degree, the pleasures of eating, but as a means of preserving his health and prolonging his life almost indefinitely.

Elements of Food Lost in Cooking.

In another chapter (page 16) it is shown that food must contain three classes of elements, those which will feed the brain and nerves, those which feed muscles and tissues, and those which furnish heat and fat. These elements may be found combined so as to be soluble in water, cold or hot, or both, and therefore, if cooked in water, are lost. The muscle-feeding elements of all meats and fish consist in fibrin and albumen (see tables, page 77), and in the flesh of all young animals, as veal and lamb, and in all kinds of fish albumen predominates.

Albumen is soluble in cold water, but coagulates and becomes solid in hot water. For example, the white of an egg, which is albumen, may be dissolved and lost in cold water, but on being dropped into hot water immediately coagulates and becomes insoluble. All meats, therefore, lose a portion of their nutrition, and some a very large portion, by being soaked in water, or by being put into cold water to boil, and if boiled at all, should be put into boiling water, unless the water in which they are boiled is to be saved as soup. In that case, the flavor and nutritive properties of the soup are much better by being first soaked in cold water and boiled in the same water.

Besides albumen, other valuable elements are lost in water, whether hot or cold, as is shown by chemical analysis. If the flesh of animals or fish be cut up fine, and washed and filtered, the water is found to contain not only the albumen, but the osmazome which gives the flavor, the phosphates which feed the brains and the nerves, and all the soluble salts of the blood, while there remains nothing nutritious but fibrin and the insoluble salts, which constitute the basis of bones. By boiling, instead of roasting or frying meats or fish, we lose therefore that which gives them relish, much of the true nourishment, and some other valuable elements.

On the other hand, by soaking in cold water, and boiling gradually, and retaining the liquid, we get all the valuable properties of meat. The liquid contains all the soluble properties, and indeed all the important properties necessary for sickly or sedentary persons; and the solids contain the fibrin and lime which are wanted for muscular power and strength of sinew and bone. Another practical error in regard to soups, relates to the nutrition in the gelatinous portions of soup obtained from the cartilages and tendons of the joints of meat, which are usually selected under the impression that the more gelatinous the more nutritious the soup, whereas it is found to be true that gelatine is in no sense nutritious. Its only use in the living system seems to be mechanical, forming protection to the joints as a kind of cushion, and attaching the muscles to the bones, and, as food, answering as waste material to keep the bowels in action. This is true of all animal jellies, as calf's foot, isinglass, &c.

Portable Soup, or Extract of Beef.

Thirty-two pounds of beef, without bone or fat, if put into cold water, gradually heated and boiled for a long time, and finally strained, and the liquid boiled down to dryness, will make one pound of true extract of beef, containing all the nutritive properties necessary for one who is sickly or sedentary. One ounce of this extract, with a little salt, will make a quart of soup or beef tea, which is rich and palatable, retaining the natural flavor of well-cooked beef, and which may be otherwise seasoned to suit the taste. This extract will keep, in a dry place, for an indefinite time, and if made, as it may be and is in the Western States where beef is cheap, need not be very expensive; and by the saving in expense of transportion, might be made a profitable way of disposing of beef.

It is kept by almost all apothecaries, and if it could be depènded on as genuine, might be the best, surest, quickest, and most economical mode of supplying wholesome animal food to the sick and feeble; but uufortunately a cheaper and far inferior article is sold under the same name, which contains only enough of the genuine extract to give it flavor, all the rest being gelatine, which contains no nourishment.

The genuine may be known from the spurious article by the following test: Of the pure extract about eighty per cent. is soluble in eighty-five per cent. alcohol, while that made from gelatine will yield to that menstruum only from four to five per cent.

Portable soup might be used, and to some extent is used, for provisioning ships on long voyages, where fresh meat and vegetables cannot be had. This idea was first suggested by Professor Liebig, who ascertained by chemical analysis that the brine in which beef is salted contains the soluble constituents of the beef, even to a greater extent than concentrated soups. Salted beef, therefore, especially after it is boiled, contains nothing but fibrin, which is not much wanted in sedentary life, as that of a sailor on a long voyage. With such meat and hard bread let us see what he gets and what he loses of necessary elements.

He gets in the meat fibrin, which is but little wanted while inactive, and some insoluble salts, as phosphate of lime, which are needed also only in proportion to active exercise, and in the hard-tack he gets little but starch, which contains carbonates for breathing, but almost no food for the brain and nervous system, and none of the acids and alkalies that are necessary to eliminate the impurities from the blood and give life and activity. The system, consequently, becomes dormant and inactive, and filled with scorbutic sores, and other diseases, such as are induced by food destitute of the principles found in fresh meats and vegetables, especially if used without taking much muscular exercise.

Another excellent substitute for fresh food is found in desiccated vegetables, which saved many a life from diarrhœa and other scorbutic diseases in the late Southern rebellion, and which are still more useful at sea, where fresh food cannot be obtained. Of these, potatoes are best, but carrots, turnips, pumpkins, and squash are all good, and many families dry them for use in that season of the year in which green vegetables are not easily kept fresh.

Beef Tea.

The best and quickest mode of preparing nourishing beef tea is to chop up lean beef into fine pieces, first broiling it lightly to develop the osmazome, add to it an equal weight of cold water, slowly heat to boiling, and after boiling three minutes strain and season to taste. In this manner the elements are retained and the natural flavor, and a soup is obtained of as much strength and better flavor than by boiling the same piece of meat for hours.

Acidulous Drinks.

The juices of all fruits, and some vegetables, contain acids which are useful in eliminating from the system various alkaline impurities, by combining them and making them soluble, and they may have some other uses in the system which are not perfectly understood; but they never enter the system as an element of nutrition, but seem to act on chemical, or perhaps chemico-vital principles. Different fruits contain different acids, as malic, oxalic, tartaric, citric, &c., but so far as is known they are all alike useful.

Oxalic acid exists in a number of plants, as common sorrel, wood sorrel, &c., but the only plant employed at the table containing this acid is garden rhubarb, or pie-plant, whose leaf-stalks are used for tarts, puddings, sauce, &c., which are perfectly wholesome, notwithstanding the fact that oxalic acid in a disorganized state is very poisonous; which is another example of the principle I have endeavored to bring out, that an element may be wholesome or poisonous as it is or is not organized in some vegetable. The oxalic acid of the shops is obtained by the chemical action of nitric acid on sugar or molasses, changing them from nutriment to poison.

Citric acid.—This acid is a constituent of the juice of the lemon, the orange, the lime, the citron, the shaddock, and other fruits, which owe their sourness to this acid. The cranberry, the red currant, the strawberry, the raspberry, the cherry, the bilberry, and the tamarind also contain it, mixed with an equal quantity of malic acid.

Tartaric acid.—This is the acid of grapes, tamarinds, and pine-apples. It also exists, in combination with potash, as bitartrate of potash, or cream of tartar, in grapes, tamarinds, and mulberries, which, collecting on the sides of the cask during the fermentation of wine, is termed crude tartar, or argol. This cream of tartar, and tartaric acid, as it is called when purified and separated from the potash, is much used as a substitute for the juice of the lemon, and if it be not disorganized in the process of purification, may not be objectionable.

Malic acid, or acid of apples, is very extensively distributed in the vegetable kingdom, being found in apples, pears, quinces, plums, apricots, peaches, cherries, gooseberries, currants, strawberries, raspberries, blackberries, pine-apples, barberries, elderberries, grapes, tomatoes, tamarinds, and other fruits, and is frequently accompanied with citric acid; and of course it is the acid of wine, cider, and beer in an unfermented state.

These acids exist in most of the fruits, in connection with a principle called pectine, which means coagulum, which gives them the property of becoming gelatinous, or of making jellies. Jellies may be made of currants (red, white, and black), apples (both sweet and sour), pears, quinces, plums, apricots, the cucurbitaceous fruits (as melons and cucumbers), gooseberries, tomatoes, oranges, lemons, guava, and tamarinds. The carrots, turnips, beets, onions, and other vegetables, also contain pectine and pectic acid. By boiling with malic acid pectine is changed into an acid that is soluble in water, and the vegetable albumen contained in fruits assists also in making the change; and this explains why the juice of a fruit, by prolonged ebullition, often loses its property of gelatinizing (or, as the cooks say, *why* it will not come). Another reason why jelly will not come is, that fruit is used before it is perfectly ripe. Unripe fruit contains very little pectine, but it is formed by the action of the acids on the pulpy matter while in the process of ripening; and if the fruit be gathered early, this process goes on afterwards till it becomes soft. Currants, for example, will not make jelly when they first turn red. It is then that the pectine begins to form, and this formation continues till decomposition commences. Vegetable jellies afford the means of making agreeable acidulous drinks, and are useful in sickness. They afford but little nourishment, but are not objectionable.

Animal jellies, as calf's-foot, &c., are nearly worthless, containing no nourishment, and no flavor except what is imparted to them while being made.

Acetic acid, as I have explained, is the product of fermentation. It is not found in any sound fruit, and not in the juices of any of them, as wine, cider, &c., till they have first undergone the process of vinous fermentation, which produces alcohol, and the acetous fermentation, which changes the alcohol in vinegar or acetous acid. Whenever, therefore, fermentation is prevented, as it can be in a preservator such as I have described in a preceding page, we might have in the juices of the grape, apple, pear, and indeed of any fruits or berries, the most delicious beverages, containing acids in their natural state, and other elements, refreshing and useful both in health and sickness, without the disorganized and unhealthy principles of alcohol and vinegar.

This thought has not before suggested itself to my

mind; but it impresses me as very important in connection with the use of the conservator. Let us examine this subject, and see what is in it.

Fermentation.

All matter is under the control of vital or chemical laws. While life continues, either in animal or vegetable matters, vital law is supreme, but when life ceases, chemical law assumes control; and in all matter that has had life chemical law manifests itself in fermentation, either vinous, acetous, or putrefaction, and the conditions in which these chemical changes take place are the same in each. There must be present, and in contact with, or a part of, the substance to be fermented, oxygen, hydrogen, carbon or nitrogen, or both. And these must be in an atmosphere above a temperature of 32°, and to have the process go on with any degree of rapidity the temperature must be above 60°.

A well-constructed preservator prevents the presence of oxygen and hydrogen, and keeps down the temperature almost to 32°, and thus three of the conditions on which fermentation depends are wanting; and experiment has shown that it effectually prevents the putrefactive fermentation. The inference, therefore, is irresistible, that it will prevent the vinous and acetous fermentations. Why not, then, every man have his cask of Catawba or Isabella wine, or his cider, from the most fragrant and delicious apples, or pears, or the juices of currants, cherries, gooseberries, strawberries, raspberries, blackberries, pine-apples, peaches, quinces, or any other fruits? and, placing each in his preservator, with an arrangement to draw them through the side, have, the year round, his choice of fifty different beverages, all of which would be delicious and wholesome, containing in their natural condition the acids which the system requires, without the addition of alcohol, or vinegar, or any other disorganized or deleterious elements?

DIET IN SICKNESS.

HAVING examined the laws that are to guide us in the selection of food in health, for the different conditions, employments, and temperatures in which it is our lot to live, let us now see if there may be considerations which will be of service in sickness.

The first hint in regard to food in sickness, we have in the fact that the appetite is taken away, which is a clear intimation that food will no longer be beneficial, but injurious; and if sudden sickness occur while the stomach contains food, or if a serious accident occur, which would be followed by inflammation, Nature guards against the evil by causing the stomach to throw off the food, and thus stop the supply of nourishment that would keep up the inflammation.

A man falls on his head, or accidentally receives a blow that jars the brain, or a wheel runs over his foot and crushes it, or any other serious accident occurs, that would naturally result in inflammation, and the first efforts of Nature for protection and cure are seen in vomiting, which relieves the stomach of all food, and thus cuts off the supply of blood from the affected organ. Can we have a clearer intimation that in such cases all food should be withheld?

In the first stage of any serious disease we have,

therefore, no question of duty, and can see the absurdity of urging sick friends to eat, when food is not only not desired, but absolutely loathed, as it generally is in all serious illness; and we find that such advice, if followed, is always succeeded by evil consequences.

In the mean time there is generally strong thirst, that is best satisfied with pure cold water; and this also is a clear intimation that pure cold water is the best thing, and the only thing, that Nature in such cases requires; and I have never seen a case in which the slightest harm came from gratifying this demand to the fullest extent, — not by filling the stomach at once, especially with very cold water, but by gratifying the desire in a more effectual way: by constantly sipping it, however cold it may be. And I have indulged many a patient, and have found great advantage in keeping up, without five minutes' cessation, the cooling influence of cold water on the tongue and in the stomach.

After a time, longer or shorter, according to the violence of the fever, Nature becoming exhausted, demands a little nutriment; but the stomach cannot digest food for want of gastric juice.

Dr. Beaumont had for many years a young man who had the stomach opened by a cannon ball, which carried away the surrounding integuments and left it open for inspection, by simply raising a kind of trap-door made by folds of the integuments that remained. This gave him an opportunity, which no other physiologist ever had, of witnessing the processes of digestion under all circumstances, in sickness or health, and noting many phenomena not before known in regard to the use of the gastric juice, and its effects on different substances, liquids and solids, the time required for digesting different articles, the first process of digesting liquid nourishment, &c.

Dr. Beaumont says, "In febrile diseases very little or no gastric juice is secreted. Hence the importance of withholding food from the stomach in febrile complaints. It can afford no nourishment, but is actually a source of irritation to the organ, and consequently to the whole system." In another place he says, "The drinks received are immediately absorbed, or otherwise disposed of, none remaining in the stomach ten minutes after being swallowed. Food taken in this condition of the stomach remains undigested for twenty-four or forty-eight hours, or more, increasing the derangement of the whole alimentary canal, and aggravating the general symptoms of the disease." The first process of digesting liquid food is to absorb the liquid and leave the solid in the stomach; indeed, both liquid and solid food is digested by first being brought into a semi-fluid state. If too liquid, by the process just described of carrying off the liquid; if too solid, by bringing into the stomach from the system, unless they are supplied from without, the liquids necessary. But there are some forms of nourishment which are absorbed without digestion, and go directly into the system to supply the demands of nature. Of this class of nutritive articles in common use, are barley-water, toast-water, beef-tea, and infusions of any of the grains.

In all of these articles the elements abstracted and appropriated are evidently the nitrates and soluble phosphates, the carbonaceous elements not being soluble; and the only carbonaceous or heat-producing element that seems capable of being directly appropriated to the supply of heat without digestion is sugar.

Here, then, we have a clear indication of the diet which nature requires in febrile diseases — and these indications are corroborated by the natural appetite. At first, there is a loathing of everything but pure cold water; and anything but cold water, even barley-water, is disagreeable to the stomach. Then, after a while, a little barley or toast-water is agreeable and refreshing; and then, after a little longer time, the luscious fruits are relished, and the sugar in them is appropriated, without taxing the digestive powers, to sustaining the necessary heat, and checking the absorption of fat. At first the heat is supplied from the absorption of fat from the system, and the patient rapidly loses fat and becomes emaciated, the adipose matter of the body being absolutely burned up to keep up the heat while the digestive powers are prostrated, and unable to digest the farinaceous food on which the system generally depends. After a while the gastric juice is secreted sufficient to digest starch, which next to sugar is the most digestible carbonaceous food, having only to undergo the process of being converted by the saliva and gastric juices into sugar, as it always must be to be prepared to supply the lungs with fuel; and then the appetite will demand gruel made from some of the farinaceous grains, and thus we shall find, by watching the appetite, that it will call for the right thing at the right time, as long as its calls are heeded; but if physicians or nurses act on their own judgment, and give farinaceous food before the system is ready for it, the disturbance and flatulence produced will prevent the natural calls, and we lose all the advantage of the natural appetite. Adopting these ideas more than twenty-five years ago, I have never since refused a patient a little of anything which the appetite really demanded, even to the most indigestible substances, as cucumber, dandelion greens, cheese, &c., and have never seen a case in which they were injurious even temporarily. A careful discrimination must, however, be made between the fitful whims by which a perverted appetite will by turns desire a thousand things, and lose it again before they can be obtained, and the steady desire by which it craves the same thing hour after hour and day after day if not obtained, and judgment must always be used in regard to the quantity given at first; at least I have always feared the consequences of indulging the appetite to the fullest extent after long abstinence, but have been astonished at the impunity with which it may be indulged for any particular article of food, however inappropriate it might seem to be.

I had at one time the care of an old nurse sick with pneumonia, and so sick that for weeks she would take scarcely a particle of nutriment, and for a long time was reduced so low as not to be expected to live from one day to another. I told her, as I had frequently told patients of whom she had the care, to take a little of anything the appetite demanded, but gave no particular directions. One day, after an abstinence from food for nearly four weeks, I found her decidedly better, and for the first time able to talk and exhibit her usual vivacity. She told me that soon after my visit, twenty-four hours before, she felt a strong desire for a cucumber with salt and vinegar, and ordered her daughter to get a good large one, which she ate with a feeling that it was just the thing required; and, not being satisfied with one, she obtained another, and another, till she had eaten three or four, and she assured me she felt not a pain or any inconvenience from the repast, and from that day she took other food and rapidly recovered. There was less danger, indeed, from that indigestible article, which contained very little nourishment, than would have been from eating immoderately of more concentrated nourishment, though it might have been much more digestible.

This statement is illustrated by another case: —

A young man, recovering from a fever, seventeen miles from home, was urged by his parents to go home before he had been able to take but very little nourishment. Contrary to advice, while stopping to rest seven miles from home, being overcome by the demands of his appetite, and having no one to restrain him, he obtained and ate heartily of beefsteak, pota-

18

toes, bread and butter, &c., and in one hour was dead. A restoration so suddenly of the natural elements of the blood probably produced apoplexy. These cases forcibly illustrate the statement on page 128, that any article of food may be wholesome or poisonous according to the circumstances under which it is taken. The cucumber was wholesome — the beefsteak a deadly poison.

These cases also show that while the appetite may be trusted in regard to the article to be eaten, it cannot be trusted in regard to the quantity, especially after the system has been exhausted by disease; so that though the unperverted appetite may in health be trusted with natural food to the extent of its demands, in sickness it can only be trusted in relation to the appropriate article to be eaten, and not in regard to the quantity required.

We therefore need some dietetic rules by which to regulate the diet of the sick. In almost all hospitals patients are divided into classes, and have a diet for each under different names.

In St. Thomas's Hospital of London

They have

	Full diet.	Milk diet.
Breakfast. .	2 pints beer, 14 oz. bread, water gruel.	12 oz. bread, 1 pint of milk.
	Dry diet.	**Fever diet.**
	14 oz. bread, 2 pints of beer, water gruel.	12 oz. bread, 2 pints of beer.

	Full diet.	Milk diet.
Dinner. . .	½ lb. beef, when dressed, twice a week; 4 oz. butter, or 6 oz. cheese, thrice a week; 1½ lb. mutton, when boiled, twice a week.*	1 pint of milk four times a week; rice puddings thrice a week.
	Dry Diet.	**Fever diet.**
	4 oz. butter four times a week; rice pudding and 4 oz. butter thrice a week.	¾ lb. beef for tea.

	Full diet.	Milk diet.
Supper. . .	1 pint of broth, four times a week.	1 pint milk.

In London Hospital

They have per day

	Common diet.	Middle diet.
Breakfast.	12 oz. bread, 1 pint porter men, ½ pint porter women; gruel.	Same as common.
	Low diet.	**Milk diet.**
	8 oz. bread; gruel.	12 oz. bread; gruel.

	Common diet.	Middle diet.
Dinner. . .	8 oz. mutton, with potatoes, five times a week; 8 oz. potatoes and soup, with vegetables, twice a week.	The same, except 4 oz. meat instead of 8 oz.
	Low diet.	**Milk diet.**
	Broth.	1 pint milk.

* All the London hospitals have, when ordered by the physician, in addition, chops, steaks, fish, wine, spirits, porter, &c.

Supper...	Common diet.	Middle diet.
	1 pint of broth.	–
	Low diet.	Milk diet.
	Gruel or broth.	1 pint milk.

In St. Bartholomew's Hospital

They have

Daily.	Common diet.	Broth diet.
	Milk porridge, 12 oz. bread, 6 oz. mutton or beef, 1 pint broth with peas or potatoes, four times a week; 2 pints beer for men, 1 pint for women; 1 oz butter thrice a week.	Milk porridge, 12 oz. bread, 2 pints broth, 1 pint beer, 1 oz. butter.
	Thin, or fever diet.	Milk diet.
	Milk porridge, 12 oz. bread, 1 pint milk, with tapioca, arrow root, sago, or rice, as may be prescribed; barley water.	Milk porridge, 12 oz. bread, 2 pints milk, with tapioca, arrow root, sago, or rice; barley water; 1 oz. butter; bread pudding 3 times a week when ordered.

In Guy's Hospital

They have

	Full diet.	Middle diet.	Low diet.	Milk diet.	Fever diet.
Daily.	14 oz. bread, $1\frac{1}{2}$ oz. butter, 1 qt. table beer, 8 oz. meat when it is dressed.	12 oz. bread, $1\frac{1}{2}$ oz. butter, 1 pint table beer, 4 oz. meat, and $\frac{1}{2}$ pint broth.	12 ounces bread, 1 oz. butter, tea and sugar.	12 ounces bread, 1 oz. butter, 2 pints of milk.	6 ounces bread, 1 oz. butter, tea and sugar.
	For each diet, gruel or barley water, as required.		$\frac{1}{2}$ lb. beef for beef tea, or arrow root, or sugar when ordered.		

At St. George's Hospital

They have

	Extra diet.	Ord'y Diet.	Fish diet.	Fever diet.	Broth diet.	Milk diet.
Daily. . .	12 oz. bread, 2 pints beer for men; 1 pint of beer for women.	12 ounces bread, 1 pt. beer.	12 ounces bread.	12 ounces bread, barley water ad libitum.	12 ounces bread.	12 ounces bread.
Breakfast.	1 pint tea, 1¼ pints milk.	1 pt. tea, ¼ pt. milk.	1 pt. tea, ¼ pt. milk.	1 pt. tea, ¼ pt. milk.	1 pt. tea, ¼ pint milk	1 pt. tea, ¼ pint milk
Dinner. .	12 oz. meat, with bone, roasted, 4 days; boiled, 3 days; ½ lb. potatoes.	6 ounces meat, ½ lb. potatoes.	4 oz. plain boiled white fish, as plaice, haddock, flounders	Arrow root, &c., as directed.	1 pt. br'th, 6 ounces light pudding.	1½ pints rice, milk 4 days, ½ lb. bread or rice pudding 3 days.
Supper. . .	1 pint gruel, ¼ pint milk.	1 pt. gruel, ¼ pint milk.	1 pt. gruel, ¼ pt. milk.	1 pt. tea, ¼ pint milk.	1 pt. gruel, ¼ pint milk.	½ pt. milk.

In Westminster Hospital

They have

	Full diet.	Middle diet.	Low diet. Fixed.	Low diet. Casual.	Spoon, or fever diet.	Incurables' diet.
Daily. . .	12 oz. bread.	10 ounces bread.	½ pound bread.		¼ pound bread.	¾ lb. bread, ½ lb. meat, ½ lb. potatoes, ¼ pt. milk, 1 pt. porter.
Breakfast.	1 pint milk porridge, or rice gruel.	1 pt. milk porridge, or thin gruel.	1 pt. tea, with sugar and milk.		1 pt. tea, with sugar and milk.	
Dinner. . .	½ lb. meat, roasted, broiled, or chops; ¾ lb. potatoes.	¼ lb. meat, roasted or boiled, or chops; ¾ lb. potatoes.	No fixed diet.	1 pt. broth or ½ lb. bread, or rice puddings, or 1 pt. beef tea, or fish	Barley water.	
Supper. . .	1 pint milk porridge, or rice gruel.	1 pt. milk porridge or gruel.	1 pt. tea, with sugar and milk.		1 pt. tea, with sugar and milk.	

In the Middlesex Hospital

They have

	Meat diet.	Soup diet.	Milk diet.	Simple diet.	Cancer diet.
Daily....	12 oz. bread.	12 ounces bread.	12 ounces bread.	6 oz. bread.	12 oz. bread, ½ lb. meat, ½ lb. potatoes, 1 pt. milk.
Breakfast.	1 pint milk.	1 pt. milk.	1 pt. milk.	1 pt. barley water.	
Dinner...	Physicians' Patients. 1½ lbs. potatoes, 4 oz. dressed beef or mutton, roasted and boiled, alternately, 4 days; 4 oz. meat in soup 3 days. Surgeons' Patients. ¾ lb. potatoes, 4 oz. dressed beef or mutton, roasted and boiled alternately.	1 pt soup, made with 4 oz. beef, alternately with 1 pt. of broth, with barley water.	½ pint milk with rice puddings four days, and batter pudding three days.	1 pt. gruel.	
Supper...	1 pt. gruel alternately with 1 pt. barley water.	1 pt. gruel.	½ pt. milk, or 1 pint gruel.	1 pt. gruel or barley water.	

In King's College Hospital

They have

	Full diet.	Middle diet.	Milk diet.	Low diet.	Fever diet.
Daily....	1 pint beer, or ½ pt. porter; 14 oz. bread.	14 oz. bread.	1 lb. bread.	8 oz. bread.	
Breakfast.	1 pt. milk porridge.	1 pint milk porridge.	1 pt. milk.	1 pt. gruel.	1 pt. gruel.
Dinner...	½ lb. meat, ½ lb. potatoes.	¼ lb. meat, ½ lb. potatoes.	1 pt. milk.	1 pt. broth.	2 pts. barley water.
Supper...	1 pt. milk porridge.	1 pint milk porridge.	1 pt. gruel.	1 pt. milk porridge.	1 pint milk porridge.

In North London Hospital

They have

	Full diet.	Middle diet.	Low diet.	Milk diet.
Daily. . .	16 oz. bread, ¼ pt. milk, ½ lb. meat, and ½ lb. potatoes, four days; 1 pint of rice or soup three days.	16 oz. bread, ¼ pt. milk, 1 pint soup or rice.	8 oz. bread, ¼ pt. milk, oatmeal gruel.	17 oz. bread, 2 pints milk.

According to Pereira, from whose treatise on dietetics the above tables are taken, and who was connected with one of these hospitals, these several diets are employed for the following reasons: —

Full, Common, or Meat Diet. — "On many occasions where it is desirable to restore or support the powers of the system, patients are permitted to satisfy their appetite for plain vegetable and animal food. In many indolent diseases, in scrofula, in some affections of the nervous system, as chorea and epilepsy, and in the stage of convalescence after acute maladies, &c., this kind of diet is frequently directed. In these cases beer and sometimes wine are permitted, and spirit is occasionally required. In some diseases of, and accidents occurring in confirmed drunkards, it is frequently found injurious to withhold the stimulus to which the patient's system has been long accustomed, and thus wine, gin, rum, or brandy are ordered according to circumstances."

This full or common diet is in general founded, I think, upon correct general principles, as understood at the time of its adoption; but in the light of some new scientific revelations might be greatly improved.

For example, in each table of full diet for all the London hospitals is given from twelve to sixteen ounces of bread, and from the remark of Pereira, page 149, that "the fine bread, prepared from flour only, is the most nutritive and digestible," I conclude that fine white bread is the article prescribed, and this conclusion is favored by the remark on the same page, that "notwithstanding that bread is denominated the *staff of life*, alone it does not appear to be capable of supporting prolonged human existence. Boussingault came to this conclusion from observing the small quantity of nitrogen which it contains; and the reports of the inspectors of prisons, on the effects of diet of bread and water, favor this notion."

These remarks are true of flour bread, but not true of bread made from wheat in its natural state, as is seen by analysis, page 24. That a great improvement in this diet would be made by substituting unbolted wheaten bread, or cracked wheat in part, I think will not be disputed by any one who will consider the facts already referred to. (See pages 26 and 27.) It is difficult also for us in Boston, who have pure water, and have never seen beer or porter used with meals to any extent, in sickness or health, to understand the necessity or advantage of giving in sickness two pints of beer to men or one and a half pints to women habitually, especially as in almost all kinds of sickness patients desire to return to primitive food and drinks, whatever their habits when well, and prefer pure water; but with such water as the best that can be furnished with their best arrangements in any hospital in London, we should realize the necessity of some beverage which would at least cover up the taste and smell of the water. Considering, therefore, the advantages of pure water which Boston possesses, and the little excuse we have for giving any substitute, our use of alcoholic beverages is much more obnoxious to criticism than that of any hospital in London. By the diet list it will be seen that no alcoholic beverages are given out regularly; but by the superintendent's report of disbursements, we see that in the year 1866 the sum of seventeen hundred and forty-nine dollars and seventy-seven cents was paid out for liquors, and seven hundred and seventy-one dollars and eighty-one cents for ale and porter — twenty-five hundred and twenty-one dollars and fifty-eight cents. Nearly fifty dollars a week for one hundred and twenty-eight patients.

Now, considering the effects of alcoholic drinks on the human system, according to the views of Professor Carpenter, who is the standard authority in the college under whose auspices this hospital is conducted, I venture the assertion that less than one dollar a week would cover the expense of alcohol in all forms in which it would be of any essential service to the patients. Carpenter says, in his Physiology, page 77, "The operation of alcohol upon the living body is essentially that of a *stimulus*, increasing for a time, like other stimuli, the vital activity of the body, and especially that of the nervo-muscular apparatus, so that a greater effect may often be produced in a given time under its use than can be obtained without it, but being followed by a corresponding depression of power, which is the more prolonged and severe in proportion as the previous excitement has been greater. Nothing, therefore, is in the end gained by their use, which is only justifiable where some temporary emergency can only be met by a temporary augmentation of power, even at the expense of an increased amount of subsequent depression, or where (as in the case of some individuals whose digestive power is deficient) it affords aid in the introduction of aliment into the system which nothing else can so well supply. These exceptional cases, however, will be less numerous in proportion as *due attention is paid to those other means of promoting health which are more in accordance with nature.*"

Will any physician contend that from seventy to one hundred applications of stimuli are necessary daily to "goad" the flagging powers of nature in these one hundred and twenty-eight patients up to their duty? A stimulus is literally a goad, and, according to Carpenter, and every other sensible physiologist, alcohol is a stimulus, and is never to be used only as a discreet horseman would use a goad or a whip when other inducements fail to excite the necessary exertion; and will any one contend that "these exceptional cases" in a year are so numerous as to require an expense to meet them of twenty-five hundred and twenty-one dollars and fifty-eight cents?

But the expense, it seems to me, is a trifle too insignificant to be mentioned (except as a means of estimating the extent of the practice) compared with other evils resulting from such practice. Professor Jacob Bigelow, in a lecture to a class of young men in Harvard Medical School, in 1825, of which I was one, uttered words on this subject that have so influenced my practice, that in forty years I have never used or recommended as much alcohol to be taken internally as is prescribed in the Boston City Hospital in one week; and while I have the pleasure of knowing that I never made a drunkard by precept or example, I have equal assurance that no patient of mine has ever had an additional pain or an additional hour of sickness for the want of alcohol in any form.

Dr. Bigelow's words were these: "Alcohol is highly stimulating, heating, and intoxicating, and its effects are so fascinating, that, when once experienced, the danger is that the desire for them may be perpetuated. Many patients have become gradually and imperceptibly intemperate under the sanction and guidance of a physician."

These assertions are denied only by those whose practice makes a denial necessary for justification, and they are as true in relation to hospital as to private practice; and being true, the inference is irresistible that scores of intemperate drinkers are made every year by the practice of giving convalescents alcoholic beverages.

They feel better for a while after a glass of wine, or ale, or whiskey, and, having "the sanction and guidance of a physician," they continue the habit after leaving the hospital, with a determination, perhaps, to discontinue it as soon as they recover their strength;

but, unfortunately, they never recover so as to be able to do without their beverage, or at least so as not to make ill health an excuse for continuing the habit, and it grows upon them till they go down to a drunkard's grave, cursing, perhaps, the doctor who first set them out on the road to destruction. Such cases I have frequently seen, and have heartily thanked God that such an awful responsibility never rested on me.

Boston City Hospital. Diet List.

Dinner.

Mondays. .	Soup, potatoes, bread (wheat, Graham, and brown), and puddings.
Tuesdays. .	Boiled corned beef and vegetables, bread (three kinds).
Wednesdays.	Fresh fish (fried and boiled), potatoes, bread (three kinds), and puddings.
Thursdays. .	Roast beef, or mutton, vegetables, and bread as above.
Fridays. .	Salt fish and potatoes, bread as above, and puddings.
Saturdays. .	Stewed meat and vegetables, bread as above.
Sundays. .	Roast beef or mutton, vegetables, bread as above.

Breakfast and Supper.

Each day of the week tea and coffee, at the discretion of the physician; shells, cocoa, bread (wheat, Graham, and brown), milk and sugar, butter, &c. Cold meat, steak or chop, if ordered.

Bread always in abundance; potatoes always; other vegetables in their season. In addition, broth, either of mutton or chicken, is made each day, that it may be in readiness for patients, if prescribed by the physicians.

The above is what is called the House Diet, which takes the place of the "Full Diet," "Ordinary Diet," or "Common Diet," of the London hospitals. But there are no tables of "Middle Diet," "First Diet," "Milk Diet," "Low Diet," "Fever Diet," or "Broth Diet," as in the London hospitals. But in every ward is a bill of fare, which is filled up every morning and evening by the nurse, under the direction of the physician, and generally according to the wishes of each patient, thus: —

Orders for Food for Patients. Ward —.

Date.		No. of Patients.	Date.		No. of Patients.
	House Diet.			Baked potatoes.	
	Beefsteak.			Eggs.	
	Mutton chop.			Milk.	
	Chicken.			Boiled rice.	
	Oysters.			Toast.	
	Broth.			Coffee.	
	Mush.			Tea.	
	Gruel.			Shells.	
	Farina.			Cocoa.	

The foregoing diet list and bill of fare may be considered the best dietetic arrangement in this country, the City Hospital being the last great establishment finished in the country, and the trustees having taken great pains to examine the diet tables of all, and make improvements on them. Like every other hospital, its diet is modified by the habits of the community in which it is situated.

The great dietetic fault of Boston consists in using much too large a proportion of carbonaceous food, which is the result of the use of superfine flour, butter, and sugar, instead of the natural combinations of these elements, as found in the grains, and fruits, and milk, from which these principles are separated. On page 34, I have estimated the proportion of white bread to all other bread used in Boston to be ninety-five per cent. The cook in the hospital estimates the proportion of bread used by the patients to be ninety per cent. of flour bread, while the proportion used by the other members of the family is much greater, making the estimate nearly the same as that for the whole city. A great improvement would undoubtedly be made by substituting bread made from unbolted wheat, ground from selected wheat, — that which is denominated Graham bread being generally an inferior quality of flour, mixed with bran, which is a different and very inferior article. Of twenty-six hundred and forty-eight dollars and fifty cents paid for bread, probably two thousand dollars are lost in the excess of carbonaceous food, which does much harm by creating a tendency to inflammations and fevers, and by prolonging this class of diseases. Of the twenty-nine hundred and seventy-eight dollars and eighty-eight cents paid for butter, all that part of it used with flour bread is lost, and worse than lost, adding only to its redundant carbonates, and increasing its heating qualities; but any part that may be used with lean meats or vegetables, may be useful, being more digestible than the fat of meats, and being useful in supplying the carbonates, which are deficient both in lean meats and green vegetables. The amount of sugar used does not appear, being included with other groceries, but probably enough to add considerably to the superabundant carbonates.

The amount of milk used in this hospital is very great, being, in the whole year, thirty-nine thousand nine hundred and fifty-two quarts, at a cost of twenty-nine hundred and seventy-six dollars and seventy cents, or four and one half quarts a week for every inmate. This is an excellent investment; and if, with all this milk used, there were as much of unbolted wheat bread, or cracked wheat, or hominy from southern corn, as the appetite demanded, the improvement would be very great.

Adaptation of Food to different Diseases.

In order to make a general adaptation of food to different diseases, and different conditions of the sick, it will be useful to recur to the table of the representative articles of the four different classes of alimentary substances, which will be found on page 134. The leading articles of the first class (the carbonates or heat-producers) are, the fat of meats, butter, sugar, and fine flour, all of which, and the last especially, are used in Boston in excess sufficient to account, undoubtedly, for many of the inflammatory diseases to which we are so liable, keeping up the steam, and heating up the timbers constantly, to the point almost of ignition, and making it more difficult to quench the flames when once started (if I may be allowed again to recur to the figure already once employed to describe the condition of the system induced by a diet unnaturally heating). This figure is also suggestive of the diet adapted to inflammatory diseases. Remove the combustible material and use water. This treatment Nature strongly suggests also, by the loss of appetite for all carbonaceous food, and the demand for cold water in all fevers and inflammatory diseases. The first effect of following these intimations will be to cause emaciation, the adipose substance being used to supply the lungs with fuel, which they must have every moment; and at the beginning of sickness it is certainly not an evil to lose this fat, and thus prepare the system for fresh, clean, and new clothing whenever it returns to a condition to need it. We need not be anxious to retain our old clothes if we can be sure of new ones, without extra expense, whenever we are able to make good use of them.

One source of that delightful sensation which constitutes the luxury of convalescence, is that sense of freshness and newness of every part, as the body is being reclothed with newly-formed adipose and muscle. This anxiety, therefore, which we so often see manifested lest we or our friends should lose flesh when sick, is at least unnecessary. Of this we can judge by adverting to our experience or observation of the difference between the luxury of convalescence from a fever, in which the flesh has been removed, to be again restored, and that from dropsy, or rheumatism, or gout, where the effete old body of flesh still clings to us. In all attacks of inflammatory disease, then, the first direction is to stop the supply of fuel, and let Nature supply the necessary heat, burning up the rubbish and cleansing the premises at the same time.

If we need no supply of carbonaceous food in the first attack of inflammatory diseases, we certainly need none of the nitrates or phosphates, for the muscles and mind both need absolute rest, and therefore need not be supplied with elements which are only necessary in muscular or mental activity. And here, too, we have but to follow the intimations of Nature, not only in regard to the supply of nutriment, but also in regard to the rest which is demanded, both for mind and muscle.

In regard to the exercise of muscles in sickness we are not much inclined to err, as we seldom use the muscles, or urge our friends to do so, in that state of lassitude which accompanies inflammatory diseases; but forgetting or not knowing that the mind is subject to the same laws as the muscles, the mind is not left to enjoy that absolute rest which it requires, and nurses, and mothers, and friends tire patients with talk on all sorts of subjects, if they do not insist on answers from them to all sorts of questions; but, by reference to pages

87, 88, and 89, it will be seen that the brain requires nourishment as well as the muscles, and is as much exhausted by efforts of the mind as the muscles are by active exercise. While, therefore, phosphatic food cannot be borne, the mind should be permitted to have absolute rest, being exercised only in making known the necessary requirements of the system. That friend is, therefore, kindest who keeps out of the sick chamber till her services are required.

Nor is it right to consult the patient on the subject of seeing friends or neighbors. The very efforts necessary to decide the question are injurious, and until after decided convalescence, and both mind and body have been recuperated by appropriate nourishment, the world, and everything pertaining to it, mentally or physically, should be absolutely shut out of the sick chamber, and when again admitted, should be admitted very carefully and gradually. Another important consideration is to CONSULT THE FEELINGS, WISHES, AND TASTES OF PATIENTS IN EVERYTHING.

Mind is the motive power of the world, and everything in it, mental or physical. And the human system, sick or well, is more dependent on the harmonious action of the mental faculties than all other influences combined beside, not only for its health and efficiency, but for its comfort when sick, and for its recovery to health.

First, then, put the mind of patients at ease in regard to everything in which they are interested, — the doctor, the nurse, the room, and everything in it, — allowing nothing in it disagreeable. Then allow them to take a little of anything they desire to take, and to taste of nothing disagreeable, of food, drink, or medicine. I have already alluded to the fact that in health the appetite and sense of taste are placed as guardians to protect the system from injurious substances (page 12); and can we believe it to be duty, when suffering from pain and sickness, to add to our suffering by taking disgusting drugs, making no effort to render them palatable and innoxious? But the argument in favor of this practice is, that Nature has furnished drugs which, in their crude state, are disagreeable, but which, nevertheless, do sometimes relieve suffering and cure disease. Does this argument prove that we should take drugs in the crude, disagreeable state in which they are naturally provided? If so, it proves too much, and, therefore, nothing.

Our food is furnished us mostly in a crude, unpalatable condition, but we were provided with intellects to show us how to cook it and adapt it to our tastes and requirements; and when we rightly use our intellects, and rightly prepare our food, we both relish it and are conscious of its adaptation to our wants. So God evidently intended we should use our brains in preparing medicines, and in adapting them to our taste and requirements, and when we do so we are rewarded by the same evidence of its adaptation to our requirements. If instead of relief we find the system disturbed, we may be sure we have mistaken the remedy, or have given it in an improper condition or quantity, just as we are always sure we have taken improper food, if, instead of gratified appetite we get disturbance from it.

Other animals are furnished both with food and medicine in a state adapted to their wants, because they have not sense to prepare them. The sick cat takes with relish the simple catnip provided for it, and it does good and not harm; but the sick child must swallow drugs which it shudders to think of, and which disturbs all its functions for days and weeks, and sometimes for life. All animals, in their natural state, take with impunity whatever they desire, sick or well, and nothing else; and until our appetites are perverted by unnatural food, we also can take and give our children everything, in a natural state, which they desire, sick or well; and when prostrate with sickness, however perverted our tastes may have been, we return to our primitive appetites and desires. The drunkard loses his desire for alcohol, the smoker for his cigar, and the gormand for his rich food. All come down to the same simple demands of nature, and all can be trusted to eat and drink what they choose, and will all be benefited by rejecting everything offensive to their tastes.

Is it reasonable that our heavenly Father should be at such infinite pains to adapt the world to the comfort and happiness of man, and give him a natural relish for everything that is best for him to have in health, but when sick and in pain, should intend to add to his suffering by consigning him to the torments of blisters, hot irons, cataplasms, and disgusting drugs?

Our reason, therefore, as well as our humanity, experience, and common sense, accords with plain deductions from Nature's common laws, and demands that everything offensive to the patient, whether of diet, regimen, or medicine, should be excluded from the sick chamber.

Following these intimations, we shall find that articles of the second and third class (page 134) will not be demanded till there is decided convalescence, and then the soluble portions. These sustain life without furnishing fibre for the muscles or solid phosphates for bones, and are, therefore, called for before the muscles can be used. Beef tea, or broth from lean meat or chicken, for example, in which are infused the albumen and soluble phosphates, the one furnishing food for the dormant tissues, and the other nervous or vital power; while the appetite for solid meat or fish will be reserved till the muscles shall require fibre for use, and the bones the solid phosphates. Liquid food, therefore, is all that is needed in severe sickness of any kind, and such food is generally all that the appetite craves or the stomach will receive. Sometimes, however, the appetite, having been blunted by some interference in giving nutriment in spite of her remonstrances, ceases to demand the right food at the right time, and we are obliged to use judgment in adapting the nutriment to circumstances. In that case great assistance may be obtained from the Dietetic Tables; when there is too much heat, abstaining from the carbonates, except as nature has combined them with cooling acid, as in the succulent fruits, and when cold and lifeless, giving some easily-digested carbonate, as starch, or some of the life-giving nitrates and phosphates, as in the broth of meats, or the phosphatic flesh of the active fishes or birds.

The fourth class of representative articles of food, being in its characteristic effects rather mechanical than vital, is to be selected with reference to the condition of the digestive organs. If there is inactivity of the stomach, or bowels, or liver, and constipation is the consequence, then this class of food should be freely used; but if, on the other hand, there is irritability of these organs, and diarrhœa, dysentery, or cholera, then these organs should be permitted to rest from the natural influences of waste, which are necessary in health, and nutriment be taken, like the juice of beef, flour porridge, &c., which contain no waste; just as in inflammation of the eye, we shut out the light, and give it rest and time to recover, or in inflammation of the brain, we prohibit all exciting influences, and abstain from all phosphatic food, using only common sense in the application of the laws of our being to our particular circumstances, as the farmer uses it in supplying the necessary elements for the crop to be produced, and allowing the land to rest when overworked and sick.

The Development and Preservation of our Faculties

Demand appropriate food and drink, taken at proper times and in suitable quantities; appropriate sleep and rest for all the faculties, alternated with regular and appropriate exercise; suitable protection from the cold, purity of the air night and day, personal cleanliness, avoiding sudden changes of habits or temperature, keeping out of the stomach everything injurious, and the right use of the means which God has provided for restoring to health the organs and faculties which may become diseased.

On each of these subjects might be written an elaborate treatise, but I propose to write a chapter only, to show as clearly and familiarly as possible the indications of Nature as to the principles which are to guide us in these important matters. First,

The Laws of Nutrition.

Every living thing requires nourishment, and every living thing is provided with food within its own reach, just adapted to its own peculiar wants; and every living thing but man is provided with instinctive powers to appropriate to its use just the elements that are needed, and, under ordinary circumstances, to reject every element that is not needed or is hurtful, as I have already explained. It is interesting to notice the wonderful provision of Nature, by which every creature, from the elephant to the minutest animalcule, comes into life just where and when its natural food is ready for it.

See the *paterfamilias* of the canker-worm family, tugging up the trunk of the apple-tree with his helpless wife on his back, to place her where she can deposit her eggs beside the buds out of which is to come the tender leaf by the influence of the same degree of heat that will hatch its eggs, so that the young worm will have food fitted for it at just the right time! And the provision by which a similar result is effected with other creatures is still more remarkable.

The larva of a species of gad-fly can live and grow only in the intestines of the horse, and the whole life of the fly after it has obtained wings, which is only a few days, is devoted to the task of depositing on the legs of the horse its eggs. These eggs are covered with gluten, by which they adhere to the hairs, and binding them together produce an irritation, and, trying to relieve that tickling with the teeth, some of the eggs adhere to the teeth and are swallowed, and thus arrive at their destination; and it is remarkable that the eggs are never deposited on any parts of the horse except those which can be reached and relieved of irritation by the teeth, otherwise they would lose all chances of arriving at their destination.

Another species of fly can be produced only in capsicum (Cayenne pepper). The fly is, of course, exceeding scarce in this country; but I have seen, in a neglected pepper-box, a flourishing family luxuriating and developing into perfect flies on their natural element.

But the most remarkable example of complicated and far-seeing provision of nature to bring a living creature into the situation where its natural food is provided, which has yet been brought out from Nature's great storehouse of wonderful things, is found in the tapeworm. The facts on which this statement rests were developed by a learned and persevering German, whose name is Küchenmeister.

It has long been known that small sacks, or cysts, containing, together with serum, a rudimentary form of animal life, are sometimes found in the liver and other organs, and sometimes in the flesh of the hog and other animals; and hogs thus infested are said to be "*measly*." If this pork is eaten uncooked, as it frequently is in Germany, in Bologna sausages, and in ham made into sandwiches, and sometimes in this country in uncooked fat pork, and one of these cysts enters the stomach, the sack is broken, and the young tape-worm, having arrived at its natural home, commences life in its own peculiar way. At first it has only a head and four suckers, through which it draws its nutriment from the coats of the stomach, and a double circle of hooks, with which it attaches itself firmly to the side of the stomach on the mucous membrane. Here it remains during its lifetime; but its body, consisting of joints like pieces of tape, from one quarter to one half inch in length, grows, one joint after another, from the head extending itself in the stomach and among the intestines, till it reaches the length of ten, twenty, thirty, and sometimes forty or fifty feet, new joints being constantly formed from the head, and pushing the old ones away, and thus the joints farthest from the head are oldest and most mature. These joints, after a while, break off in pieces, sometimes of fifteen or twenty feet long; each joint containing numerous eggs or germs, are cast off, and if they find a lodgment on the grass or in water, where they may be taken into the stomach of another animal, are hatched in their stomach, and in their first form have the power of crawling through the integuments into the liver or flesh, forming new cysts or sacks, and thus are prepared again to be taken into the human stomach, to go again their rounds. The eggs will not hatch except in the stomach of a quadruped; and the developed animal cannot live except in the human stomach. The only chance, therefore, of perpetuating itself is, first, the chance that some animal which is eaten by man shall get an egg into its stomach, and that some man shall get it after the first process of development into his stomach, which chance would seem to be very small in this country, where so little raw meat is eaten, and where so few animals have access to the means of obtaining the eggs.

While, therefore, every tape-worm may, in the course of its life (sometimes of many years), cast off as many eggs as there are inhabitants on the face of the earth, the chances of the conditions being fulfilled, on which their perpetuation depends, are so small that, in this country, it is very rarely found. When once it gets hold, however, it is very difficult to dislodge it. I once gave two ounces of spirits of turpentine, which brought away twenty-five feet of the worm; but the head remained, and the creature still lived and flourished.

To prove that the tape-worm is developed from the cysts taken from measly pork, Küchenmeister performed the following experiment on a criminal condemned to death: He administered, during three days, seventy-five of these cysts, giving them time to develop before execution. After execution he found ten young tapeworms in the intestines, six of which were destitute of hooks; but the remaining four were attached by their hooks to the mucous membrane.

And to prove the other part of the theory, some pigs were fed with segments of tape-worm, and subsequently killed. The flesh was filled with the cysts in different stages of development, from the first commencement to the perfect formation, in proportion to the amount eaten and the time which had elapsed, while a pig of the same litter, not so fed, was entirely free from this formation.*

And that interesting parasite, called *louse*, can live only on its own animal or plant, and if transferred to any other species will soon starve; and thus every living thing is provided with its appropriate food, and with means of getting it in its own limited sphere.

But man has no limits to his range of enterprise, and no limit to the variety of food on which he can subsist; and yet no animal has such a struggle with difficulties, not only in selecting food suitable for his powers of digestion, but in adapting it to his varied circumstances.

What is the Natural Food for Man?

When God created man, he gave him for meat "every herb bearing seed which is upon the face of the earth, and every tree in the which is the fruit of a tree yielding seed;" and when, afterwards, he blessed Noah

* See Küchenmeister's Manual of Animal and Vegetable Parasites.

for his faithfulness, he gave him, in addition to his bill of fare, "every beast of the earth and every fowl of the air," "and all the fishes of the sea," and told him that "every moving thing that liveth shall be meat for him, even as the green herb."

This would enable him to fulfil his destiny, and have dominion over all other creatures, and to live with the polar bear almost at the north pole, or with the monkey at the equator, having in each of these extremes of temperature food adapted to his wants. Wherever he chooses to live, in a cold, or hot, or temperate climate, he finds prepared at his hand the kind of food best adapted to his wants, and has a relish for just the article best fitted to supply his wants. If he lives in Greenland, he desires and has the heat-producing fat of whales and seals, the very thought of which would disgust him in Africa; and if in Africa, he desires and has the cooling fruits and vegetables which would freeze him to death in Greenland; and in the climate where cold and heat alternate, he has all the variety best adapted to his changing circumstances.

To comprehend the necessity of this variety of food, and to understand the principle on which we can adapt our food to the different conditions and employments of life, it will be necessary first to understand the physiological necessity for food. Besides the necessity of providing for the growth of the young, food is necessary, principally, for three essential purposes: —

1. To supply the waste which is constantly going on in the tissues, especially in the muscular or moving part of the system.

2. To supply the fat and the animal heat of the system.

3. To supply food for the brain and nervous system, the bones and solid tissues, and some essential elements in pure red blood.

Now, if we examine any one article in its natural state in the whole bill of fare which God has given us, either of the vegetable or animal kingdom, we shall find these three classes of elements, but find them combined in different proportions, and find them mostly, also, in a condition to require some cooking to fit them for digestion, and thus find exercise for our mental faculties, both in selecting food and cooking it, so as to adapt it to our varying circumstances.

In this respect man, and all other animals, are placed in very different circumstances. All animals but man are endowed with instincts to direct them to the right food which is prepared for them, and which requires no cooking and no preparation; but the destiny of man was, that he should use his intellect to study Nature's laws, and to use them in the selection of appropriate food, and in preparing it for digestion.

What his condition in regard to food was before the fall, is not clearly revealed; but even in the garden of Eden he had something to do, for it is said, "And the Lord God took the man and put him into the garden of Eden, to dress it and keep it."

But after the fall, his condition is clearly revealed to Adam in these awful sentences: "Cursed is the ground for thy sake. In sorrow shalt thou eat of it all the days of thy life." "Thorns also, and thistles shall it bring forth to thee, and thou shalt eat of the herb of the field." "In the sweat of thy face shalt thou eat bread till thou return unto the ground."

After that sentence, whatever his variety of fruits and vegetables might have been before, he seems to have been almost literally driven to the herb of the field, including, perhaps, some farinaceous seeds of the grasses, and some wild fruits and berries, that out of them, by the use of his wits and by the sweat of his face, he should cultivate the grains, and fruits, and vegetables, and to the end of time increase their variety, improve their taste, and fit them, not only to become the necessaries, but also the choicest luxuries of life. And it is interesting to trace, as far as we may, our grains, delicious fruits, and succulent vegetables, to their original wild fruits and green herbs.

Many of our grains and vegetables were so early changed by cultivation that their history has not been preserved, and their original grass, or tree, or herb cannot now be found or recognized; but enough have been traced to their origin, and the wonderful changes noticed which have been wrought by cultivation, to warrant the belief that farinaceous grains, and our valuable vegetables and fruits, which cannot be found wild in any part of the world, are so changed by cultivation that their original grasses or plants are not recognized.

Cabbage, in all its varieties, cauliflower, broccoli, &c., have all been traced to, and cultivated from the kale, colwort, &c., which grew in a natural branching way, without forming a head at all.

Celery is cultivated from a very disagreeable herb, called *apium*. All the delicious varieties of apples came originally from the crab apple, which grows wild in every part of England, and in many parts of this country, — a bitter, sour, disagreeable fruit.

And the peach is a still more remarkable example of the effects of cultivation and change of climate.

When first introduced into Europe from Persia its pulp was hard, disagreeable, bitter, and sour, resembling the pulp of a walnut in a green state; and it is generally supposed that by some change of climate or culture the green pulp of the fruit, or nut of the almond, the pit or kernel of which it almost exactly resembles in appearance and taste, and the botanical character of which it also very nearly resembles, was prevented from drying into a shell or nut, and by continued culture has come to be a delicious fruit. At any rate, since its history was first known it has changed from a disagreeable substance, which afforded no nutriment, to a very valuable and delicious fruit.

Rye, barley, wheat, oats, &c., have all the characteristics of the grasses, and the seeds of all our common grasses, as well as all the grains, contain alike the nitrates, the carbonates, and the phosphates, and these elements of food are found in all in nearly the same proportions, and in nearly the right proportions, to supply all the wants of the human system in ordinary temperatures and circumstances. But neither of these grains is found wild in any part of the world, and the inference is fair that they were changed from their original grasses so early and so radically that their identity has not been transmitted to us.

Our maize, or Indian corn, has also the characteristics of the gigantic grasses, and must have come from the same source as the sugar-cane, the sorghum, and broom-cane. And this suppostion, I think, is corroborated by a very curious circumstance which came under my own observation. More than twenty-five years ago some officers in the United States service brought from Egypt a mummy, in the integuments of which were found some peculiar grains of maize. It had not probably been exposed to the air for three thousand years, and on being planted it grew; but the season proved too short, and it was not so perfected as to be capable of being perpetuated. Some which was planted in my own garden grew like common Indian corn, tasselled out, and grains of corn were formed, not on a cob, but on a bundle of small stalks, as if the stalks of the top of broom-corn had been firmly tied together, and had adhered, and the grains of corn grew around this bundle of sticks in a conical form. The inference to my mind was, that at the period at which this corn grew, the ear of corn was undergoing a process of change from the large seeded umbelliferous plant, like the broom-corn, to the solid, cylindrical ear, on a cob, as we now find it.

The potato is a still more recent and interesting illustration of the power of climate and cultivation to transform a useless bulbous root into a valuable article of diet.

The plant from which the potato is cultivated is now found growing wild in Chili and Montevideo, and is a useless, gnarly root; but within the last two or three centuries it has been changed into a standard article of diet in all Europe and North America, supporting, to a great extent, in some places, thousands of working people.

Thus, if we will build on Nature's own foundations, we can improve almost every living thing, animal or vegetable, and add to our bill of fare indefinitely, not only the necessaries but the luxuries of life, still retaining all the elements needed by the system; but when we attempt to improve our natural food, by abstracting what we call the best parts of any article, we make sad mistakes, and have to suffer the consequences, as we have before explained.

Besides the appropriate supply of the elements required for all the organs, functions, and faculties, other considerations demand our attention in regard to the selection of articles of food.

Some articles of food contain more nourishment and less waste than others. Some require more and some less powers of digestion than others, &c.

Is that article most wholesome which contains most nourishment? Certainly not in this country, where we all get too much nourishment. Food containing waste is absolutely necessary every day, not only to produce the necessary distention of the stomach and intestines, but to produce the natural stimulant for which this waste was intended; and one of the prominent evils, and perhaps the greatest next to the evils produced by the want of essential elements, in the use of our fine flour, sugar, and butter, in their various combinations, is the evil of constipation, which is the natural consequence of the too constant and too exclusive use of these articles, which contain no waste materials.

Are those articles which are most easily digested the most wholesome? Certainly not, for the stomach, like every other organ and faculty, needs exercise to acquire or keep up its energy and healthy action; and therefore, on the contrary, that article of food is best, other things being equal, which most fully exercises the powers of digestion; but that article is not wholesome which overtaxes these powers; just as that muscular exercise is best which most fully develops the powers of the muscles, but does not overtax them.

Beans and rice, for illustration, contain nearly equal amounts of nutrition, each containing from eighty to ninety per cent., and each containing some of all the elements of nutrition required, but in different proportions, as we see by the tables; but the power and time required for digesting these articles differ materially, beans being one of the hardest and rice one of the easiest articles to be digested.

Now who can say, abstractly, which is most wholesome, beans or rice? To the laboring man, who has powers of digestion sufficient for beans, they are more wholesome than rice, which is too soon disposed of, and too soon leaves a desire for other food, and gives too little strength of muscle; but to the sedentary invalid, whose powers of digestion are feeble, rice would be wholesome, while beans might be distressingly unwholesome, and for a permanent article of diet, to be eaten alone, both would be unwholesome, as each contains too little waste for the healthy action of the bowels.

Osmazome.

The taste and appetite are placed as sentinels to guard the portals of the stomach, and, through the stomach, the whole system; and, under the direction of instinct, in all animals in their natural condition, are absolutely or very nearly infallible, both as to admissions and rejections. Offer an elephant a piece of tobacco or a glass of whiskey, and he will not only reject it, but reject you with disdain for the insult; but give him his natural food, and he will take all that his appetite demands, and all that would be good for him, and no more.

The same thing is true of man till his taste is perverted. The little child always relishes its natural food, and may be safely trusted to take of it all he wants; but offer him unnatural food, or unnatural drugs or medicine, and he rejects it. A perverted appetite, however, cannot be trusted, as it demands and relishes articles which are positively hurtful.

It is interesting to notice the great variety and exquisite delicacy with which Nature has flavored the different articles of food, no two articles having the same flavor, although in other respects almost exactly alike. Beef and mutton, for example, contain the same elements, and are almost exactly alike except in regard to the osmazome, which constitutes their distinctive flavor; but this difference is of very considerable importance practically, when we consider that that which relishes best always digests best. We should therefore never allow ourselves to eat that which is disagreeable to our own taste, whatever others may think of it. And this is true of every article of food in the animal or vegetable kingdom, and other things being equal, and they generally are equal, that which we love best *in its natural state* is best for us.

Another noticeable fact is, that this osmazome is in its perfection only when the food is in a perfect condition for digestion. Those articles which require cooking have their flavor most perfectly developed just at the time when they are properly cooked, and ready to be eaten and easily to be digested, and any considerable delay, or a second cooking, always diminishes the flavor. Beefsteak, for example, is much more palatable and much more digestible when first cooked, than when it has been exposed, and its osmazome evaporated, or when warmed over; indeed, all meats are better when once well cooked, to be eaten cold, than to be warmed or cooked over, and this is understood by all cooks, who always add some spices to make meats palatable on a second cooking.

Soups from meats and vegetables have a much more delicious flavor when made from raw meat and vegetables than when made from meat and vegetables previously cooked, and the most delicious soups are made without other spices than are found in vegetables and meats. Most meats and vegetables become, by frequent cooking, so insipid as to be unpalatable and unwholesome, as I have elsewhere explained, merely from the loss of the osmazome; and this natural stimulant of digestion can be only very imperfectly supplied by aromatic condiments. On the other hand berries, and the rich fruits which need no cooking, have their most delicious flavor already developed, and any attempt at improving them by cooking only makes them less palatable and less digestible.

We have, therefore, a clear intimation that we should consult our appetite and taste, both in regard to the kind of food and to the manner of preparing it.

No one can realize till he tries it, what an amount of real enjoyment can be added to life by simply studying Nature's laws in regard to food, and by applying them to every-day life, in the mere enjoyment of meals, as well as in the freedom from sickness and pain, and in the increased value of all our faculties. And these laws are very simple and easily understood.

In every variety of food furnished for man on the face of the earth, every article contains in its natural state, with all other essential elements, that peculiar element called osmazome, which is in correspondence with the wants of the system at all times, and induces an appetite and relish for just the article most needed. The osmazome of whale oil, for example, would be very disgusting to a man living under the equator, while to a man exposed to the cold of Lapland nothing could be more agreeable; and the orange, which is so delicious in warm climates, would have no attractions for one living in cold climates.

Condiments.

In view of the fact, so clearly revealed, that food, to be well digested, must be made to relish, condiments are of no small importance in the philosophy of cooking; for, though Nature has furnished to all suitable food in its natural state, when properly cooked, all that is needed, except salt, to make it palatable and digestible, still it is quite impossible always to get our food in just the right condition, and to eat it while the osmazome remains. We often need a substitute for the natural flavor, and Nature seems to have furnished that substitute in the aromatic herbs, and seeds, and flowers. Certain it is, that mixed food, or re-cooked food, as minced meat, or sausages, or soups from re-cooked meats and vegetables, are made more digestible by being made palatable with condiments; but in this, as in everything else, that cooking is best which best imitates Nature. The flavors of all natural and valuable food are delicate, not strong or pungent, except in the onion, and other worthless articles; and to all but perverted tastes food is most agreeable which is only delicately flavored, and nothing can be more certain than that the pungent spices, as horse-radish, mustard, cloves, red pepper, &c., any one of which, if applied to the skin, would produce inflammation, must be injurious to the delicate stomach, as they are generally used. This, indeed, has been proved beyond all doubt. All condiments, indeed, must be used as a choice of evils. If we could at all times get the requsite elements of food, either from the beasts of the field, or the fowl of the air, or the grains, and vegetables, and fruits, just when they have their natural osmazome fully developed, we should need no condiments; but if we cannot get appropriate food till after its natural flavor has evaporated, or has been dissipated by re-cooking, then some delicate condiments are useful to make it palatable and digestible. When obliged to dine on food that is not relished, the stomach is oppressed, and the food remains undigested till we take a bit of cheese, or a few nuts or raisins, or some agreeable condiment, which, though indigestible in themselves, will arouse the stomach to action, and the dinner will be digested.

Some part, at least, of every meal must have an agreeable flavor in order to be well digested. For this reason, a small cup of aromatic coffee will sometimes make amends for a very poor dinner; but a little is better than more.

Salt.

Salt has some characteristics peculiar to itself, differing from all other elements or compounds, organic or inorganic. It is not in any sense nutriment, as it does not furnish support to any organ or function, and does nothing towards sustaining life, as has been often proved in the shipwrecked and famishing sailor, who, instead of relieving his sufferings, has added to them by taking salt water, even in very small quantities. Neither is it a chemical agent, combining with some other element in the system to effect a necessary change, as the acids combine with alkaline bases and remove effete matter from the system in the excretions. It is chloride of sodium, wherever found, in the stomach, in the blood, or in the excretions, and what its office is in the system, is not known; but undoubtedly it has some beneficial influence besides its use as a condiment. This seems to be indicated by the fact that other animals seem to require salt, and have a natural desire for it, and seem to suffer if for a length of time they are deprived of it.

And this is not confined to domesticated animals, as the buffalo and the deer of the western prairies make paths to the salt licks by their frequent visits after salt.

Still it is not an absolute necessity in the animal economy, at least not farther than may be met by the chloride of sodium, which is found in almost all animal and vegetable food, as whole nations of men and their domestic animals live without salt, except as it is found in food; and this relieves us from the apparent exception which salt furnishes to the law which I have endeavored to develop, that all elements to be incorporated into the human system, or any other animal system, must first be organized in some vegetable.

There is enough salt in common, natural food, to account for all the salt actually incorporated in the system; indeed, it is yet an unsettled physiological question whether any salt is actually incorporated in the blood or in any of the organs.

But whatever else is accomplished in the system by salt, its essential use is that of a condiment, exciting the secretory organs to do their duty. Certain it is that it does incite to action the salivary and other glands. Take in the mouth a bit of salt fish, or bacon, or any other savory article, and the mouth is immediately filled with saliva; and when it is received into the stomach, the gastric juice also immediately gushes out. Of these effects on the glands of the mouth and stomach we can have no doubt, as they are under the observation of our senses; but of the effects on the liver, the pancreas, and the other glands, we have only to judge by inference; but the inference is certainly fair if the glandular system, as far as we can know, is stimulated to action by salt; the other glands, whose action we cannot observe, but whose duties are also connected with the process of digestion, may also be affected by the same agent. My conclusion, therefore, is, that salt, like other condiments, promotes digestion by exciting the glands and inducing the production and flow of their secretions. And the principal value of the salt is in its savor; so that the question, "If the salt have lost its savor, wherewith shall it be salted?" like all other questions from the divine Master, contained a philosophical truth as well as an apt illustration.

Like all other condiments, salt is useful or injurious, according as it is taken in large or small quantities. A little gives a better relish than more, and therefore is more useful, while the larger the quantity the more injurious. The only rule, therefore, for the use of it is to use as little as will give to food a relish; and the amount necessary for that depends very much on habit, except in regard to that which is found in plants and the flesh of animals. Salt is an inorganic substance, and the only one demanded and extensively used as a condiment, and the only one so universally and so abundantly furnished; and this fact alone would indicate its importance in the animal economy; but some nations of men, and some animals in every nation, do not require salt; and to some, as the birds, it is a poison, in quite small quantities; and this fact, on the other hand, would indicate that it is not, like the nutritive elements, necessary for the support of animal life.

Other condiments are from the vegetable kingdom, and mostly from tropical climates; and, from the very narrow range of temperature to which the most aromatic are limited, we may infer that they were not intended for universal use; but each probably possesses some medicinal quality adapted to some peculiarity of the diseases of its own locality.

The *cinnamon* is said to be indigenous only to the Island of Ceylon, and even there is confined to a small district in the south-western part of that island.

The *clove* is a native of the Molucca Islands, and the *nutmeg* of the same islands. *Ginger* is a native of the south-east coast of Asia and the adjacent islands. The *pimento* or *allspice* grows spontaneously in Jamaica, and one writer says, "it is purely a child of Nature, and seems to mock all the labors of man in his endeavors to extend or improve its growth: not one attempt in fifty to propagate the young plants, or to raise their seeds, in parts of the country where it is not found growing spontaneously, having succeeded." These spices, therefore, were evidently not intended for universal use; nevertheless, upon the principles which I have elsewhere explained, they may be useful in promoting the digestibility of food which is destitute of, or deficient in osmazome; not by any special virtue in them, but upon the general principle, that whatever agrees with the taste excites the glands to secrete the fluids necessary for digestion.

Sometimes a deficiency in these digestive fluids is the cause of a want of appetite, and the appetite craves something savory; and, taking a hint from this instinctive demand of Nature, I have, for the last twenty-five years, practised giving a sick patient, especially after passing the crisis of disease, a little of anything which the appetite demanded. Salt fish, smoked ham, pickles, anything else savory and agreeable at the time to the patient, by only being chewed and held in the mouth will excite the secretions, and then the stomach will be prepared for simple and natural nourishment, and will call for it.

This practice may be carried too far, and is frequently, in warm weather and warm climates, where carbonaceous food is not needed. The appetite is then stimulated by the pungent spices, which do harm not only by their own exciting influence, but by inducing the taking of unnatural and stimulating food. In this way the people of our Southern States prepare themselves for the bilious fevers and other diseases which carry off so many; and this has been proved by the fact that those among them who have sense enough to abstain from alcohol, spices, and pork, and live on the cooling fruits, and vegetables, and grains of their own climate, are exempt from these diseases.

Those spices are best which are best relished, as their value consists in gratifying the taste, and thus exciting the secretions. Of course no one can judge for another in regard to the spice to be used; and cooks must not consult their own taste, but the taste of the family for whom they cook; for a spice that may be highly relished by one, and therefore wholesome, may for another be disagreeable and unwholesome. The rules, therefore, for selecting and using spices are very simple: First, use none at all with food that can be relished without it. Second, use that which best agrees with the natural taste. Third, use the smallest quantity that will be satisfactory to the unperverted taste, and never allow the quantity to be increased. Our gustatory pleasures, like all other pleasures of life, are best enjoyed by the moderate use of the good things that are kindly provided for us. And the greatest sufferings which come from them, come, as do most of our physical sufferings, from deceiving ourselves with the idea that if a little of any good thing will give us pleasure, the pleasure may be increased by increasing the quantity. Instead, therefore, of being contented with the delicate and wholesome flavor which may be imparted by a very little pepper or any other spice, we are inclined to increase the amount, till we take into the delicate stomach these spices of strength sufficient to draw a blister on the skin if applied to it, — and can they fail to be injurious?

Cinnamon.

Cinnamon is the bark of twigs or young shoots of a tree which grows in Ceylon to the height of twenty or thirty feet. It has been the source of a great trade for more than three hundred years, and its fragrance has been admired from time immemorial. By a report of the Royal Asiatic Society, made some years since, it is stated that the number of people engaged in the cinnamon department of trade was from twenty-five to twenty-six thousand persons, and that the amount exported was two hundred thousand tons.

At one time, when under Dutch government and monopoly, the degree of rigor with which this monopoly was maintained was so great that "the selling or giving away the smallest quantity of cinnamon (even were it but the single stick), the exporting of it, the peeling of the bark, extracting the oil either from that or the leaves, or the camphor from the roots, except by the servants of the government, and by their order, as well as the wilful injuring of a cinnamon plant, were all made crimes punishable with *death*, both on the persons committing them, and upon every servant of government who should connive at it." *

* Bertolacci's Ceylon, p. 241.

And in order to keep up the price when the supply was greater than the demand, the government ordered the destruction of all the surplus. "M. Beaumere relates that on the 10th of June, 1760, he beheld, near the admiralty at Amsterdam, a blazing pile of these aromatics, which were valued at eight millions of livres, and an equal quantity was burnt the next day. The air was perfumed with this incense; the essential oils, freed from their confinement, distilled over, mixing in one spicy stream, which flowed at the feet of the spectators; but no person was suffered to collect any of this, nor, on pain of heavy punishment, to rescue the smallest quantity of the spice from the wasting elements." *

Cassia.

Cassia is supposed to be an inferior quality of cinnamon, and to come from a variety of the same species of tree; but botanists consider it a distinct species. It is not brought from Ceylon, but principally from China, and both the bark and buds are used. They have the same kind of aroma as cinnamon, but inferior in degree of flavor.

Clove.

Europeans are said to have known this spice for more than two thousand years. It is a product of the Molucca Islands, and was for a long time under the

* Lankester's Vegetable Substances used for the Food of Man, p. 202.

control of the Dutch government, who monopolized the trade in this as other spices, having driven off the Portuguese, who first discovered the source from which it came to Europe. It is the product of a beautiful tree, every part of which is fragrant; but the only part used is the calyx of the flower, which, while in the form of an elongated bud, is beaten from the tree and dried for the market. It has an exceedingly pungent flavor, and should therefore be used only in very small quantities.

Nutmeg.

The nutmeg is the kernel of the fruit of a beautiful tree, a native also of the Moluccas; but now cultivated in many islands, and in the southern part of the peninsula of India, the mountains, and some other places. The tree furnishes two spices, the nutmeg or kernel, and the mace, which is the membranous tunic or covering of the shell in which the nutmeg is contained.

The flavor of the nutmeg is much less pungent than that of the clove, and therefore is less stimulating and injurious.

Ginger.

Ginger came originally from Southern Asia, but at an early period was transplanted in South America and the West Indies, from which places it was exported to Europe as early as 1547. (Edwards' West Indies, vol. ii.) It comes from the tuberous joints or roots of the ginger plant, and in commerce is distinguished as black and white ginger; both kinds, however, come from the same plant, the difference of color depending on the mode of preparatiou.

Pepper.

There are said to be at least sixty varieties of pepper, some of which are found in every part of the world. The black pepper of commerce, which is the most extensively used, is found native on the mountains on the coast of Malabar, and is cultivated to a great extent in Sumatra and Java, and forms the principal article of export in these places. It grows on a creeping or climbing plant, and resembles, when the leaves are off, very closely the grape vine.

Pimento, or Allspice.

This spice is the unripe fruit of a large and beautiful tree. The berries are gathered just after the flower has fallen off, as they lose their fragrance and become valueless if suffered to ripen. The crop, in a favorable season, is sometimes enormous, a single tree yielding one hundred weight of dried fruit after losing one third in curing. The allspice has a flavor which seems to combine the properties of many other spices, and that fact is the origin of its proper name.

Capsicum

Is a native of India, but has been acclimated in this country and England, of which there are three kinds, the cherry pepper, the guinea pepper, and the bell pepper. The green pods of all these varieties are used for pickles, and the ripe ones for seasoning pickles, &c.

Vanilla.

Vanilla is a native of Mexico and some parts of India. It is a parasitical plant, with lanceolate leaves, eighteen inches long and three inches wide, and bears slender pods, containing, besides numerous seeds, a substance which is black, oily, and balsamic when recently gathered, and its odor, when strongly inhaled, produces a kind of temporary intoxication. These pods are gathered and dried, and constitute the vanilla which is used for making chocolate, and for flavoring ice-creams, cakes, blanc-mange, &c.

These foreign spices, together with many seasoning herbs, which grow spontaneously or are acclimated in this country, such as parsley, fennel, purslain, horse-radish, mint, spearmint, thyme, sage, marjoram, &c., are used for seasoning meats, cakes, soups, broths, &c. They owe their fragrant and spicy qualities to volatile or essential oil, each having its own, which may, by distillation, be collected, and, being dissolved in alcohol, are called essences. In that form they are generally kept and used instead of the crude spices and herbs from which they were taken.

Clothing.

All animals but man are furnished with protection from the cold, adapted exactly to the range of temperature in which they are destined to live. The polar bear and eider duck, and all other animals in the most northern climates, are clothed with thick, porous, compressible material, the interstices of which, being filled with confined air, are non-conductors of heat, and therefore are adapted to confine within the animal the heat that is generated in the lungs by a process almost exactly resembling combustion; as elsewhere described, it is said that a ball of eider down, which, as imported, is compressed into the size of a fist, is expanded by the gentle application of heat into a mass sufficient to fill a bed-tick.

And this gives us an idea of the quality of material best adapted for winter clothing. It should be soft, porous, and compressible, as these qualities distinguish the clothing of all northern animals. The animals of the tropics are not clothed at all, or clothed with thin, short, straight hairs, which offer no resistance to the escape of animal heat, while animals in temperate climates, with a cold winter and a warm summer, are provided with a change of garments for summer and winter.

But man, destined to control all animals, and therefore to live in every variety of temperature, is left to the exercise of his wits in the appropriation of materials furnished from animals in cold climates, and from fibrous vegetation in the silk-worm in warm climates, which he can best cultivate in just the climate where they are best adapted to supply his wants; and they are wisest who most perfectly imitate nature, and in cold climates and cold weather cover themselves with a loose, porous texture, of which loosely spun and loosely-woven wool furnishes the best material, not only as protection from the cold, but also to admit the free escape of perspiration, constantly going on in every healthy system.

And then in summer, or in warm climates, to use the materials which, by being closely spun and closely woven, so as not to confine air in their interstices, are not adapted to prevent the escape of animal heat, as cotton, flax, or silk. But how shall we dress in a climate where we are exposed to frequent changes? The fact is well known, whether we understand the philosophy of the thing or not, that if the skin be exposed to a temperature to which it is not accustomed, an inflammation is followed in some part, generally in one which has been weakened by disease, and this we call catching cold; and this occurs from sudden changes of temperature, or from sudden changes of dress. In a changeable climate, therefore, this subject is important, especially as most of our inflammatory diseases are induced by catching cold. (See Fig. 16, p. 327.)

How to Avoid Catching Cold.

To avoid colds, as to avoid all other diseases, we must consider the predisposing as well as the exciting causes.

We may be strongly predisposed to any disease, and yet escape it by carefully avoiding the causes which excite it; or, on the other hand, we may fortify ourselves against the exciting causes of disease by removing all predisposing causes of it. Or we may be doubly secure by removing and avoiding both the predisposing and exciting causes.

Among the predisposing causes of colds, there is probably no one so important as error of diet, which I have more fully discussed in another chapter, viz., the error of taking too much of carboniferous or heat-producing food, of which the representative articles are butter, fine flour, and sugar, which keep the tissues of the system in a state ready for the slightest exciting cause of inflammation, just as the sheathing around a steam-boiler is made ready to ignite by the slightest spark of fire; and as the greatest care must be taken to keep the spark of fire from such inflammable boards and timbers, so those who live on this unnatural, inflammation-producing food, must be scrupulously careful to avoid the exciting causes of cold; and common observation will support the assertion that those who live most exclusively on food as Nature furnishes it, are the least subject to colds, and best able to resist their deleterious influences.

Another predisposing cause is unnatural tenderness and susceptibility of the skin from want of friction or bathing, which will be explained in a chapter devoted to the subject of bathing and external friction. The most prominent exciting cause of colds, and the inflammatory diseases connected with them, is exposure of a part of the skin to cold or moisture in a manner to which it is not accustomed.

This exposure, by causing contraction of the pores, prevents the natural circulation of blood and perspiration, and throws them back on some other parts of the system. This increases the heat of the other organs, and, if weakened by previous disease, or otherwise predisposed to inflammation, proves to be the spark to "touch off" the heated sheathing of the lungs, or nose, or throat, or any other organ which proves to be most ignitible. To prevent these evils, then, we must avoid currents of air, or standing still on the cold ground, especially with thin shoes, or making great and sudden changes of dress, especially when tired, or weak, or exhausted from any cause, and, in our variable New England climate, take a lesson from the animals, and make no material change but twice a year, wearing the same thickness of dress all days from spring to fall, and from fall to spring, — only thicker in winter, and more porous, but never trying to conform our dress to cold or hot days.

Bathing and Friction.

Some animals bathe, others do not. Those that bathe seem to do so for purposes of cleanliness; but all animals, whose skin is made for the same functions as those of man, whether they bathe or not, have the means of applying friction to every part of the skin. Fowls and birds sometimes bathe, but more generally keep the skin free and clean by the use of the bill, and where the bill cannot be applied, the toes can be, so that every point in the skin, and every feather, is kept clear and clean. The cow not only keeps her own skin clean by the use of her moist, rough tongue, but she assiduously applies her crash towel to every part of her calf, and no "mother's darling" is made cleaner every morning; and I am not prepared to say that soap and Cochituate water, with a towel, have any superior advantages, either for cleanliness or for healthy friction.

From every part of the skin, as I have elsewhere explained, sensible and insensible perspiration are constantly exuding, carrying off waste materials, which must be thus disposed of, or some disease is the consequence. It is, therefore, very important that the skin be kept clean and free from all obstructions; but it is not of great consequence whether this be done by general bathing, by sponging, or by dry friction with a rough towel, hair mitten, or flesh brush.

One quite important object, however, is gained by the use of water to the whole surface: it is thus rendered less susceptible to cold and moisture, so that those who are habituated to cold bathing, within proper limits, are less liable to catch cold on exposure to cold or damp air. But to derive benefit and not harm from cold bathing, or cold sponging, certain conditions must be observed. The cold bath must be followed by a reaction, which gives a pleasurable glow of heat, or it does harm and not good; and to insure that reaction, we must not bathe at night, or at any time after exhaustive exercise, or directly after a full meal, and, until we are accustomed to it, must not be exposed to cold but for a very short time, but we can gradually learn to bear more and more exposure. Without these precautions, cold baths are dangerous.

Our Free Public Baths may be invaluable as a means of cleanliness for the neglected poor; but unless used with discretion, according to rules above suggested, will be the means of sacrificing many children. Cold bathing, or cold sponging, should always be followed with friction by a coarse crash towel, the advantage of which will be seen by reference to the important functions of the skin.

The Functions of the Skin. — The advantages of bathing and friction will be seen and understood by considering the structure of the skin, which cannot be explained by a verbal description. I therefore insert a cut, drawn from a section of skin as seen under a

Fig. 16.

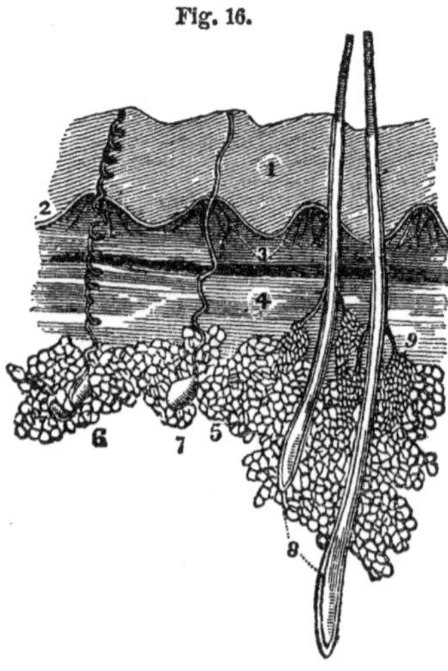

1. Cuticle, or Scarfskin.
2. Rete Mucosum, or Mucous Web.
3. Corpus Papillæ.
4. True Skin.
5. Cellular Membrane, or Fat Cells.

6 and 7. Perspiratory Glands and Ducts.

8. Roots of Hairs.
9. Oil Follicles.

microscope, and clearly delineating the different parts of this complicated and important organ, and showing the necessity of cleanliness in order to the perfect performance of its functions.

1. *The Cuticle or Scarfskin* is the dry, membranous outside covering of the body, consisting of laminæ of hardened mucus, or albuminous matter, without nerves or blood vessels, and therefore without feeling or life, except a kind of vegetable life. It is, when kept clean and fresh, as it may be by daily ablution or friction, spongy and porous, so as to admit through it freely the perspiration, &c., which exudes from beneath, but when neglected becomes hard, and filled with concreted impurities, which obstruct the natural secretions, and become the source of much derangement of the system, and of many diseases both of the skin and other organs. It constantly exfoliates in scales, as we can see at any time by applying friction or a moist cloth to any part of it, and is separated in blisters on the application of heat or irritating substances, as Spanish flies, mustard, &c.

2. *The Rete Mucosum, or Mucous Web*, in which resides the coloring matter which constitutes the complexion, and which, in the Ethiopian, is black. Like the cuticle, it is not organized with nerves and blood vessels, and therefore not absorbed, and being covered with the cuticle, is not exfoliated. It therefore remains almost permanent, and letters and figures inserted with coloring matter like India ink, remain during life. It is this inertness that renders diseases of the skin so

difficult of cure. In the cure of disease absorption is necessary; therefore those parts in which the absorbents are inactive, as in the cartilages, bones, and rete mucosum, when once diseased are very slow of cure, the irritating matter being out of the reach of the absorbents.

3. *Corpus Papillæ*, or that sensitive part of the skin in which resides the sense of touch. It consists of a collection of papillæ formed by the extremities of the nerves and vessels, which, after having passed the true skin beneath, are grouped in little pencils or villi on a spongy erectile tissue. These villi are disposed in pairs, and when not in action are soft and relaxed, but start up erect when employed in the sense of touch. They are very readily seen when a blister has removed their covering, and give the acute sensibility which in that case is felt to the touch, the scarfskin being necessary to modify and blunt the sensitiveness of the uncovered papillæ.

4. *The Deeper Layer, or True Skin.*—This consists of a dense collection of fibres, forming a firm stratum, interspersed with holes for the passage of nerves and blood vessels, and is mostly composed of gelatine; and the skin of animals is therefore used for making glue. Gelatine, when united with tannin, forms a substance which is insoluble in water, and constitutes the leather for our boots, &c.

These four strata constitute the skin, which is united to the structures below by cellular membranes, which contain more or less adipose matter, or fat, which is represented by the little globules under the skin, marked 5.

6 and 7 are the perspiratory glands and ducts, which are so exceedingly small that, according to the calculation of Wilson, the standard authority on the anatomy of the skin, there are twenty-eight hundred to every square inch of the body. The number of square inches in a man of ordinary stature is about twenty-five hundred, so that the number of glands and tubes would be about seven millions, and the length of tubing through the skin about twenty-eight miles. By this delicate and complicated apparatus are performed some of the most important functions of the system. The amount of liquid carried off through this apparatus in insensible perspiration, and the effects of it in removing the impurities from the blood and in regulating the temperature, I have elsewhere described. It is estimated to be, on an average, eleven grains every minute. The amount of course varies very greatly according to the dryness of the atmosphere, the degree of activity of the circulation, the temperature to which the body is exposed, the amount of liquids previously taken, &c.

Dr. Southard Smith, of London, tried experiments upon eight workmen at the Phœnix Gas Works, engaged in "drawing" and "charging" the retorts, &c., during which they were exposed to intense heat, accurately weighing the men and their clothes immediately before they began their work, and after they had finished, they taking nothing and ejecting nothing in the mean time.

Experiment 1. November 18, 1836. — Day bright and clear. Temperature of the air of the apartment in which the men worked, 60°; barometer, 29.25 to 29.4. Duration of labor, 45 minutes. Average loss of weight, 3 lbs. 6 oz. Maximum, 4 lbs. 3 oz. Minimum, 2 lbs. 8 oz.

Experiment 2. November 25, 1836. — Day foggy, with scarcely any wind. Temperature of the air, 39°. Barometer, 29.8. Duration of labor, 75 minutes. Average loss of weight, 2 lbs. 2 oz. Maximum, 2 lbs. 15 oz. Minimum, 14 oz.

Experiment 3. June 6, 1837. — Day exceeding bright and clear, with little wind. Temperature of the air, 60°. Duration of labor, 60 minutes. Average loss of weight, 2 lbs. 8 oz. Maximum, 3 lbs. Minimum, 2 lbs.

Experiment 4. On the same day, two men worked in an unusually hot place for 70 minutes, and the loss of weight of one was 4 lbs. 14 oz., and the other 5 lbs. 2 oz.

Besides this function of eliminating perspiration, and with it the impurities of the blood, the skin secretes an oil, which lubricates the hair, &c., as seen in the little glands at 9, and also secretes in different parts of the body odor peculiar to each part, and also peculiar to each individual.

This distinctive odor is not in many instances sufficiently strong to be recognized by human olfactories; but the dog, whose olfactories are much more acute, can recognize his master, and follow him through a crowded city, by the effluvia which is transmitted through the leather of his boot to the sidewalk, — a fact that would seem incredible, but is nevertheless well known.

By the aid of this cut we shall be able to understand the importance of friction and ablution. The scarfskin is made up of laminæ, which are constantly exfoliating to make room for new laminæ formed underneath. They are placed obliquely on each other, like the shingles on a roof, and serve as valves to prevent the access of air to the sensitive papillæ and skin beneath, and when contracted by cold, or the interstices filled with concreted and dried effete matters from within or dust and dirt from without, the mouths of the delicate ducts through which the perspiration is evolved are filled, and thus the important process which I have described is obstructed.

Johnson, in his Elements of Agricultural Chemistry, makes the following statement: "Six pigs were put up together for seven weeks. Three were currycombed and cared for, the other three left to themselves. The former three consumed five bushels of peas less, and had gained two stones and four pounds more, than the uncurried three." And he adds, "The skins of pigs fed in the forest in the season of acorns are white and shining."

This last fact is important, showing as it does that even a pig will keep his skin clean if he can get access to the means of friction; but the fact that pigs will eat less and gain more with clean skins than with neglected ones, is a fact, the practical value of which, if rightly considered, cannot, it seems to me, be overestimated. The construction of the skin of the pig and that of man is the same, and the effect of friction is of course the same.

Let us just look at the subject in the light of economy. A currycomb saved, on three pigs, five bushels of peas, say $10, and gained twenty pounds of pork, say $2.40 = $12.40, about 60 cents a week on each pig. Suppose a flesh-brush, well applied every day, would save as much on a man as a currycomb saves on a pig (and no one will say this estimate is extravagant), he would save in one year $31.20 — the interest on more than five hundred dollars. A bathing-tub and crash towel might do as well, but no better, so far as relates to the skin, and the daily use of it would cost much more trouble; and besides, every one can afford a flesh-brush and time to use it. But the pecuniary consideration, in comparison with others, is too mean to mention, only that it forcibly shows the influence on the system of keeping the skin in healthy working order.

Let any one who has never enjoyed the luxurious sensation of a thorough friction of every part of the skin, try it some night when he comes home tired and dusty, and the pleasurable glow of health, and the refreshing sleep that will follow, will make him wonder that he has so long neglected a duty so simple, and one that so manifestly does him good. Why, everybody curries his horse, and knows that neither oats, nor corn, nor hay, nor all together will keep him in good condition without that operation. Can he give a good reason why he should not curry himself?

The Lungs, and their Functions.

The lungs occupy an air-tight chest which includes the heart, having no external opening, except through the trachea or windpipe. The lungs occupy a much larger space than is generally supposed, extending from a point almost on a level with the top of the shoulder to the edge of the lowest ribs, the main body of them occupying the back of the chest, and their edges lying over the heart in front. Their office is to change and purify the blood by burning up the waste particles which are constantly being removed from the system, and out of these waste materials furnishing the necessary animal heat, and to supply the new particles of nutriment with oxygen, which is necessary to convert them into pure blood. To accomplish these complicated functions a very delicate organization is required. The air and the blood, which are of very different density and temperature, must meet in cells so fine as that the liquid blood shall come in contact with the gaseous oxygen, and in these gossamer cells is carried on a process so important that if for a single moment it should stop, as in fainting, strangulation, or drowning, all vital forces cease, and, unless immediately renewed, life is hopelessly extinct. And to the physiologist the wonder is perpetual that such a process can be carried on by machinery so exquisitely delicate, hour after hour, and day after day, sleeping and waking, for threescore years, without stopping for a single moment for repairs. And the wonder is increased when we consider the abuses to which this delicate structure is submitted. Of course, the delicate membranes are subject to the same laws as other organs of the human system. They must have nourishment containing the elements necessary to give them health and strength, including the nitrates and phosphates, or they cannot have firmness of texture and power to resist the pressure of the circulation; and yet the articles of food on which many depend are composed mostly of fine flour, sugar, or butter, which increase the work of the lungs, but diminish the strength of their tissues, being almost destitute of these elements. Then, again, they must be freely and perfectly exercised by doing their natural duties in order to retain their vigor, according to the universal law of Nature; and yet how common it is, by compression of the dress, especially with ladies, to exclude from some parts of the lungs so entirely every particle of air that they are never allowed to have appropriate exercise! The wonder then is, not that so many die of consumption, but that any live and attain the vigor sufficient to perpetuate the race. And the wonder is still increased by consideration of the fact that so little regard is had to the purity of the air we breathe.

Ventilation.

Within the last forty years many facts have been brought to light showing the necessity of breathing pure air, night and day, in order to enjoy health. Till then, in fact, open fireplaces, with wood fires, which changed the air of the closest house every few minutes, rendered all attention to the subject unnecessary; but the introduction of stoves, and the necessity of economy in fuel, brought an entire change, and made it necessary to institute some plan for artificial ventilation.

In 1830, some scientific men instituted a new system of ventilation in the Foundling Hospital, in London, and also in the Zoölogical Garden of that city, and the result was astonishing, and awakened the attention of scientific men of the whole civilized world to the subject. In two years the average length of life of infants had increased more than one hundred per cent., and the average length of life of monkeys had increased in about the same proportion; and it is remarkable that infants and monkeys in these institutions had, before this change, both died of nearly the same diseases, both children and monkeys having generally developed tubercles of the lungs or bowels; and this fact to me is a strong intimation that scrofulous diseases are developed, if not induced, either directly by carbonic acid, or by the absence of oxygen, as it is well known that the air of a room in which is going on the process of combustion, or the process of breathing, until ventilated comes to contain too much carbonic acid and too little oxygen.

There are undoubtedly other causes of consumption, as I have before intimated, but I think the influence of soil, and climate, and temperature, have very little responsibility directly for the disease which carries off so large a part of our population. Northern climates are more subject to consumption only because the necessity of artificial heat, and of economizing in fuel, has induced a disregard to ventilation; while in southern climates, all dwellings are open to the fresh air. Every room that is shut close, in which is combustion from lamps or gas, or in which is carried on the process of breathing, or in which at night are growing plants, must be ventilated frequently, as the oxygen, under these circumstances, is being consumed and carbonic acid gas being generated every moment.

Muscular Development.

Every organ and every faculty, physical and mental, must be exercised to be developed, or to retain its normal condition, and, within certain limits, the strength and perfection of those organs and faculties are in proportion to their exercise or material use. This principle is particularly manifested in the development of muscles. The right arm, especially that of the blacksmith, or other artisans who use it almost exclusively, is manifestly larger and stronger than the left, and the extent to which this development of power and control of the muscles can be carried is truly astonishing. Muscles are only the red flesh of animals which make our tender steak, and yet, when endowed with vitality, a little bundle of these delicate fibres will sustain and move the weight of tons. A man of ordinary size has brought up his muscles to the power of sustaining a weight of nearly three thousand pounds; and all this weight, besides the weight of his own body, must come upon a few bundles of red flesh in the back and also in the legs.

How astonishing also is the control of the will over the muscles, as shown in the gymnastic feats, which a long course of training enables men to perform! A man will lie on his back, lifting with his toes a long ladder into the air, on the top of which is another ladder, and on the top of that his own son, cutting up his pranks as fearlessly as if standing on the ground. Another man will trundle a wheelbarrow over Niagara River, on a single rope, knowing that if he should fall, death is certain.

On the other hand, we see men, otherwise in good health, who have so neglected muscular exercise that they are scarcely able to carry the weight of their own bodies; indeed, many a silly girl, in order to bring herself to her own ridiculous standard of beauty, has so weakened the muscles of the chest and back as to be unable to sustain her head and shoulders without artificial support.

And I once saw a woman, who, merely in gratifying a pervérse will, disabled herself from walking or standing for more than four years. When her husband was about going to sea for a year, she demanded some extravagant purchase, with the threat that unless it was made she would go to bed and stay there till he returned; and this threat she carried out literally. When the husband returned, she could no more stand or walk than a rag baby, and the husband, naturally, abandoned her forever. Having no means of support, she tried to recover her lost powers; but the pain of trying to use the neglected muscles and joints was so great that she abandoned the effort, and remained in that helpless condition for four years, when she was obliged to be carried to the almshouse, of which I then had the medical care. Being there under my control, I set about restoring the wasted muscles by walking her daily, between two strong women, regardless of her screams and imprecations; and very slowly the muscles began to grow and assume their power, and in four or five months she was discharged, able to walk and get her own living.

These illustrations show more clearly than a long dissertation on gymnastics, the necessity for muscular exercise, and the principles upon which to regulate it. Every motion exercises the muscles adapted to make that motion. If, therefore, we make every motion we are capable of making, we exercise every muscle. To do this, we need no complicated machinery. Every one has in his own room the means of exercising every muscle of his body. By standing erect, unencumbered with any clothing which shall embarrass the action, and making the motions of rapid walking without advancing, at the same time extending the arms, expanding the chest, and lifting up and letting down the shoulder-blades, we bring into action nearly all the voluntary muscles of the body; and then, to give tension and strength to the muscles, we may lift some article of furniture, according to the strength, as the end of the sofa, the bureau, or the foot or head of the bed, and thus get every practical benefit that can be had from the most complicated gymnastic apparatus. If the exercise has been neglected till the chest has become contracted and the lungs compressed, we may need the assistance of some pulleys on the wall, attached to weights, or springs, so that by placing the back to them, and taking hold and pulling forward with the hands over the shoulders, the chest is expanded, and for a time, till we have acquired sufficient tension and strength of muscle, we may derive advantage from raising, in a proper position, graduated weights; but having acquired the necessary tension and power for ordinary purposes of life and health, nothing is gained by bringing the muscles into fuller power or activity. All the instructions which any man of common sense needs, can be given in five minutes; indeed they are all included in the hints given above. An intelligent mother, therefore, in her own house, can develop the form of her daughter much better than a professional gymnast; and if mothers, when their daughters are beginning to develop into womanhood, and to feel the restraints of society, would just regard these hints, and insist, as a matter of duty, that they should exercise every muscle of the body every day, and conform in other respects to the hygienic laws elsewhere described, Nature will do for them all else that is necessary to develop perfect forms and perfect health. If this is neglected, it is folly to expect that a few months of tuition at a gymnasium will do much for them. At most it can only prepare the way for domestic exercise in such as have waked up to a sense of duty when the health of their daughters has already suffered from neglect, and then can be of use only as exercise is afterwards continued.

What we want is a clear conception of the object to be gained by exercise,—"a sound mind in a sound body,"—and this desirable condition can only be attained by the harmonious play together, every day, of our mental and physical faculties. It cannot be attained by an effort to ascertain how much we can lift or how far we can jump. On the contrary, such efforts tend to destroy that harmony, and to induce degeneracy and brutality of mind; and this for the obvious reason that it develops the faculties which constitute the highest glory of the brute at the expense of those which constitute the highest glory of the man. He who has no higher aspiration than to be the strongest or most athletic man, must be humbled by the thought that many an insect, which is esteemed of so little value as to be crushed under foot without compunction or thought, can lift, in proportion to its weight, a hundred times as much, and jump a hundred times as far. (See page 83.)

Rest and Sleep.

Every faculty and every organ of the body require exercise, that is, it must be used for the purpose for which it was made. To maintain a sound mind in a sound body we must expand our vital energy every day, partly on the intellectual, partly on the muscular, and partly on the digestive faculties, and also every day allow these faculties to rest. We may so overwork either class of faculties as to burden and depress the other classes, and disqualify them for rest.

We may so burden the digestive powers, by inappropriate food, as to be unfit either for muscular or mental exercise; or we may so exhaust the vital powers by violent and long-continued muscular exertion as to be unable to digest food or use the mind; or we may so work the brain as to exhaust our vital energy, and be unable to use the muscles or digest food. In either case we cannot enjoy quiet rest, or good refreshing sleep, which can only follow appropriate exercise of all the faculties in accordance with the laws which govern these faculties. The stomach, not being under control of voluntary muscles, can work while other organs rest; but it requires rest: and as from three to five hours are required for the digestion of a meal of food, and as good refreshing sleep can only be enjoyed when the stomach is at rest, our principal meals should be taken early in the day, the simplest food only being allowed after the fatigues of the day, and that not within three hours of sleep; indeed, all our faculties and organs require rest before sleep. Our evenings should, therefore, be devoted to social or religious enjoyments, and to these simple requisitions we need nothing added but implicit trust in God, a conscience void of offence, and obedience to all of Nature's laws.

www.ingramcontent.com/pod-product-compliance
Lightning Source LLC
La Vergne TN
LVHW010205110826
845151LV00002B/609

* 9 7 8 1 4 2 5 5 3 5 7 5 9 *